Smith

v.

Jones, Vol. 3

Even More **Interesting Cases
In the Magistrate's Court**

Robert F. Simms

© 2016 by
ROBERT F. SIMMS

ISBN: 978-0-9858233-7-5
Printed in the United States of America

To My Wife,
Who for more than forty years
encouraged me as I tried to
live and work honorably,
and didn't ride me too hard
when I screwed up.

CONTENTS

INTRODUCTION (AGAIN)

What keeps me interested in my job is the infinite variety of human stories in cases when they're filed and in the courtroom when trials take place. Many people go to work and push the same papers, fill the same orders, make the same products, mail the same boxes—you get the picture. The judge's work makes him part of many a human drama going on all the time all around us, dramas most people aren't aware of.

Admittedly, most cases that come through the magistrate court aren't quite the stuff of a hit TV series or a blockbuster movie, but all of them are poignant, exciting, distressing, confusing, challenging, troubling, or heartbreaking events for the people who live them. They are stories that someone will tell with regret, another with victory, still another with bitterness, and yet another with thankfulness. The magistrate—I hope this one, anyway—tells them with fascination, intrigue, and often a bit of empathy.

In these volumes of *Smith v. Jones,* I selected highlights from typical cases filed in my court. While magistrates in South Carolina also deal with criminal matters, I encounter more drama in civil work. In my experience civil proceedings are more lengthy than criminal ones, where defendants often plead guilty and the facts are cut and dried. In a civil matter, however, a trial is often like a play, starting off matter-of-fact, developing suspense, revealing conflict, and featuring a denouement and perhaps a surprise ending. Even without surprise, magistrate court cases still make good storytelling, and, I hope for your sakes, good reading.

What follows are two dozen more stories of real life drama in my courtroom. As in the previous volumes, I have changed all the plaintiffs' names to Smith and all the defendants' names to Jones, and now and then I have had to alter a few other insignificant facts to protect the guilty as well as the innocent. Other than that, as the narrator of TV's "Dragnet" used to say, "The story you are about to [read] is true."

1
SAD BUSINESS

At a judicial education seminar in September one year, two presenters who did not attend each other's sessions independently mentioned a judge's need to be aware when sentencing someone that sometimes a minor jail sentence will cascade into major catastrophe. Consider a person already on the brink of economic disaster who makes a bad decision that puts him in jeopardy of jail. It very well may be that if the judge puts him in jail for thirty days, he will lose his job. If he loses his job, he may well lose his apartment or house. If he loses his home, he may lose his wife. Down he goes until he is truly at bottom, and may well turn to criminal pursuits again in order to survive.

The fact is, many people live paycheck to paycheck in the most precarious way. While the judge cannot ever, *ever* let sympathy affect the determination of guilt, he should *often* let his knowledge of the defendant's circumstances influence sentencing, if the judge has any discretion in the matter.

Similarly, in civil issues the judge cannot require a plaintiff to "go easy" on a defendant. Tenants being sued for eviction for nonpayment of rent, for instance, often ask the court to give them more time to move, but the judge has no authority either to give him that time or to tell a landlord that *he* has to give him more time. The emotion involved in some eviction cases, however, engulfs the parties and the judge in a brief drama about real life consequences, sometimes about lives spiraling down into depressing depths.

Few court situations tug at the judge's heartstrings like an eviction filed against someone who just can't seem to catch a break in life. The judge strains against his obligation, under the law, to eject someone, because he knows that the person has few if any choices left about where to go, and little if anything left to go to.

Such was the plight of a man of about forty who appeared one day as a defendant against an eviction.

THE PLEADINGS

Smith Meadows Apartments filed for eviction against Fisher Jones over the sole issue of unpaid rent. Smith alleged that Jones owed $830.00. Not many tenants ask for hearings, especially when unpaid rent is the only issue. Jones, however, wanted a hearing, and my clerk advised him of state law requiring him to pay into the Court the amount of rent allegedly owed, if he wished to present a defense. He differed with the amount alleged, however, which necessitated a hearing just to determine the amount of rent first. When the date arrived, I was prepared to hear testimony only on the amount of rent owed and to make a determination of what that amount actually was. At that point, Jones would have to pay the money to the Court to be heard further.

THE EVIDENCE

The parties entered the courtroom together after I was already seated and making notes. Defendant hobbled in wearing a Bledsoe brace on his right leg and a similar device on his right arm. I knew what a Bledsoe brace was only because I had worn one myself three months ago after having crushed my knee horrifically in an accident. I had empathy for Jones as soon as I saw him, and I was alerted inwardly to the danger that I might develop a bias.

Plaintiff

Teresa Smith appeared for Smith Meadows and testified that Fisher Jones was indeed in arrears in rent for the month of August, and it was now September. Jones's lease had run out at the end of July, and Smith said that if he had paid August's rent on time, she was going to allow him to go on a month-to-month lease term. He didn't pay on time, however, and she decided to go ahead and file to have him evicted. She said the rental amount was $750.00, that a late fee for August was $40.00, and that she included the court filing fee, also $40.00, in her figure of $830.00 that she put on the Application for Ejectment.

Defendant

Fisher Jones wanted to stand for his testimony, so eager was he to present his case, and I had to remind him that I was interested for the moment only in the amount of rent in contest, and to assure him that he could, and probably should, remain seated because of his injury.

Jones showed me postal money orders for August's rent, which he offered to Smith on the 31st of the month, nearly a month late. He said he tried to pay what he owed but that Smith refused to accept it, saying that she was going to file for eviction. Jones didn't think Smith should be able to evict him if he had offered payment for the amount she said he owed. He was ignoring the fact that he was late in offering it, in addition to his having been late many of the preceding months of his lease.

The bottom line was that the figure of $750.00 for rent was not in contest, and Jones conceded that he owed the late fee of $40.00. While Smith could sue Jones for the other $40.00, she did not have a lease with Jones that said she could require him to pay the eviction filing fee as part of the late rent if she wanted to accept late payment and not go through with the eviction. The amount of rent due, therefore, was $790.00.

At this point, I told Fisher Jones that he would have to pay $790.00 into the Court in order to offer defenses, bits of which he had been trying to slip in between testimony about the amount of rent owed. So far, I had gathered that:

- Jones was married;
- He had seven children;
- He was unemployed;

- He received disability checks;
- He depended on his wife's meager wages for the rest of the family's support;
- He still had the greatest of difficulty in meeting monthly obligations;
- He had moved to Smith Meadows a few months ago hoping he would not be forced to find even more meager lodging;
- He was afraid he was going to be homeless;
- Nevertheless, since July he had been trying to find another place to go, because he thought he might be evicted;
- His injuries appeared to have something to do with an encounter at Smith Meadows, over which there was some sort of gag order;
- He wanted desperately to ignore the gag order and divulge the salient facts to me, in at least a roundabout way, if he could only present his defense.

All this I had picked up from interspersed comments.

As much as I had tried to remain both sanguine and reserved during the proceeding so far, on the third time Jones interjected that he was disabled, I interrupted him to say calmly, Mr. Jones, don't play the disability card anymore with me." He apologized, as he knew that's what he was doing. In reality, he didn't have to take any extra steps to evoke at least a basic sympathy from me; it was evident he was deserving of it.

When I put the question to him as to whether or not he wanted to pay the rent into the Court, Jones paused, uncertain, conflicted. He then held up papers and said that he understood me to have said that if he paid the rent he could present his case. I wanted to ask if there were an echo in the courtroom, because that's what I just told him. Instead, I merely confirmed that he had understood me correctly, and I put the issue to him again:

"Mr. Jones, I have determined that the amount of rent you owe is $790.00. You have that in your hands right now. You can give that money to the Court right now and I'll hear your defense. Otherwise, I will determine the case on the basis of the pleadings and the evidence offered to this point. Do you understand?" I felt as if I were hosting "Let's Make a Deal."

Jones put up his hand as if to signal that he wanted me to wait for him to answer. He then acted as if he had something stuck in his throat and was trying to swallow it. I asked if he needed some assistance, and he managed to say quietly that he had trouble swallowing, that he had epilepsy, and that he was having a seizure. I asked if he needed me to call someone, and he shook his head and simply asked for a minute to get through the episode. The minute turned into about five, while he nodded his head, occasionally putting it down on the defense table, and fought off his petite mal.

I had an informed sympathy for Jones. In college I had a fraternity brother, "Bill," who had epilepsy, controlled well with medication. He had the bad habit, however, of skipping his meds, thinking that eventually he would overcome his disorder through the sheer force of will. One day in the "Pit," the college cafeteria, while Bill was eating with three of us brothers, he had a seizure and threw himself over backwards on the floor. The other three of us at the table calmly knelt beside him to keep him safe for the next few minutes, after which Bill got up, seated himself and resumed eating as if nothing had happened. It was just life, for him.

While Jones was working through his difficulty silently, Plaintiff Smith offered that Jones had indeed come to her with his money orders for August's rent but that he didn't have quite enough to zero his balance in the books. With a warm and compassionate expression on her face, Smith said that since Jones had been late numerous times, she gave him back the money, suggesting that he keep it to help him move to another place. Under our law, she could have taken the money and still evicted him, but she was genuinely trying to help him.

Presently, Jones recovered and looked up with tears welling up in the corners of his eyes. I asked him once again what he wanted to do:

"Mr. Jones, you heard Ms. Smith say that she gave you your

money back so you could more easily move. You *have* that money in your hands. You can give it to the Court so you can present the defense you have hinted at. You should understand that if you pay it into the Court, I will give it to the prevailing party. I'm not recommending anything to you, but I want you to be clear that if your defense is not sufficient, you will not be getting that money back. Knowing that, what do you want to do?"

Jones struggled to make this decision but finally said, "Well, I guess I'll just leave it at that."

I then announced that the Court found for Plaintiff Smith Meadows Apartments and I approved the Application for Ejectment. I turned to Ms. Smith and said to her, "I am going to leave this case open for fifteen days for you to apply for the Writ of Ejectment anytime within that period. Do you understand?"

Teresa Smith understood that I was allowing her to give a little extra time to Mr. Jones if she wanted to. I felt that from her compassion for him, she might give him most of that two weeks to find a place and move, before taking out the Writ and then having him set out on the street twenty-four hours later—the hard facts of life under the law.

Instead, Smith went straight to the clerks' window and paid for the Writ of Ejectment on the spot. Sometimes a sweet face masks a no-nonsense lady. Business is business, sad or not.

2
ANGER MISMANAGEMENT

People sometimes say that *"things* got out of control," or that "the *situation* escalated," as if it were the circumstances themselves that were the blame. Of course, it's people who make things get worse and blow up. Sometimes, it is apparent on its face that a minor conflict grows into a major one because one person is a hothead. Sometimes two people who face off are both hotheads. What is surprising, however, is how little it takes to set off a firestorm of anger in some people, and how inexplicably that anger continues to burn, even without further provocation. The fact is that some people have anger issues deep inside them that are just waiting to be exhibited, and woe be to him who sets off the flood of pent up rage!

THE PLEADINGS

Dillard Smith appeared at the courthouse window to file a Motion for Restraining Order against Wallace Jones. Smith and Jones lived in the same neighborhood, several blocks apart, but they had not known each other until the events that gave rise to Smith's filing. According to Smith's brief complaint, Jones had driven his work truck past Smith's house one afternoon at too great a speed for safety in that residential area. When Jones did so again, Smith noted the signs on the truck identifying a business. He wrote to the business, advising them of one of their employees' dangerous driving. It happened that Jones was the business's owner. He emailed Smith in response and said he wanted to come by and resolve the issue. What happened after that was a remarkable series of events leading to an episode six months later where Jones threatened Smith at his own house, Smith called police, and police ended up seeking a warrant for Jones's arrest on a charge of stalking.

In my court, Smith wanted a Restraining Order against Jones. I had issued a Temporary Restraining Order and summoned the parties to a hearing. Jones was served with the Order at the jail shortly before he made bond on the stalking charge.

THE EVIDENCE

Dillard Smith appeared with his wife and his attorney, Carla Williams. Wallace Jones came with his wife as well, and a newly acquired attorney, Bill James. Several other adults, including Jones's father, were in the gallery, as were two police officers, both of whom had been subpoenæd by Plaintiff Smith.

I was accompanied by my constable that day. The Defendant's allegedly having threatened the Plaintiff's life several times, I wanted my officer present, as well as the deputies, who probably would depart shortly, leaving me with no courtroom security unless the constable attended. Normally I carry my own handgun, but I had left it behind that day, rather inexplicably.

Williams and James wanted an *in camera* hearing before testimony. It turned out to be over a concern that Mr. James had about profanity in a voice mail Williams wanted to bring into evidence. In a phone message to Smith, Wallace Jones had laced a single sentence with the F-word. I told both lawyers that there were no children present in the courtroom and the Judge had heard it all: the voice mail would come in.

Plaintiff

Ms. Williams first called Deputy Thad Means, who had served the arrest warrant for stalking on Wallace Jones just a few weeks before this hearing in September. Means didn't know Smith and had no knowledge of his and Jones's confrontations. He wasn't even the responding officer the evening of the incident that resulted in the stalking charge. He just served the warrant.

However, he testified that on the way to the jail while in the deputy's cruiser, Jones offered that he wasn't going to kill Smith unless Smith didn't "give it up." At the jail while Means was booking Jones, Jones repeated that if Smith "kept it up," he, Jones, would kill him.

With this dramatic opening to the case, Jones's attorney, Bill James, cross examined by trying to get Deputy Means to admit that people sometimes say things they don't mean. Means declined to endorse the idea that in this case Jones was being insincere. Instead, said Means, Jones was enraged and seemed undeterred by his being arrested for stalking. Means said he was a little startled by Jones's insistence, at the jail and in the presence of deputies no less, that he would kill Smith. Attorney James gave up the line of questioning and sat down.

Ms. Williams then called Plaintiff Dillard Smith. Mr. Smith was a slight figure of a man, slender and fair, who talked in a soft tenor voice with measured tones. As part of his testimony he was to reveal that he was a runner, a man with two elementary school children, and somewhat incongruously, I thought, a motorcycle rider. In spite of this last bit of information, I couldn't escape the impression that he could be afraid of his own shadow.

In lengthy testimony, Smith rambled and delivered many an excursus on his psychological state and that of his children, even crying at one point as he told how upsetting it all was. He recounted the story of being out in his yard one late afternoon in February of that year as a white pickup truck came barreling down the street well above the speed limit. It distressed Smith that someone would endanger the children in the neighborhood, where the speed limit was 25 m.p.h. When the event recurred the next day, Smith was able to read the sign on the back of the truck, which included a website of a business.

Smith promptly went inside and emailed the company, informing them politely that one of their employees was speeding through his neighborhood. He also accessed his neighborhood's Facebook page on the Internet, which he had started and hosted, and he left a post there suggesting that everyone be on the lookout for a speeding white truck.

Later that evening, Smith got a reply to his email. It was from Wallace Jones, the owner of the company whose logo appeared on the truck, who also happened to be the driver of the truck, and who lived several blocks away. Jones said in his reply, "I just tried to call and left you a voice mail. I need to meet with you to discuss getting the slander on Facebook removed. I am ready to solve this issue in any way possible. Please respond soon so that we can settle this tonight. I would really like to become your friend. I think that once you meet me you will regret slandering me and you will remove it." Obviously, something had tipped him off to the post on the neighborhood Facebook page. His email reply sounded vaguely like Don Vito Corleone's famous threat, "I'll make him an offer he can't refuse."

Smith replied right away: "I said nothing slanderous about you. I merely complained about speeding. I also didn't mention your name."

The next day, Jones sent a text message to Smith's phone, which stated succinctly and ominously that the time for Smith to remove the Facebook "slander" was now past. What was implied was that Smith had blown his opportunity to resolve the issue "amicably." What followed in another exchange of email clarified Jones's intentions to make Smith pay for complaining about his driving.

Smith said the voice mail from Jones was menacing. Having previously agreed not to object to it, Mr. James did not object now, and the voice mail was played. Williams held Smith's iPhone up to the microphone at her table, and the courtroom was treated to a message that did, indeed, sound like a thinly veiled threat. He said he didn't want to resolve things on some "girly Facebook page." His intonation was not friendly, and the F-word punctuated Jones's malicious intent.

Smith said in the next six months, between February, when all this trouble began, and September, when it reached another peak, Jones's primary offenses toward Smith were slow, drive-bys in his white pickup truck, as he returned home in the evening. In spite of the fact that Jones could have gone home through the neighborhood by a different route, Smith said Jones drove by his house very slowly, and that he took it as intimidation. Smith would see him from inside the house as Jones conducted these slow-speed drive-bys, as if conducting some kind of menacing surveillance.

Then in early September one afternoon, Jones cruised by slowly as Smith was just opening his garage door. He was getting ready to back his motorcycle out, to wash it. When Jones saw Smith, he stopped, backed up and blocked Smith's driveway. Opening his window, he began to speak threateningly to Smith, challenging him to fight, telling him they were *going* to have it out. Smith remained some distance away, he said, though he did come about halfway down his short driveway.

Smith told the Court he had just bought a handgun and that at the time of this incident he had just completed the required course for the issuance of a concealed weapons permit, which he did because he was increasingly scared of Jones. He didn't actually say that he had the gun with him at the time, and the Court concluded he didn't, because there hadn't been time enough for him to receive his CWP card since his training. I reasoned that Mr. Smith was not one to carry his new weapon concealed in violation of the law before having his license in his pocket.

Whether he had the pistol or not, Smith said his instructor emphasized in class that the CWP holder should not escalate a situation of confrontation. Acting on that warning, Smith stayed up in his driveway while the argument progressed.

Within a minute or so, as Smith refused to fight Jones and still denied slandering him, Jones became more and more enraged, eventually telling Smith he was going to kill him. Twice more he said, "I'm going to F-ing [he used the word] kill you!" Smith's neighbor from across the street came over to try to calm down Jones, and Smith himself soon retreated to his garage and closed the door. His wife and children inside were frightened. He called the police, and when they came and took his statement, they went to Jones's house and questioned him. That led to their seeking a warrant for stalking, which a judge issued that day.

On cross examination, Jones's attorney tried valiantly to soften the evidentiary impact of Smith's story. Mostly he tried to make the recent encounter in the driveway into something that Smith had provoked in some part. He asked if Smith hadn't violated the very principle he said he was trying to follow, by approaching the truck aggressively. Attorney James couldn't get Smith to testify in such a way as to make himself look like a willing participant at all, much less an antagonist.

Mr. James asked Smith on cross whether or not his children had seen the incident in September at the driveway. He didn't know, but Smith had asked his children how they felt and they had told him they were afraid. Smith said, "I asked them to write down their feelings. Our counselor—we've been seeing a family counselor about all this—she told us it would be good for our children to write about their feelings."

Without impugning the value of counseling (I've done my share of it) or the importance of helping children not to repress their feelings, I must say that this bit of information reaffirmed my impressions of Dillard Smith's constitution.

Williams then called the neighbor from across the street, Bud Green, who inadvertently had taken video of some of the drive-by episodes. Green had set up a surveillance camera that took frames at about ¼ second intervals, and he had aimed it at the end of his driveway. His mailbox had been vandalized recently, and he wanted to catch the culprit if it happened again. One morning just before dawn he checked his video and saw something happen in Dillard Smith's driveway. A white pickup truck pulled into the driveway with lights off, stopped, went closer to the garage door, stayed for a minute or so, then slowly backed out and drove slowly out of the neighborhood. Green went over to Smith's house to show him the video. After that, Green was able to capture several other videos of either Jones's white pickup truck or his red Mustang cruising past Smith's house very slowly, early in the morning. The whole thing seemed ominous to Green, and he said Smith seemed concerned about it as well.

Carla Williams introduced one of the DVD videos that Green

had shot. She had it on her laptop. The witness was going to be asked to identify the vehicle in the video. Williams, James and I crowded around the laptop computer and watched the video. A time stamp on the video showed it was taken around 6:30 a.m. The light from a lamp on Green's house made the foreground bright but the street was murky black. The vehicle that approached and went by the end of the driveway was in only about four frames. What I saw was mostly the blur of red tail lights. Nothing else could be identified: type of vehicle, model of vehicle, or its color. Green was silent, and Williams sheepishly admitted she couldn't make out anything from the video either. She withdrew the motion to move the video into evidence.

On cross, Mr. James went after witness Green, asking if, when he went over to defuse the driveway confrontation, hadn't Mr. Jones then desisted and gone away? Yes, that was true. Mr. James looked smugly satisfied with the answer. In my mind, I saw Leslie Nielson in *Naked Gun,* standing in front of an ongoing scene of fire and carnage, telling the crowd, "Move along! Nothing to see here!"

When Mr. James was finished, Green stepped down, and Ms. Williams rested the Plaintiff's case.

Defendant

When I turned to Mr. James for the Defendant's case, he immediately moved for a directed verdict for the Defendant, "or whatever it would be in this circumstance, your honor" he said. He was cognizant of the fact that the term, "directed verdict" more strictly applies to a judge's directing a jury to reach a given verdict when there is no evidence or fact in dispute that may support anything but that verdict. When there is no jury, a verdict isn't really "directed" but the term has stuck for a motion that the judge decide the case without a defendant's having to present any defense at all. Many lawyers always, *always,* move for a directed verdict, hoping the judge can be manipulated by their confidence that the case is a slam dunk for the defendant.

I denied the motion, and Mr. James immediately called Heather

Jones, Wallace Jones's wife.

Mrs. Jones was a shy and demure woman, and under soft questioning she described her husband as a gentle and courteous man. Mr. James began a series of questions about her husband's personality, his community involvement, his charitable activities, etc. When he began asking her if her husband were a courteous person, Ms. Williams objected.

"This is irrelevant, your honor."

"Your honor," said Mr. James, "it goes to the state of mind…"

"Mr. James," I said, "this is fundamentally character testimony, generally inadmissable except to rebut testimony in which character has been impeached. The testimony so far has been about what the Defendant did, but it has not besmirched his character *per se*. The objection is sustained."

Mr. James continued in another vein, asking Mrs. Jones if she drove either or both vehicles she and her husband own. Yes, she said, she drove both of them, though more often the red Mustang. Had she driven the Mustang to school to drop off her children early in the morning? Yes, she had. How fast did she drive up the street? She said she drove 25 m.p.h., which was, after all, the speed limit. Did she have any knowledge of her husband's having an ongoing feud with Dillard Smith during the period of February to September of that year? No, she didn't.

Mr. James then asked Mrs. Jones what was going to happen this very afternoon, the day of the hearing. She and her husband were closing on a house, she said. They were moving. Where? To the northern part of the city, about seven miles away. Mr. James sat down.

On cross, Ms. Williams tried to get Heather Jones to say that she didn't drive by the Smith's house quite as early as the video had shown. James objected, "What video, your honor? There's no video in evidence," he said with a wry smile.

"Quite right, Mr. James. Objection sustained." Williams didn't have anything else, and I dismissed Mrs. Jones.

Not surprisingly, Mr. James did not call his client Mr. Jones to testify. If even *half* of what the Plaintiff had testified was even *half* true, Mr. James did not want to subject Wallace Jones to Ms. Williams's cross examination.

With no more testimony to be given, Mr. James said, "I don't know if you want closing arguments at this point, your honor, or what." I said that was up to the parties. Normally, closing statements in civil cases were in this order: plaintiff, defendant, plaintiff; however, James launched right into his closing statement. I glanced at Ms. Williams and she shook her head slightly with closed eyes, indicating she didn't care that he was going out of order. She would get the last word anyway.

Closing Statements

James argued passionately that for a restraining order to be issued, the Court must find a pattern of harassing or stalking behavior. (He didn't attempt to argue that any of the other elements of harassment or stalking were not present, because they clearly were.) In this case, he said, there was no pattern, because for six months there had been no incident. James argued that the incidents complained of by Plaintiff had to have taken place in a ninety-day period.

Ms. Williams rose to object, which is usually not done during opening or closing statements, but she wanted to ask the Court if there were any mention of a ninety-day period in the statute. I inferred that she might have doubted that I knew the statute well, and she wanted to make certain that I was apprised of the fact that the statute *doesn't* say anything about ninety days. In fact, I was well aware that the statute didn't say such a thing. Mr. James was referring to a time period that some older case law had mentioned and that some courts accepted as definitive with regard to "a pattern of activity." I told both sides that I was intimately acquainted with the law, having frequently applied it and having that very morning consulted it in regards to this case.

Mr. James took the hint and dropped that part of his argument, but he continued to pound away at the idea that there was no pattern of harassing activity. He then emphasized to the Court that his client was already under a no-contact order from the bond court in the matter of the stalking charge against his client. In other words, he implied, a restraining order would be superfluous. He concluded with what he hoped would be the convincing argument that the Joneses, after all, were moving beginning today and that the situation, whatever it had been, would resolve itself right away. He sat down.

Ms. Williams rose and began by smiling sweetly and assuring the Court that she would very briefly offer her summation. She was acutely aware that it was now well past the lunch hour. Perhaps she had heard my stomach growl from behind the bench. She put together the case from beginning to end, argued strongly for the Court to take seriously the oral testimony about drive-by intimidation, and she rounded out her case with a plea for the Court to give the Plaintiff "some measure of protection against this kind of behavior that had no justification whatsoever."

THE JUDGMENT

I had been making notes for the Judgment during the proceedings, trying to make it look as if I were just recording testimony, which I also did. I didn't need to deliberate further.

For the benefit of both parties I will say first that the Court did not need to consider the numerous drive-by incidents as part of a pattern. The statute defines "a pattern" as "two or more acts occurring over a period of time, however short, evidencing a continuity of purpose." Even without the alleged drive-bys, more than two acts exist that may be considered in the determination of a pattern. I considered the first email of Defendant on February 26, the voice mail of the same date, Defendant's email on the 27th, his part in the exchange of text messages on the 27th and 28th, and the incident in the Smith's driveway on September 6. In addition, I considered testimony of the officer that Mr. Jones has been charged with stalking based on probable cause from the same evidence as offered here today.

The Court sees a definite pattern of intensifying anger and threats. A pattern need not be restricted to ninety days or any particular time period. A person may repeat a harassing or menacing act only once a year on the anniversary of some event over which he holds a grudge. The interval may be longer. A pattern is a pattern. In this case, there is a pattern of harassment at the very least, and every other element of harassment as defined in §16-3-1700(A) of our state statutes.

What I see is a case of anger mismanagement by the Defendant. Nothing in the testimony suggests that what the Plaintiff did or said in any way justifies the Defendant's exhibition of escalating rage. Threatening repeatedly to kill someone for complaining about your speeding is intolerably irrational.

The issuance of a Restraining Order does not add to the no-contact order issued by the bond court. It is not, however, superfluous. It guarantees that the Plaintiff will have some protection for a year, should the criminal matter be resolved before then and should no similar order be extended by the criminal trial court.

Nor is the Defendant's imminent move to another neighborhood a reason for the Court to consider any less valid the Plaintiff's motion for an Order based on previous acts. Separating combatants often merely delays incidents instead of preventing them.

The Court therefore issues the Restraining Order, extending the temporary order to one year from its issuance date.

Mr. Jones, I order you to have no contact whatsoever with Mr. Smith or his family, whether by physical presence, phone calls, electronic contact, or written message, or any other mode of communication designed to make its way to the Smiths' notice. It is my hope that you will exercise self control and not violate the order.

It is also my hope that you, Mr. Smith, will not for any reason make contact yourself with Mr. Jones, and that you will not make further posts on Facebook or any other place that directly or indirectly refer to Mr. Jones and that might provoke further incidents. (Both parties were nodding: the Plaintiff and his attorney in ready agreement of the two-way-street nature of a Restraining Order; and the Defendant, as if to say, "Yeah, you too!")

In light of this urging, Mr. Smith, I want you to consider specifically that your interpretation of Mr. Jones's alleged, slow, drive-bys of your house may be mistaken. They may not have been anything more than the lawful passage of a resident of your neighborhood, who has the right to take the most efficient route in and out of that neighborhood, driving at the posted speed limit. Incidentally, you can't have it both ways: you cannot complain of someone's driving too fast and then complain that they drive too slowly when they may in fact be going the speed limit of 25 m.p.h. —even if they do it to rub it in to someone who complained. In itself, that is no act of harassment. (Both parties were nodding: the Defendant as if I had cleared him of some wrongdoing; and the Plaintiff in humble acknowledgment of the point.)

I instructed the parties to leave separately by a few minutes. As my constable and I left the courtroom and walked down the back hall, I asked him if he didn't wish he were in the courtroom more often to see the fascinating little dramas that played out there.

He remarked that the Defendant was just a bully. I said I was thinking more "hothead," but bully would do. Not only that, he said, but the Plaintiff was something of a weenie, in spite of his decision to buy a gun.

Our both being motorcycle riders, my constable asked me what sort of motorcycle might a fellow who is frightened by his own shadow actually ride.

"Probably a moped," I replied.

3
THIS VACUUM SUCKS

Door-to-door salesmen have a general reputation that isn't altogether good. Like used car salesmen, the door-to-door man often uses high pressure tactics, engages in questionable sales practices, and is difficult to find if the homeowner has an issue to be resolved later. Not surprisingly, door-to-door sales generate lawsuits.

THE PLEADINGS

Harold Smith came to the Court to file a Summons and Complaint against Jason Jones, d/b/a Sunny Day Vacuum Company. Smith said Jones had sold him and his wife a vacuum system for $2,000.00. However, when Smith made a good faith attempt to give notice of cancellation within the time specified by law, which is three days, Jones refused to refund the money and take back the returned vacuum. Jones filed an Answer denying that Smith had returned the vacuum within three days.

THE EVIDENCE

Harold Smith, a man in his mid thirties, was a lawyer, and sitting at his table to my left he looked the part. I hadn't seen him in my courtroom, and I didn't know in what area of the law he practiced, but his Complaint was several pages long and was typical of filings by attorneys in the Magistrate Court, detailed and thorough. He came with his wife, who was his co-Plaintiff in the matter. Jason Jones sat at the defense table, leaning on his elbows, a man of slightly scruffy appearance, who wore a look of irritation and almost belligerence. He resented being there.

Plaintiff

Smith told a simple story of having been visited on a Wednesday evening at his home by Jones, who sold Sunny Day Vacuums. Smith said Jones stayed about two hours, talking and demonstrating his product, and that after that time Smith and his wife narrowly decided to buy the vacuum. They paid Jones by check.

The vacuum cleaner didn't suck—or actually, it did, because it worked properly. However, two days later, with other bills pressing, they decided to return the vacuum. Smith knew the law, and he knew he had to give Jones written notice of cancellation by midnight the third business day after the sale. He wrote a letter and went to the post office, finding it already closed on that Saturday afternoon. He and his wife were going out to eat that evening, so they decided to go to Jones's place of business and hand deliver the letter of cancellation. If Jones didn't happen to be there on Saturday, Smith said he was going to put it in his mail slot or mailbox.

However, Smith couldn't find the business. He went to the address shown on the sales receipt, which functioned as the contract in the purchase, and couldn't find such a business there. People at surrounding businesses said they hadn't heard of the Sunny Day Vacuum business and that if it had ever been there, it had been a long time ago.

Smith noticed that the phone number on the receipt (but not the address) was crossed out, and a call to the number anyway verified that it was not in service. He decided to pursue the matter on Monday. When he did, he found a number, called it, and got Jones on the phone. Jones gave him another address for the business and said something to the effect that he would give him a refund.

Smith mailed his original cancellation notice, still in the unopened envelope, to the new address, along with another letter cancelling the purchase. The letter also asked for Jones to come pick up the vacuum or tell Smith where to return it. Days passed. Smith finally called Jones again, and Jones dismissively told him it was too late to return the vacuum. Smith said Jones told him, "I never got no letter."

Smith said he told Jones, "I sent it May 7." Smith said Jones replied that he didn't get it. "Anyway," Jones added, "the money's already gone. You're too late."

Smith showed the court an image of his canceled check, telling me that Jones had deposited the $2,000.00 instrument in the bank on Thursday. He argued that Jones *did* have the money. I found the argument odd, since anyone would cash or deposit a check promptly, even if he didn't spend it. Smith seemed to be suggesting that the deposit proved that Jones did have the money; I had assumed, conversely, that what Jones meant by telling Smith the money was "gone" was that he had spent it already. Even if I were right, however, Smith's case was no less strong.

When Smith realized he was not going to change Jones's mind, he put together a Complaint and filed it in my court. He said service had been difficult to accomplish on Defendant, as Jones was hard to locate. He had to hire a process server, who himself had difficulty but finally served Jones. Smith had paid $150.00 for service of process.

Smith said he really didn't want to have to sue Jones. (I thought this statement, coming from a lawyer, was remarkable, but I didn't sense anything disingenuous about Smith at all. I thought it likely that his practice was not in trial law.) However, Smith said, the money was not really the issue; it was the principle of the thing. He thought it likely that Jones could and would repeat this practice of getting out of making refunds, if he were allowed to get away with doing it to him.

Smith had nothing more, and Jones didn't have any questions for him. I sensed that Jones was uncomfortable squaring off against a lawyer.

Defendant

Jones wanted to tell his side of things, however, and he was very brief. His defense was first that Smith didn't return the vacuum within three days. He referred to "returning the vacuum" several times, revealing that he didn't understand fully what the requirements of the law were, that Smith only had to give notice of cancellation within three days, not actually return the unit within that time.

Jones also claimed that he had told Smith when he was demonstrating and selling the vacuum system that the address on the receipt was wrong, and that he gave Smith a new address while at his house. Out of the corner of my eye I saw Smith sit up, startled and incredulous, though he withheld any interruption or response.

Then Jones held up the letter he had gotten from Smith. (—Wait: I thought he hadn't gotten a letter!) He said it didn't come until the 9th of May, well after the three days Smith had to change his mind.

Finally, Jones gave a more generic defense: "Your honor, I've been doing this fifteen years. I run a small business, and I don't have money sitting around. I sell a unit and buy another one. I have to keep turning around the money. I've had people cancel on me before, and all they have to do is call and say they've changed their minds, and I'll give 'em the money, but Mr. Smith didn't do that in time." Jones seemed to be finished, but then he started up again.

"It's right there on the contract. They have three days to return the vacuum. He didn't do that. The law says he has three days. It was nine days before he told me he wanted his money back."

Plaintiff

Smith didn't want to question Jones in cross, but he wanted to rebut Jones's contention that he had told them about the old address. "Your honor, Mr. Jones never said anything about his business address having changed."

THE JUDGMENT

I had made notes prior to trial and scribbled more notes during the hearing and was ready to put them together on the fly:

First of all, the principal law governing this case is that a "buyer may cancel a home solicitation sale until midnight of the third business day after the day on which the buyer signs an agreement or offer to purchase," and that "cancellation occurs when the buyer gives **written notice** of cancellation to the seller **at the address stated in the agreement** or offer to purchase." [I emphasized the words I have written here in bold, and made certain Mr. Jones took note.]

The parties should note that the statute does not require the return of the merchandise by the third day, only the receipt of written notice of cancellation.

The Court considers business days to be Monday through Friday. The transaction occurred on Wednesday, April 30. The third day after the sale was Saturday, May 3. The third business day would have been Monday, May 5. Plaintiffs attempted to give notice of cancellation on Saturday, however, by seeking Defendant's place of business, using the business address shown on their sales receipt. Defendant had moved his place of business a considerable time earlier, however, and was negligent in correcting his address on his receipts. Plaintiffs made a thoroughly good faith attempt to find Defendant's place of business to hand deliver notice of cancellation, and their inability to do so was entirely the fault of Defendant, whose negligence prevented Plaintiffs from exercising their right of cancellation under the law.

Even if the Court were to consider the fact that some USPS offices are open a few hours on Saturday, and loosely to consider Saturday, May 3, to have been a business day, its not having been a business day for *Defendant* at the place of business specified on the *bill* or receipt of sale eliminates that day's consideration as a business day, and still places the final day for cancellation on Monday, May 5.

As to the conflict of testimony over whether or not Defendant told Plaintiff on Wednesday that his business address had changed, I note that Mr. Smith has approached this matter with organization and detail, and appears from his testimony to be a person who takes note of all facts and does not act randomly. I cannot see any reason Mr. Smith would have gone to an address he knew was not valid. Given the assertion of conflicting claims by the parties, I find Mr. Smith's statement to be factual that he had no knowledge that Jones's business address on the bill was old and invalid.

Defendant's defense of his needing to buy new product with proceeds from his sales warrants the Court's final observation. Conducting a business in a hand-to-mouth fashion may *explain* Defendant's difficulty in refunding Plaintiffs' money, but it does not *justify* the refusal to do so.

THE COURT RENDERS JUDGMENT FOR PLAINTIFFS AND ORDERS DEFENDANT TO PAY $2,380.00 IN DAMAGES AND COSTS.

4
The Importance of Being Earnest

Some people object to gambling on the premise that it's an attempt to get something for nothing. I don't have any moral objection to getting something for nothing, if it really is for nothing. If there are strings attached, it isn't something for nothing. However, I don't gamble, because if you don't get something for nothing, you'll certainly get nothing for something—you lose what you put down on a mere chance.

Putting down earnest money is not gambling. It's showing you're serious—earnest—about buying. If, however, you really don't know what will happen with earnest money, what will result in its forfeiture or what will qualify you for its return, then forking over earnest money may be more like ante-ing up in a game of chance. That's when a good contract can make the difference between a secured deposit and a lottery ticket.

The Pleadings

Tommy and Sharon Smith brought suit against Jones Homes and Ronald Jones individually, over a $5,000.00 deposit they had paid Jones to reserve a site for a new home. When they backed out of the deal, Jones wouldn't return their money. After Jones was served with the suit, he submitted an Answer saying that their "deposit" had been converted to Earnest Money, as part of a construction contract.

The Evidence

Scheduling a hearing on the matter was difficult because Jones repeatedly seemed to have a conflict. Finally, I set a date and simply informed Jones that if he didn't appear, the issue might be decided against him as a matter of default. It appeared to the Court that Jones was being evasive, and I fought the inclination to develop a mild prejudice.

The day of trial, however, both Jones and his wife, who were president and vice president of their company, appeared. They were a nice looking couple in their forties who didn't betray in any way their being defendants in three other suits either current or just disposed in my court.

Tommy and Sharon Smith were at the other table, a couple who were of similar age and appearance. After swearing in all four at one time, I adopted a relaxed approach and asked the Smiths to tell me their story.

Tommy and Sharon Smith signed a Home Reservation Agreement with Jones Homes, LLC, ("Jones Homes" or "Jones") on September 13 of the previous year, making a deposit of $5,000.00, showing their intent to purchase a home to be constructed by Jones on a particular property in the Pretty Plots subdivision, and obtaining right of first refusal on it. On the following December 9 the Smiths signed a Construction Agreement with Jones Homes ("the Contract"), which was then signed on December 10 by Jones. The deposit made to establish the Home Reservation Agreement was converted to Earnest Money by way of Item 5, "Payments," in the Construction Contract.

The Contract included a provision in Item 4, "Financing and Appraisal", whereby the "agreement is contingent on the Client's ability to obtain financing for not less than 80% of the total construction price." The Smiths said they were not able to get financing because the bank wanted the Construction Contract modified first. The Smiths gave the Court a sheaf of papers including a chronologically organized series of text messages left via the Jones Homes website, in which they politely went back and forth over the matter of financing, the changes proposed and those not agreed to, the reasons each side experienced delays, and other matters. They also submitted a copy of a letter, sent in the following January, in which they told Jones they were not going to pursue the construction anymore, in part because of Jones's not having broken ground, more than two months after the construction agreement had been signed, and also because the Smiths found themselves temporarily unable to be present to supervise and consult on the construction.

The Smiths argued that Jones should return their deposit because the Home Reservation Agreement said it was fully refundable.

Defendant

Ronald Jones didn't want to ask any questions of the Smiths, but just to skip to his defense. As courteously as the Smiths had told me their side, Jones gave me his perspective.

As I had already concluded, Jones had been experiencing financial difficulties. He was under contract for all the lots in the Pretty Plots subdivision, and he had been buying them one at a time as he got the funds, in part from the earnest money of respective buyers. He pointed out that the Construction Contract, signed two months after the Home Reservation Agreement, had converted the Smith's $5,000.00 into earnest money, and that it was no longer the mere deposit referred to by the September document.

Jones denied—again, very politely—that the bank (which he had recommended to the Smiths) actually refused to lend money to the Smiths until Brown changed the Contract. Au contraire, he said, he had worked with that particular bank many times before and although he was making some of the changes they asked for, he had no doubt the bank would finance the Smith's construction. Jones said various things, including minor surgery, did delay his work in December of the previous year, but that he closed on the Smith's lot at the end of that month, using their Earnest Money as well as other funds to pay for the land.

Jones said he didn't have any indication prior to closing on the Smith's lot that they were feeling "iffy" about the Contract. The day after Christmas he had uploaded the revised Contract to his website for the Smiths to download and sign. He didn't realize until the middle of January, when he received their letter, that they were backing out.

The Smiths had a few questions in cross examination. They pointed to their text correspondence with Jones, emphasizing their language that the bank wouldn't lend them the money until changes had been made. Wasn't that notice to Jones that they "couldn't get financing"?

Jones answered that the bank called him and didn't represent the matter that way. They wanted a change here or there, but there was no question that the Smith's qualified and that the loan would go through.

But, the Smith's said, they didn't sign the modified Contract. They pointed Jones to the clause in the Home Reservation Agreement that said it didn't bind the parties unless an "acceptable definitive" contract were signed. They asked Jones to confirm that's what the Reservation Agreement said. He agreed that it did, but he said, "But then we signed the Construction Contract. It converted the $5,000.00 deposit into earnest money. And I used the earnest money in buying the lot."

Things went back and forth a bit more, and then the Smiths wanted to offer rebuttal testimony.

The Smiths reinforced their previous testimony that the bank indicated that financing was pending upon some modification of the Contract. Further, two weeks later the Smiths notified Jones by text message on the Jones website that "the bank is waiting for the lot transaction to take place." To them, this meant that the bank *would not* lend them the money if Jones didn't change the contract. They said that Jones Homes was fully aware that they had not obtained financing throughout the month of December. Jones uploaded the revised Contract to the website, but the Smith's did not sign it. They didn't explain to me exactly why, but it was clear that their reasons for backing out of the Contract were the same reasons they didn't sign the revised version. Having not signed the revision, they *did not* obtain financing.

The Smiths believed the Contract was in abeyance until modifications had been made and a new contract signed. The Smiths argued to the Court that the bank's unwillingness to proceed with financing right away rendered the Contract less than "acceptable definitive."

At this point, I was curious about the Smiths' repetition of this matter of an "acceptable definitive" contract. I asked them, "When you signed the Home Reservation Agreement, what did you think "acceptable definitive" meant?

They both chimed in after a confused pause, saying that they assumed it meant that all the obligations of each side were laid out, that everything was covered. I followed up by asking what they thought the "acceptable" part meant. Well, they said, they assumed it meant they agreed to it.

I repeated the question to Defendant Jones. He gave an assured answer in different terms but amounting to the same thing.

Then I asked the Smiths whose signatures were on the signature page of the Contract. They said theirs and Jones's. I said, "So, the bank is not a party to the Contract."

The Joneses looked at each other as if to say to themselves, 'That's a dumb question: of course not.' What they actually said was a respectful, "No, your honor."

My dumb question had an obvious point. "So," I said, "the bank was not a party to your agreement. Isn't it then true that the bank's exceptions to the Contract's terms (or lack of terms) could not render the Contract "unacceptable?"

A look of understanding passed over their faces as I asked them the followup question: "Doesn't the term 'acceptable' in the Home Reservation Agreement refer to yours and Jones's acceptance, not the bank's?" They nodded and realized the purpose of my question. The Smiths and Jones agreed that their mutual acceptance of the terms of the Contract was all that was necessary to bind the parties to those terms. The bank could not render the Contract void by hesitating to lend the Smiths money.

The Smiths continued to argue, however, that because they didn't signed the revised contract, there was nothing to hold them to. They thought their letter in mid January was sufficient to back out of the plan to build without forfeiting the Earnest Money. In that letter they had stated courteously:

> "We realize that this decision, combined with the December 13 expiration of the 'home reservation agreement', means that lot 8 is no longer reserved for us."

When Jones didn't take the hint and return their money, the Smiths wrote a little more explicit request on January 29, in which they said they were concerned that Jones had not made any progress on the model home in the Pretty Plots subdivision and had not as of that time broken ground on their own home. Partly on those grounds, they wrote, as well as for their previously stated, personal reasons, they were "not going to proceed." They would take a "wait and see" approach about reconsidering in the future. To mollify Jones, they suggested that he keep a thousand of the five thousand dollars for his work.

Jones responded with a courteous refusal (all these folks were a model of politeness). He said in part that his company "moved forward with the purchase of [the Smiths'] lot based upon our signed construction agreement," and he stated that "the lot reservation deposit was applied as Earnest Money to the construction agreement that you signed with us." Jones took the position that his company was "willing to apply a credit for this Earnest Money to a subsequent construction agreement should you decide to move forward with us."

This response's not being satisfactory to them, the Smith's brought suit. No more Mr. Nice Guy.

I had another question for both parties. I had looked at the Construction Contract enough to see that it did not say anything about what would happen to the Earnest Money, but I wanted each party to see that for himself. I asked, first of Plaintiff and then of Defendant, "In this contract, is there any paragraph that says what happens to the Earnest Money?"

Both parties turned pages and looked. Even Jones wasn't

immediately certain. Often, *neither* party knows what's in a contract he signs. After a pause, both parties agreed there was nothing said about the Earnest Money after the simple statement that the $5,000.00 from the Reservation Agreement was hereby converted to Earnest Money.

When both parties confirmed they had said all they had to say, I deliberated and then gave a Judgment, including findings of fact as represented in the description of the case above, and continuing my ruling as follows:

THE JUDGMENT

The Court finds that the Contract, while not sufficient for the bank to proceed with the Smiths' loan on December 10 or even later, was still in force, having been signed by both parties and not having been voided by any event. The Smiths had not obtained financing throughout December, or even by mid January, but the Court finds this fact not conclusive of any claim that they *could not* obtain financing.

- They had not applied for financing anywhere other than the one bank;
- They had not invoked the Financing clause of the Contract that made the Contract "contingent on the Client's *ability* [emphasis added] to obtain financing for not less than 80% of the total construction price;"
- They had represented themselves as being financially able to obtain financing, a fact to which Jones testified and which the Smiths did not contest at trial;
- Further, Jones Homes presented an updated version of the Contract they were certain would satisfy the bank's requests, and the Court agrees with Jones's assessment that the revised contract would have been acceptable;
- Finally, when the Smiths notified Jones in mid January of their decision not to move forward with construction, they did so for reasons other than financing and made no claim

that their not having obtained financing was even involved.

The Smiths' reliance on the Home Reservation Agreement was unfounded. The Court sees clearly that the Construction Contract superseded the Reservation Agreement and that the Construction Contract contained no automatic guarantee of a refund of the Earnest Money.

South Carolina statutes provide for the resolution of disputes over earnest money by lawsuit and "order of a court of competent jurisdiction." For guidance beyond that, we must turn to the Common Law and case law:

Our case law evidences a variety of circumstances generally upholding the Common Law principle that earnest money may be retained by a seller or builder where the buyer backs out of the contract unilaterally, without encountering problems with title or unforeseen issues with land, etc., but where the builder is able and willing to perform under the provisions of the contract. While any individual contract may provide for exceptions or may generously guarantee the full return of earnest money with no questions asked, the contract in the instant case, the Construction Contract, provided only the one contingency: the "Client's ability to obtain financing." If the client were *unable* to obtain financing, the entire contract would be voided.

Whereas this Court has already found above that Tommy and Sharon Smith had not demonstrated their actual inability to obtain financing, and whereas the Contract in no other way provides for the return of the Earnest Money, and whereas in point of fact Jones Homes had applied the Earnest Money toward the first expense involved in construction, namely the purchase of the lot:

NOW THEREFORE THIS COURT UPHOLDS DEFENDANT'S JUST RETENTION OF EARNEST MONEY, RENDERS JUDGMENT FOR THE DEFENDANT, AND DISMISSES THE COMPLAINT OF THE PLAINTIFFS.

5
SENTIMENTAL VALUE

How much things are worth is sometimes relative. People often claim more value for their property than it would actually fetch if they sold it. The reason for the disparity may be dishonesty; then again, some people are just misinformed about what they have. Others enhance the monetary value of something for sentimental reasons. If you sue for the value of property someone else is responsible for losing or destroying, you may be able to get more than it was worth, as long as you can show that it had some actual value to begin with. Getting extra damages awarded for sentimental value would then depend on convincing the Court that you will be harmed by the loss of the property, beyond the actual value of it. Proving that claim may be more difficult than most people think.

THE PLEADINGS

Shaw Smith came to the courthouse to file suit against three defendants: Michelle Jones, an employee of State Title Loans; State Title Loans itself; and Blackey's Auto Auction. Smith's car had been repossessed by State Title Loans and sold by Blackey's a few weeks afterwards. In his written Complaint, Smith wove a tale about having been told by friends that he shouldn't have gotten his title loan from State, how they recommended he get another loan from a competing company, and how this other company said they would pay off his first loan and give him a better deal. Something fell through, however, and Smith believed Michelle Jones had his car repossessed to get back at him for going to another company for a second loan. When the repossession took place, in the car were several items of property that were valuable in both a real and a sentimental way. Smith said the items "had not been returned to me."

State Title Loans filed an Answer explaining what had happened from their perspective, including information from the competing loan company saying that Smith never actually got the second loan. Jones co-signed State Title Loans' document and included a statement that Smith never made the first payment on the title loan. Blackey's wrote a letter as its Answer, explaining that they always leave personal property in the vehicles they tow and that Smith never came to their place of business until after his car had been sold.

THE EVIDENCE

The parties were unaccompanied by any other witnesses on the day of the hearing, though Eddie "Blackey" Pruett was in the gallery. I knew Blackey casually. He had hosted breakfasts for two dozen or so community leaders a few times a year. Occasionally he was sued over just such a matter as today's case, and he was well aware of the law involving personal property in repossessed cars. Eddie was not called on to testify, however.

One preliminary issue needed addressing. I had noted that Shaw Smith's long, typed-out explanation of his Complaint against the three defendants dwelled mostly on the reason he had not made any payments to State Title Loans, how they had repossessed his car "illegally," how Michelle Jones had acted with "malicious revenge" toward him, and how the towing service had violated the law. However, when he got to the matter of the money he was asking in damages, curiously, none of it was for being deprived of the car. All the damages he requested were for the personal property *in* the car.

"Mr. Smith," I said, "You have asked for damages for fishing equipment, a GPS, a family Bible, a dialysis kit, numerous medications and other items. All those things you valued at a total of $3,500.00. You have also asked for $4,000.00 in damages for pain and suffering. Is this correct?"

"Yes, your honor," said Smith.

"Is that all?" I asked.

"Yes, your honor."

After a pause to emphasize that I was not encouraging an amended Complaint, and would not at this point allow one, I continued speaking to Smith.

"You did not ask for damages for the repossessed vehicle, and you didn't indicate that you would ask for any further damages at court. In fact, you have asked for the jurisdictional limit already. However, a substantial portion of your Complaint dealt with the circumstances surrounding your getting a title loan and how your car was eventually repossessed.

"In the view of the Court, the matter of your getting a title loan, the question of your having defaulted on the loan, and all the other events leading up to the night your car was repossessed, are irrelevant to your Complaint, since you have asked only for damages for the lost personal possessions. Your Complaint alleges that the reason you ultimately lost the possessions is that nobody "gave them back" to you. Even if I allowed you to tell me the story from the beginning, and even if you were to prove your contention that the car shouldn't have been repossessed, you haven't asked for any damages for the loss of the car itself. One of the classic defenses against a lawsuit is that there are no damages. Since you haven't claimed any damages for the car itself, I see no need to hear about your claim that it was repossessed 'illegally.'"

"Uh," said Smith. "Okay." He understood the logic, but clearly he had hoped to tell a lengthy tale about how some mean people took his car.

"In the interest of time," I said in conclusion, "I'm ruling that you begin your testimony the night of the repossession."

I will admit to the reader that I was taking a slight risk at this point. Mr. Smith could have argued that the reason he lost his personal property was precisely because State Title Loans had illegally repossessed the car. That would tie the damages for the items in the car to the repossession itself, not just to the alleged illegal withholding of the items, once the car had been removed from Smith's driveway.

The problem with this argument was first that even if State had repossessed the car illegally, Smith could have gotten his property back through the *same* procedures as if the car had been taken back quite *legally*. The second problem with the argument, had Smith made it, was that the pleadings made very clear that the repo was on the up and up. Not only did Defendants allege that Smith had defaulted on the loan, but Smith *himself* admitted, though without meaning to, that he had defaulted. Ultimately, I believed, the reason Smith had not asked for $2,000.00 (or whatever) for the car itself was that he knew he couldn't show that it had been repossessed illegally.

I was prepared, however, to allow him to start at the beginning and tell me all about the loan, etc., if he objected to my ruling and claimed it was necessary to his case to recount the whole story. I was not really pressed for time, and one of the working principles of magistrate court is that people just want someone to hear them out. Smith didn't object, however. Nevertheless, it was difficult keeping both him and the various Defendants on track, because they had come expecting to defend themselves against the allegations of overcharging, deceit, vindictiveness, sneakiness, and illegality.

Plaintiff

Shaw Smith began, as instructed, on the night that Quicky Towing knocked on his door at about 9 o'clock on the previous March 6, a Thursday. A burly tow truck operator with a paper in his hand announced that Smith's car was being repossessed and gave him the paper, a form from State Title Loans, which included the number he could call the next day for information about where the car would be. The car was already on the rollback truck. (As Defendants later told the Court, per their policy, Quicky didn't allow a car's owner to retrieve anything from a car during a repo operation. Smith would be able to do that later.) Smith said there was no name on the truck, however, and he went into a panic not knowing where they were taking his car.

At this point, Shaw Smith began to recount in sweeping terms with indignation, desperation and pathos: how he was unable to find out where the car was; unable to get to anyplace he needed to be; in a medical crisis; and without information about how to recover his precious possessions from his car. In fact, he said, he knew the law, and the law says that if you don't want your car repossessed, the tower has to stop what he's doing. (Oddly enough, I didn't recall this law.) I listened carefully, however, and learned that by sometime the following day he had learned from State Title Loans that his car was at Blackey's Auto Auction.

He said he contacted Blackey's on the Saturday after the repossession. He didn't tell the Court the exact exchange of words, but he represented the conversation as being unhelpful. Smith said he made a few more contacts and finally contacted Blackey's again on March 10th. Blackey's told him that they didn't repo the car, that Quicky Towing did, and that Quicky was hired by State Title Loans.

I suspected that Blackey's also told Smith that he could come get his possessions, but Smith's testimony jumped from the matter of phone calls to his inability to travel to Blackey's. Smith lived about twenty miles away. Besides, his life was now complicated: he was disabled, being in dialysis three times a week (he managed to slip in the word "disabled" about a dozen times during his testimony); he had to go to doctors' appointments, etcetera, etcetera. Moreover, his HIV medicine had been in the car, he had experienced a breakdown once he didn't have his medicine, and he had to be put in the hospital. He didn't say whether or not it was an overnight stay, a week, or a single evening spent in the ER. I found the omission revealing.

Now, Smith began telling the Court what was in the car. He described the fishing equipment, telling me it had all been his father's and was the only thing he had of his father's in the world. The fishing equipment alone was worth $2,000.00. The family Bible was actually his wife's. She had died in his arms the previous year, and the Bible was precious to him. There was a dialysis bag, a kit he took with him to dialysis containing an iPod, headphones, and blankets. The kit also contained his HIV medicine. Finally, there was a leather vest from his truck club, which he said was worth $450.00.

On the phone, Smith asked State Title Loans to give him his possessions, but they denied they had them. According to Smith, the burly towing man had said that State would have his things. Smith argued with Michelle Jones at State Title Loans, who finally lost patience with him and kept telling him to go to Blackey's. Before he knew it, Smith said, the car had been sold. He called Blackey's and learned this fact, and asked about his possessions. They said they never removed anything from the car. If anything was in it, it stayed with the car when it was sold.

Smith now began to plead almost tearfully with the Court to simply give him some compensation for his possessions, to give him some justice. He had lost his only car, he was suffering, and now, to add insult to injury, he had lost his possessions, which meant so much to him.

I questioned Smith about the value of the things that were in the car. He went down the list, giving me round figures for the various items, totaling about $3,500.00. Then Smith asked for an additional $4,000.00 for the sentimental value. He wiped away a few tears (I didn't actually see them), and spoke in a broken voice, repeating how much these things meant to him, reminders as they were of the loved ones he had lost.

Smith then began to preach to the Court, telling me he knew the law, that an owner had the right to one opportunity to get his possessions out of a towed car. On this particular matter of the law he was correct. He had read the pertinent law—probably he had read the flyer I distribute to people who question the Court about their rights in towing situations. Smith said his rights had been violated, because his property "had not been returned" to him.

Smith was finished, but I had a few questions for him.

"Why were these *valuable* items in your car?"

"Well, the fishing equipment I used. I fished with it."

"And your medicine?"

"That's just where I keep it."

The dialysis bag I understood. But, "the Bible?" I asked? I would have carried a less precious Bible for car use, but then, that's just me.

"What can I say?" he answered. He had no explanation.

"Do you work?" I asked Smith.

With a look of incredulity, he said, "No. I'm disabled. I go to dialysis three times a week."

"I see. Now, Mr. Smith, when was the first time you went to Blackey's? Was it shortly after the 10th?"

"No, actually, your honor, it was on—and he stopped to flip through papers on his table. After a minute he said, "the 9th."

"The 9th of what?" I asked.

"June."

"Wait a minute," I said. The repossession took place on March 6; you contacted Blackey's by phone on March 8 and March 10, but you didn't go there until three months later? Is that correct?"

With very little expression and in a quieter voice, Smith said, "Yes, your honor."

"I see. All right, go on," I said. But Smith was finished.

The Defendants, perhaps lost in the somewhat tangled tale, didn't want to cross examine but merely to tell their side of the story, which is often the case.

Defendants

Up first, Michelle Jones started at the beginning with the loan made to Smith the previous December. I had to remind her that we were starting with the repossession. Skipping forward, she said that acting for State Title Loans, she had hired Quicky Towing to go get Smith's car, since he had defaulted on the title loan. State had used Quicky many times and Quicky was instructed to give certain information to the client so he or she would have contact numbers for State Title Loans. Smith did call State the day after the towing, and Jones told him both where to go to retrieve personal belongings and also when a sale would take place on the car. The date of the sale was *four weeks* away.

"Ms. Jones," I asked, "did you ever see or interact with Mr. Smith anywhere outside your business?"

"No, never," she said.

"Were you always acting in your role as an agent of State Title Loans?"

"Yes, your honor."

I told her to go on and she said that was pretty much it, except for Smith's repeated calls, and that on every occasion she would direct his inquiries to Blackey's.

In addition to Michelle Jones, another man had appeared to represent State Title Loans, and he added to her testimony. He told the Court that in fact the car had been sold not four weeks, but *six weeks* after repossession, so that Smith had even longer to get his property.

Finally, Blackey's testified. Howie Pruett, son of the owner, told me in straightforward language that Blackey's gets cars , puts them on the lot, and auctions them "as is." They don't go into the cars except to drive them to a parking place and later into the bay of the main building where the auction is taking place. They don't take anything out, and they certainly don't store items that were in the cars when they were towed in. It's the responsibility of the owner of the car to come request the opportunity to retrieve personal belongings from the car, after he shows proper identification as the person to whom the car is registered.

What's more, Pruett said, Smith had testified that he called Blackey's on Saturday, March 9. "We are *never* open on Saturdays, your honor. There's no way he called us on that day."

Smith had little of importance to ask or answer in cross examination.

THE JUDGMENT

I retreated to chambers for about a half hour and returned with a Judgment, which said in part:

I have a fair amount of compassion toward Mr. Smith in his life circumstances. My constable has been in dialysis for a year and a half while awaiting a kidney transplant. Three weeks ago he got 'the call' to go immediately to Jacksonville, Florida, 400 miles away, to have his surgery. I know he has been through a lot; so I know that Mr. Smith has had it hard.

My constable is not only my friend, but my employee, and I wanted to visit him. However, I had my own troubles: I shattered my knee about the time Mr. Smith's car was being repossessed, I didn't begin driving until four months later, and I limped around on a cane after that until very recently. Because of pain, stiffness and still-healing ligaments, I had difficulty with long traveling times. But I *needed* to go see him. It was an 800-mile round trip, but I went. *When you really need to go somewhere, you find a way.*

Now to your case, Mr. Smith. I am not hesitant to say that I have sympathy for you in these matters because I am going to be quick to say firmly to you and to the three defendants that I am not going to rule on your Complaint on the basis of sympathy. My decision will be made on the basis of the law and the evidence in this case.

In my office I am surrounded by a little collection I have made of photographs, paintings and figurines of Lady Justice. In most of these artistic works, three things are featured: the blindfold on the Lady's eyes, the scales of justice in her hand, and the books of law at her feet. She is blindfolded, so she will not judge by mere appearances, but judge righteously. She holds scales in which she weighs the evidence; and she stands firmly on the law as her standard. I am charged with the responsibility of making my decisions according to law and evidence, without sympathy or bias.

The law states that the owner of a towed car "has one opportunity to remove from the vehicle any personal property not attached to the vehicle," and that "the proprietor of the [place where the vehicle is towed] must release any personal property."

Note carefully that the proprietor has no responsibility to find the owner, call him, persuade him to come down to the shop, and give him his property. The onus, the initiative, the responsibility, is all upon the car's owner. If you're going to get it back, you have to go get it.

Now, what does the evidence show me?

1. All elements of the repossession, towing, delivery of the towed vehicle, storage of the vehicle, and sale of the vehicle were carried out properly in accordance with the law.

2. Plaintiff Smith knew where the vehicle was but did not appear at Blackey's for more than three months after the repossession, by which time and to his knowledge in fact, the car had been sold, with whatever possessions were in it.

The Court finds it curious and revealing that Mr. Smith said the physical objects in his vehicle were worth thousands of dollars, and many more thousands of dollars in sentimental value; however, they were not worth enough for him to hire a cab, or to pay an acquaintance for the time and gas to take him twenty miles, to retrieve these precious things. *When you really need to go somewhere, you find a way.*

Mr. Smith's heel dragging, though explained in part by his various medical woes, is not sufficient to justify his holding anyone else responsible for the loss of his property.

3. The Court dismisses Michelle Jones from the suit, since she was at all times acting as an agent of her business.

4. The Court dismisses the Complaint and renders Judgment for State Title Loans, on a finding that at no time did they have Plaintiff's property in their possession or were in any way a bailee for Plaintiff.

5. The Court dismisses the Complaint of Plaintiff against Blackey's Auto Auction, finding as I do that they complied with the law and did not refuse an attempt of the Plaintiff to reclaim his personal property, since he never presented himself and made any such request.

Court is dismissed.

6
THE PUPPET MASTER

Some people who appear in court without a lawyer may have consulted one beforehand. *Pro se* parties may purchase only an attorney's advice, not his decidedly more expensive presence for a trial. The cheapest route of all for quasi legal advice is going to one of many websites that describe procedures and legal filings for a small fee.

Occasionally, after consulting a lawyer and paying her several hundred dollars for advice, a Plaintiff may then want to recover those fees if he wins his case. Unless the lawyer came to court with him, however, legal fees won't be awarded. Still, some people think any legal advice is better than none, and they may still pay a lawyer for a billable hour or so, and then go it on their own when they get to court.

Sometimes, however, the legal advice a person seeks is questionable. Numerous times over the years I have detected the hand of someone in the background, someone with just enough knowledge of the law to be dangerous, guiding and advising either a plaintiff or a defendant. If these shadowy figures in the background are getting any payment for their services and are not lawyers, they are operating in violation of the law; however, many of them no doubt are simply avuncular relatives or friends, or occasionally, would-be lawyers availing themselves of the vast wealth of information on the Internet.

I concluded circumstantially that a young lady facing an eviction action was being guided by such a shadowy figure behind the scenes. The existence of this person was so obvious to me that I began to refer to him as the Puppet Master. I never met him, but he was most certainly pulling the strings.

THE PLEADINGS

Plaintiff Joyner Smith Properties came to the courthouse to file an Application for Ejectment against LaShonda Jones, alleging she was in arrears in rent. The Court's constable did not find Jones at home on his first attempt to serve her, and he posted the ten-day notice. Service of an eviction action can be made by two postings at least forty-eight hours apart followed by regular mailing of the notice. That was the plan, except that LaShonda Jones called the courthouse the second day after the posting and asked for more time. Our standard answer is that we can't give her more time; only the landlord can. She was told she might want to talk to Joyner Smith Properties.

By calling the court, Jones perfected service—the effect of a helpful rule of civil procedure—her phone call verified receipt of the Rule to Show Cause. At any rate, she did not ask for a hearing and she didn't indicate she was or would be contesting the eviction. Most people being evicted simply want more time; they know they're behind in rent, for instance, and they don't plan to come to court just to be told that fact.

The court clerk informed Jones that she would have ten days from that date to move or show cause why she shouldn't have to. The ten days passed without our hearing from LaShonda Jones. On the eleventh day, Joyner Smith Properties came to get a Writ of Ejectment, and the constable posted the Writ the next day.

Then the Puppet Master went into action. The day the Writ of Ejectment was posted, the tenant, or possibly the Puppet Master himself, appeared before the Circuit Court to file an Appeal. This was a somewhat odd thing to do. There had never been a hearing.

—The Circuit Court, sitting in its appellate capacity, does not try a case *de novo*. Instead, it reviews the magistrate court's recording of the case and looks at the evidence and any objections and motions, with the sole purpose of determining whether or not the magistrate judge made any sort of error in his conduct of the trial. If he committed a legal error somewhere that, in the view of the appellate judge, changed his judgment from what it would otherwise have been, they are likely to reverse or remand the case to the magistrate for re-hearing. Unless the mistake of the judge was in finding fact without any evidence to support it, or ignoring overwhelming evidence and finding a fact controverted by it, the appellate court will not otherwise disturb the ruling of the magistrate. Further, the appellate court will generally not just go looking for errors on its own: it responds to the appellant's identification of some alleged error, and it then rules on whether or not the appeal has merit.

Every lawyer knows how an appeal works, and knows what he needs to put in his appeal in order to ensure the maximum chance of having the magistrate's decision overturned or sent back for re-trial. (When the Circuit Court remands a case to the magistrate, it often says specifically that it is sending it back to the magistrate "for a finding not inconsistent with this ruling.") If LaShonda Jones had been represented by a real lawyer, he would have crafted an appeal that contained some sort of alleged error on my part. He didn't. This was my first indication that the Puppet Master was not actually an attorney. I believed that he or she was just someone who was going to help Jones fight to stay in her rental house for as long as she could. He was going to try to use the system to benefit the tenant at a cost to the landlord.

More obvious than this was the fact that there was little on which the tenant could base an allegation of magisterial mistake, since there had been *no trial!* So far, the case file consisted only of the Application for Ejectment, a copy of the Notice to Show Cause, and an Affidavit of Service. Since LaShonda Jones had failed to show cause or ask for a hearing to do so, Judgment was entered against her by default. There was therefore nothing for the appellate court to review.

Indeed, the appeal stated merely: "Comes now the Defendant before the Circuit Court and appeals the judgment of the magistrate." The second, brief paragraph was a quotation of a section of the landlord-tenant law stating that "it is sufficient to stay execution of a judgment for ejectment that the tenant sign an undertaking that he will pay to the landlord the amount of rent, determined by the magistrate in accordance with Section 27-40780, as it becomes due periodically after the judgment was entered."

In other words, to keep the constable from setting her out, Jones had to sign a bond that she would pay the landlord the rent. Right away, I set a hearing for determining the amount of bond. We held it in a few days.

Bond Hearing

Attending the hearing was Joyner Smith for the Plaintiff and LaShonda Jones, the Defendant, who was accompanied by a man about her age who took a seat in a row behind Defendant's table. He was a hefty and tall young man wearing a well fitted, gray suit, black rimmed glasses and a nondescript tie. I had a look at him, trying to size him up as a likely candidate for the Puppet Master. I believed he must be. He avoided my gaze, however, and didn't testify during the hearing. I thought I caught a quick glance by LaShonda Jones toward him at one point, however, which she probably wouldn't have done if he had simply been a friend lending moral support.

After explaining the sole purpose of the hearing as being to set a bond, I took testimony from each party as to how much money constituted the rent, past due and also due at the first of the month. Jones tried to give testimony about her objection to the eviction. Initially, I disallowed it because I assumed it was irrelevant to the setting of bond, but it became apparent to me that her objection had to do with her claim that she didn't owe any rent when Joyner Smith Properties took out the eviction action in the first place. Since that dispute affected the bond amount for the rent already due, I allowed her to explain her point.

Jones had decided not to renew her lease, recently expired. For two months, she had gone on a month-to-month basis, which Smith allowed, and then she had given a thirty day notice.

However, when she gave notice, she also failed to pay rent. Her position was that Smith could take her $1,000.00 security deposit as her last month's rent. When Smith filed for eviction after Jones defaulted in rent, Jones was convinced that Smith Properties was in the wrong since they already had $1,000.00 in hand to cover her last month.

No doubt, Smith *would* appropriate the deposit for the unpaid rent, but that was not the point, and it was not yet the time to do so. I asked Jones if she weren't still in the property. Yes. I asked her if she knew the purpose of a security deposit. This was when she shot a quick glance back to the Puppet Master, but he imitated the Sphinx and gave her no help. I explained that the security deposit's purpose was to secure the landlord against damage to the rental property beyond normal wear and tear. Yes, the landlord could also keep the deposit for back rent, but not until after Jones had surrendered the property. If they used it before she left, they would have no money to fix damages beyond normal wear and tear, if there should happen to be any.

Jones seemed to understand, but her assent was nervous. She seemed to be trying to say little more than she had obviously rehearsed in the presence of the Puppet Master. She did not otherwise contest the testimony of Smith about the amount of rent.

Since "the amount of rent...as it becomes due" included the amount *already* due as well as what would come due in about nine days, I set the bond at $2,200.00 payable to the landlord within five business days, followed by a promise to continue paying the landlord $1,000.00 in rent each month as long as the appeal was pending. Privately, I knew it wouldn't be pending very long.

I also doubted that LaShonda Jones would pay December's rent. I closed the hearing by issuing the bond and requiring that Jones sign it. It would be ready for her at the court window in a few minutes.

After I returned to chambers, my clerk came to tell me that upon their exiting the courtroom, Jones and her mysterious companion huddled together in a corner of the lobby, and that the nameless man in gray was rapidly and intensely explaining to LaShonda everything I had said and what it meant. Actually, I thought I had been quite clear and non-technical in what I said in the courtroom, but the Puppet Master was making certain that his client, whom I was beginning to see more as his marionette, was up to speed on everything.

Jones signed the bond and went her way. In the office we wondered aloud whether or not she would make her payment of $2,200.00 to Smith Properties by the next Wednesday, which would be the last of five business days. The odds were not in her favor.

Emergency Hearing

We were surprised, however, when the very next day the Puppet Master himself returned to the court to serve, on behalf of LaShonda Jones, a copy of a Request for Emergency Hearing by the Circuit Court. It was clearly intended to look like a lawyer's work, though its type was too small and here and there were some odd or awkward phrases I thought unlikely to have come from an actual attorney. The highlights were as follows:

- Quoting another portion of the statute on a Bond to Stay, the Puppet Master—or the Defendant, if you choose to believe that she had the smarts to have written either this document or the appeal—asked the Circuit Court to modify the bond. He—or she—objected to having to pay money to the landlord. The request alleged that bond money should be paid to the clerk of court (Circuit Court was implied) and not the landlord.
- Going further, the request alleged that the magistrate had "wrongly interpreted the literal meaning of the statute."
- After these polite accusations, the Puppet Master quoted case law where a judge had written that "a court cannot rewrite the statute and inject into it matters which are not in the legislature's language." (The Puppet Master's view was that the legislature, while writing, "pay to the landlord," didn't actually mean it.)

- Next to last, the filing stated that "the Bond to Stay is being provided to the Clerk of Court for the county in the amount of $2,200.00."
- Finally, and fortunately for me, he had requested the magistrate to hold a hearing *before* any Circuit Court hearing, for the purpose of "clarifying the law."

This last request, I assumed, was either a shot across the bow, for the purpose of giving me one final chance to 'get it right,' or it was a genuine attempt to show deference to the magistrate court. I assumed it was the former.

Before the sun had reached its high point in the sky, I had set a hearing to 'clarify the law.' Then I sat down and wrote a four page paper on the relevant statutes, and waited five days to use it. Before putting the finishing touches on it, I asked my clerk to call the county Clerk of Court. What she told me was interesting.

Hearing to Clarify Law

When the parties sat down on the Tuesday before the last day Jones had to pay the back rent, the young man I was certain was operating the puppet strings came with LaShonda Jones and took a seat beside her at the defense table. He occupied the chair that lawyers usually take there, and I looked at him expectantly, my face asking the obvious question of whether or not he were her attorney. I was able to get out of my mouth, "Are you"— when he held up his hands in front of his chest and ever so slightly shook his head.

He responded in a small and soft voice, "Oh, no, I'm not— I'm just"— to which I answered:

"You're just here for moral support?" I smiled good naturedly, and he smiled back, and sat down. He was good; I'll have to grant him that. He hadn't given away his identity as the Puppet Master, if I had been looking for evidence worthy of court. I wasn't, however.

I politely gave Jones the opportunity to summarize her position on the law. By this time I knew she was not the person who had written the documents filed with the Circuit Court and that she probably would have little to say. I was not wrong. She stammered and then managed to repeat the essential objection she had to the Bond to Stay:

"I was just—it was just that I objected—that I believe that the bond should be paid into the court instead of the landlord."

I waited for more, but there wasn't any. After a long pause, I asked her if she had anything else. I said it was all being recorded and I wanted her to feel that she had made her argument plain. She didn't even look at the paper the Puppet Master had filed. She obviously hadn't been prepared to summarize it or present an oral argument for her position—after all, the document was not her words. This time, she didn't look back at her shadowy friend. She looked at me like a deer in the headlights and finally gave a little hand gesture that accompanied her words, "That's all."

"All right," I said. "You've asked for a clarification of the law, and I have prepared a ruling that I'm going to put on the record." I glanced briefly and purposefully at the Puppet Master when I said this, as if telling him that the following four pages in front of me were for him, not her. The look I got back was enough for me to tell that he knew I was onto him.

I won't include the whole four pages here, only a few excerpts:

Defendant states that "the court may have misinterpreted the literal meaning of the statute." The phrase is curious. One may misinterpret a statute, but the literal nature of something is just that: literal—the words themselves. The particular statutes in question are not obscured in the fog of legalese. Four times the statute says: "Pay to the landlord." It refers to the landlord's giving the tenant a receipt, and it speaks of paying the landlord "as rent becomes due." The *literal* language is quite clear: *pay the landlord.*

Defendant stated in her motion that the legislature intended "to afford all parties proper due process and fairness." Due process is what the law requires in its plain language, and this

Court has followed that law in a careful and exacting way. While Defendant implies by her citations of case law that this Court has rewritten the statute by requiring her to pay the landlord instead of the court, I refer her to the law where repeatedly the statute says, "pay the landlord." If the citations support anyone, they buttress the decisions of this Court.

As to Defendant's citation of a statute speaking of paying bond to the county's Clerk of Court, that statute is what we call a general provision. Where a specific statute provides otherwise, we must abide by the specific, applicable statute. The statute in this case could not be more clear: "Pay the landlord."

Finally, this Court cites the county Clerk of Court, who to this Court not twenty-four hours ago denied any knowledge of ever having received a payment on a Bond to Stay Execution of a Writ of Ejectment issued by a Magistrate Court. The Clerk informed this Court that she refused Defendant's proffered payment of $2,200.00. As of this hour, I assume that money is still in Defendant's hand.

[Parenthetically the reader should know that in fact, the Clerk had told me that the person who tried to pay her the bond was not LaShonda, but some hefty and tall young man in a gray suit. The Clerk also told me that a hearing had been scheduled for eight days away, on the motion to modify the bond. I told her I would send her the results of my own hearing to 'clarify the law.' I thought it was likely that if I then dismissed the appeal the day afterward, the Circuit Court would cancel its hearing on bond modification, which would be moot anyway.]

[Looking at Defendant] You have just a little more than twenty-four hours to make payment of bond for the past due amount of rent *to the landlord*. If you do not, then in accordance with the statute, the Stay will be lifted, the Appeal you filed will be dismissed *by me,* and the Writ will be executed.

I offered Jones a chance to ask any questions. She had none. She was overwhelmed. It wasn't my first purpose to overwhelm her, only to answer the implied accusations of my unfairness, ineptitude, and ignorance. My response was directed at her only incidentally. My real target was the Puppet Master. When Jones had whispered or muttered her surrender, I looked over at her friend, ever so briefly. I hoped I had overwhelmed him just a little bit, too.

Immediately after the hearing was over, I faxed to the county Clerk of Court the ruling I had just read into the record in my court. The Clerk had promised me whatever I sent she would put into their case file right away, so I had no doubt that the judge who had already been assigned to the appeal (who, incidentally, had upheld me recently in an appeal in another, significant case) would read my ruling.

A Waiting Game

The only thing left to do was to wait for twenty-four hours to see if LaShonda would pay the landlord, Joyner Smith Properties.

Ms. Jones's last day to pay was the Wednesday before Thanksgiving. I was taking that day off, and I asked my clerk to call Smith Properties just before closing time to see if Jones had paid them the $2,200.00 back rent owed as part of the bond. When I didn't hear from her, I assumed that Jones had paid. It was the only way for her to go forward.

However, the following Monday when I returned to work, I learned that Jones had not made payment after all. Immediately, I instructed the constable to arrange a time within forty-eight hours to set out Jones and her possessions. It did not make me happy to eject someone, especially during the holidays—it never does. However, someone who plays the system without a meritorious case, and impugns the fairness of the Court to boot, doesn't get an apologetic response from me. You mess with the bull, you get the horns.

I also wrote up a Dismissal of Appeal, citing the appropriate statute, and faxed it to the Clerk of Court. Then I had my constable take the original over to the county courthouse by hand.

The next day, after the time of their hearing, I called the Clerk to see what had been done. The circuit court judge had promptly dismissed the motion to modify the bond, and he acknowledged the dismissal of the appeal.

I learned that LaShonda Jones had gone to the county courthouse but to the wrong courtroom that day, and that the judge sent messages down the hall to the other courtrooms to try to locate her. The judge in courtroom 3, where Jones mistakenly was, told her to go to courtroom 8, but for mysterious reasons I never found out, when she left the wrong place she never showed up in the right place. It was one floor up and down the hall.

I suspect that by that point she had just given up.

The next day the constable went to execute the Writ, finding that Jones was about half moved out already. It took her another half day, and she was gone.

According to my constable, Jones lived in the rental unit with her two children and a boyfriend, who wasn't there at first but showed up later. He was a hefty and tall young man. The Puppet Master.

7
SECOND VERSE, SAME AS THE FIRST

The Magistrate Court doesn't do divorces, even though the Magistrate is empowered to do weddings. Once you're hitched, no matter how humble the officiant, it takes a Circuit Court Judge, in the Family Court, to unhitch you.

A Magistrate, however, occasionally does get a case involving people who used to be married, or who live together as if they're married, or who just about got married but didn't. Two out of three of these possibilities describe a case between a couple who came before the Court one winter.

THE PLEADINGS

Tamara Smith filed a Summons and Complaint against Deon Jones alleging that he had broken their engagement after she had spent a lot of money and gone to a lot of trouble to relocate from Maryland to South Carolina to marry him. As damages she wanted: expenses for moving to South Carolina; reimbursement for money she gave Jones to pay bills; moving expenses from the South Carolina apartment to another apartment of her own in the same city after the breakup; anticipated expenses for moving back to Maryland; the cost of the marriage license; and the balance of the Magistrate Court monetary limit for "embarrassment and emotional distress."

Deon Jones's Answer said that he admitted to breaking off the engagement; however, he stated that after he broke up with Tamara he offered her about $2,700.00 to move back to Maryland, but she refused it. He agreed that because of her justifiable expectations he owed her something, but not everything she was asking. The Court scheduled a trial.

THE EVIDENCE

Tamara Smith was a stylish woman of about forty-five who appeared to be composed and organized as she sat at the Plaintiff's table with several files full of papers. Deon Jones was a hefty truck driving man who appeared dressed for work. He had nothing in front of him but his propped elbows.

Plaintiff

Tamara Smith gave the Court a brief story of her having lived in Maryland, her original home, where she was taking care of her mother who was dying of cancer. By phone she and Defendant Deon Jones, who lived in my county, were moving toward a possible engagement. Smith explained that she and Jones had been married formerly. (I didn't know this until trial.)

I asked Tamara to tell me something about that, and she said she and Deon had been married about ten years and had lived here in South Carolina. They divorced about fifteen years ago and within two months he married some younger woman in their church, but the new couple had the marriage annulled within six months. Within a year or so Tamara and Deon established communications with each other and over the years they re-established a comfortable relationship, principally by phone.

In December of the previous year, Tamara's mother died. Not long afterward, Smith's sister, who also lived in Maryland, died as well. Having no family left to keep her in Maryland, Tamara began to think about returning to South Carolina. She and Jones arranged for her to visit briefly, and while she was in South Carolina, Deon Jones proposed to her and gave her a ring. Before she returned to Maryland, Tamara and Deon went to the county building and got a marriage license. Tamara paid the fee.

Back in Maryland, Tamara set about winding things down and preparing to move. In the interim she sent Deon money now and again to help with household expenses, looking at it as an investment. By May, she was ready to leave her job. She testified specifically that she gave the required two-week notice at work that she would be leaving. Once she left her company she was free to move, and she did so in a short time, arriving in South Carolina the first of June.

Here's where the story gave rise to the suit. Tamara Smith moved in with Deon Jones. An actual wedding date was not set, but they planned to take vows within a very short time and without hoopla. They might even have gone to a Magistrate to do the deed.

There were a few bumps in the road, as she called them. One was a disagreement about church. She said Deon wanted her to go to church with him, at the same church they had both attended before the divorce. He was still a member there. Tamara said, "No, huh uh, I wasn't gonna go where that woman was, no way! I told him we would just have to agree to disagree about some things."

However, eight days after she moved in, she said Deon came to her one morning before he went off to drive his truck for several days, and he said, "What are we doing?"

Tamara thought that one comment summed it all up, but she filled in a few blanks by saying that Deon explained that "things weren't going to work," and he wanted them to be "just friends." She said that she told him she had moved and given up everything to come marry him and now he wanted to be just friends? She was incensed and hurt.

Deon left for his long haul truck trip. When he came back, Tamara had moved out, into an apartment nearby. She filed her suit against Deon within two months.

Smith moved a number of documents into evidence showing amounts of money spent on moving and the like. About $3,500.00 of her alleged damages were for these things. The other $3,500.00 she wanted for emotional distress. I asked her about that, thinking to myself that she didn't seem very distressed today. She briefly spoke about her embarrassment and added some tautological comments about being hurt. Interestingly, she gave this summary, as she did all her other testimony, in a matter-of-fact manner with a very pleasant look on her face.

Defendant

Deon Jones didn't want to question Tamara, but he did want to tell his side of things. His tale matched Tamara's in the major facts of their deciding to get married, her visit, the proposal, her moving, the eight days, and even his terse, quizzical announcement: "What are we doing?" However, Deon wanted the Court to know *why* he had decided to get married again, *what* had happened with Tamara's work in Maryland, and *why* he had broken things off after just eight days together again in his apartment in South Carolina.

First, Deon gave me a thumbnail sketch of their previous marriage, which had produced two children and a lot of heartache. Deon said Tamara used all sorts of tactics to get her way in the marriage, including withholding sex. With her it was always her way or the highway. However, it wouldn't have been Deon who hit the highway: he told the Court that Tamara had left him no fewer than seven times in their ten years of marriage.

Deon told several little stories about their married life that led the Court to the following conclusion:

While Tamara had been controlling by nature, Deon was not easily controlled, and when they fought and he wouldn't give in, she went out the door. When he relented and begged her to return, she did, and the cycle repeated.

When Tamara left the last time, she filed for divorce. Then she moved back to Maryland to be with family. (The two had met at a nearby, South Carolina university when they were in school.)

Over the next decade or so as they kept in touch, the long distance relationship seemed to improve, especially as Tamara's mother became ill. During the entire previous year, Deon and Tamara seemed to come to a more mature understanding, albeit at a distance. By the time Tamara's mother was at death's door, Deon said he believed Tamara had changed. He believed they could make things work this time if they remarried.

On the strength of that hope, and in response to Tamara's initiative, not his (which I found entirely credible), he agreed to move toward getting married.

Deon interrupted his account of his and Tamara's reunification saga to comment on her work situation. From what Tamara had told him on the phone, work was not Shangri-La. She didn't get along with her supervisor and she had underlings who didn't like her. When she gave notice at work, they wanted her to train her replacement. When she balked, they fired her and walked her out of the building. Tamara had not given me the whole picture, and Deon wanted to tell it like it was, because, as I thought, he wanted me to get a little different impression of the kind of personality Tamara had.

From Deon's account, together with little clues from Tamara's attitude and her editing of her story, I was able to gather that Tamara could be very difficult to live with. She was putting on a very good act for the Court, but subtle body language now and then, plus the cold hard facts—not contradicted by her, by the way—began to reveal what she was probably like at home.

Back to the tale of not-so-blissful pre-marital life, Deon said that the very day Tamara moved back in with him after fifteen years apart, he realized that in fact she had not changed at all. He had thought she had mellowed and matured, but she hadn't. She came in with a bang, beginning to run his life the way she had tried to do before. Her skills at manipulation had improved, if anything. They argued about things great and small. The matter of what church they would attend was just one thing. All in all the situation was like a lyric from a Herman's Hermits song: "Second verse, same as the first." He saw the same old trouble coming at him again, fast.

On the church matter Deon backtracked to tell me about his brief marriage to a woman who was in their congregation. The rapid union had been a great mistake, he said, that he made simply because he was trying to fill the great gap left by his divorce. The two had not been involved before Deon and Tamara's divorce (a fact that Tamara did not dispute) and Deon and this other woman had not been involved since they had their marriage annulled. In fact, there had been no one in Deon's life romantically since his divorce from Tamara. He tried to convince Tamara there was no reason they had to find a different church because there was no issue with this other woman, but Tamara was intractable. He also said she was "incapable of loving."

Deon said with a huff, "Agree to disagree, huh! Your honor, it was an all out fight. There weren't no agree to disagree about it. She wanted her way about everything. I realized after just a week that there weren't no way it was gonna work, no how. That's why I axed her that day, just before I left for work, 'What are we doin'?' I knew it wasn't gonna work." Deon then rested his chin on his interlaced hands and turned his face away toward the wall, as he had done repeatedly throughout Tamara's testimony. He was barely controlling his emotions, trying not to cry.

After composing himself, Jones added to his testimony that he had told Tamara she didn't have to move out right away, though he understood she might want to move back to Maryland soon. He said he told her there was plenty of room and she could stay until she was ready to return to her family home.

Plaintiff's rebuttal

I gave Tamara the opportunity to give me rebuttal testimony, and she made a few defensive comments about her resignation, trying to spin things back her way, but without much credibility. The matter was not really relevant anyway. Then she revisited the disagreement about church and insisted that she would have felt very uncomfortable being around Deon's second wife. Finally, she waxed moral and said firmly that living with Deon after the breakup was unthinkable; she had to have her own apartment until she might move back to Maryland.

What was significant about her rebuttal was what Tamara Smith did *not* say about Deon Jones's testimony. She did *not* attempt to contest his depiction of her being argumentative or controlling; she merely nitpicked little incidents.

When she was through, I asked Tamara Smith about the ring. She had pawned it, she said. "The man told me it wasn't even a diamond, either," she said, with a hostile glance at the other table. "I got maybe fifty dollars out of it."

The parties were finished. The early afternoon hearing had gone on for two hours and I wanted to look at everything and think it over before sending my decision to them in a day or two.

THE JUDGMENT

The written Judgment was long; I wanted to explain my findings in great detail, because I threaded a line between the two sides like the Mississippi works its way through the hills and valleys of the Midwest. To summarize the major findings:

First, I found that a contract between the parties existed, namely the engagement agreement, and that Defendant Jones had breached that contract. As a result, Plaintiff Smith had incurred some damages. The damages were foreseeable and directly consequential. Plaintiff's moving expenses from Maryland were the simplest and clearest damages she incurred. I awarded her moving expenses.

I dismissed Plaintiff's contributions to Defendant's household; they were not required by the terms of the engagement, and nothing Smith said justified awarding her their repayment. Smith had argued that she would not have sent Jones any money if not for the engagement. I said in my Judgment, however: "The obligations of the engagement contract cannot be seen as continually expanding over the period of the engagement or as covering a widening network of activities under the theory that they were occasioned in some way by the anticipation of marriage."

I awarded Plaintiff the cost of the marriage license, but I dismissed the prospective moving costs back to Maryland. However, I gave Plaintiff the cost of moving out of Jones's apartment. "Defendant as a reasonable person should have been aware that breaking up with Plaintiff would result in the emotional necessity of her moving out," I said.

Finally, I dealt with the claim for "emotional distress:"

> Plaintiff's request for damages for emotional distress is understandable. Given no more facts than a couple engaged for a year then going through a breakup, one might anticipate that a party innocent of the breakup would be aggrieved and that emotional distress would be expected. However, the facts of this case, as the Court took pains to find, are that Plaintiff contributed materially to the disagreeableness that disturbed Defendant and pushed him towards breaking off the engagement. There was no hint in testimony that Defendant had another romantic liaison or any other motive for discontinuing the marriage plans. The conflict that Plaintiff wanted to waive off as "needing to agree to disagree," Defendant characterized as fundamental conflicts of personality and harbingers of serious discord. The Court's impression of the couple's brief lives together in June of this past year aligns with Defendant's description. It does not appear to the Court that Defendant's breaking up with Plaintiff came entirely out of the blue as a capricious and totally unwarranted decision, violently destroying Plaintiff's emotionally sunshiny day and joyous outlook. A real relationship is almost always more complex than that, and the Court believes that it was so in this case.

> As well, the Court was profoundly aware that, of the two parties in the courtroom, Defendant was the person clearly under a severe weight of emotional distress. While the Court was not present to observe the parties in the weeks just after the breakup, the parties' respective disclosures of their mind-sets, their emotions, and their actions during that period lead the Court to find that Plaintiff did not suffer a level of distress that is actionable. The Court therefore denies the request for damages for emotional distress.

The total award I made to the Smith was $2,750.00, almost the same thing Jones offered her when he broke off the engagement, to cover her move back home. I suspect he paid her quickly and hoped to put this matter to rest. He probably regarded it as far less expensive than the cost to his life of going through "deja vu all over again."

8
NOWHERE TO GO

Federally subsidized housing has its own set of rules that sometimes are more daunting to live by than many private leases. One of the rules that bite fast and hard is that tenants can be evicted for illegal activity, even if they haven't been convicted of the alleged illegal activity in a court of law. The owners of federally subsidized housing do not have to meet the standard of proof that applies in the court in criminal matters—"beyond reasonable doubt." Being arrested and charged with a crime is sufficient. However, a tenant doesn't even have to have been charged with a crime; if the owner determines to his satisfaction that illegal activity has taken place—such as drug use—he can terminate the lease. The tenant has a right under Federal law to a grievance hearing, but that hearing is private, between landlord and tenant. The landlord can still end the lease.

That's where the court comes in, however, because a landlord cannot forcibly remove a tenant without going through the court. By the time an eviction action is brought pursuant to a claim of illegal activity, usually all the proper procedures have been followed, and it's all over but the crying.

Sometimes, the crying takes place in court.

THE PLEADINGS

Smith Grove Apartments did business with the Court in the form of a dozen or more filings at a time, month after month. Its tenants were mostly Section 8, persons who have a voucher for all or a substantial portion of their rent and who owe only the balance to the owner. Gladys Smith brought her usual armload of cases to the Court one winter's day, including one against elderly Sybil Jones, who recently had been charged with malicious damage to private property. Smith wanted her out.

Once the papers were served on Jones, someone, not Jones, called on her behalf saying he represented her and she wanted a hearing. The Court was led to believe the representative was her attorney, and as a matter of routine, the clerk scheduled a hearing.

THE EVIDENCE

Plaintiff and Defendant and their respective witnesses filed into the small, alternate courtroom on the day of trial, lending a slightly less formal feel to the proceedings. There was insufficient space for everyone involved, however. Plaintiff Gladys Smith appeared with an assistant at her table. Defendant Sybil Jones, a man about her age leaning on a cane, and another man and woman, positioned themselves at the other table, the younger man remaining standing for lack of a seat. There was no attorney for Ms. Jones; apparently the younger of the two men on her side was the one who had called the courthouse, and he was not a lawyer.

I had been at the county building and was late returning to the courthouse, one of those rare instances in which I was not on the bench by the precise hour of a hearing. I decided to begin with an apology and a little levity to relax the little crowd.

"Folks," I said, "You were here when the Court summoned you to be, and I apologize for being late, myself. It's a rare occasion, and I'm sorry you were the exception to the rule. I was in the circuit court a few weeks ago for a roll call due to begin at 9:00 a.m., and it didn't begin until 10:30. I patted myself on the back for having a higher standard, and now, I'm late by almost thirty minutes." Everyone smiled forgivingly. "The worst part of it is," I continued, "you might begin to think this was your doctor's office or the E.R."

That got an outright laugh by all present, and I felt everyone relax. I swore in the Plaintiff and listened as she quietly got down to business.

Plaintiff

Ms. Smith took barely three minutes to review with the Court her testimony, summarized already on her Application for Ejectment. Smith said Sybil Jones had been arrested at her apartment door for having vandalized her husband's truck. Police responded to a call, interviewed Mr. Jones and others, and then went to Sybil Jones's apartment, where they spoke with her briefly and then put her in handcuffs.

The apartments have a lengthy and detailed lease with each of their occupants and they operate under Federal guidelines as well, both of which list criminal activity as justification for termination of a tenant's lease. Smith gave Jones notice of termination. Jones asked for a grievance hearing before the apartment's board and was granted it as required by law. She appeared by herself at that hearing. The board determined after a hearing of both parties that it would continue to pursue the eviction on the basis of the State's charge of malicious damage against Sybil Jones. There was no doubt she had committed the offense: she admitted that she had written obscenities in magic marker on her ex-husband's truck.

Smith had nothing more to add at the moment, and I asked if Ms. Jones would like to ask her any questions.

Defendant

Sybil Jones was a somewhat elderly woman, perhaps seventy-five, short of stature, with a screwed up face that seemed to descend from all points into a tightly pinched mouth. She appeared to have no teeth. She had sat mute until this point, and while at first I thought it was because she was angry—she looked it—I began to think that it was instead because she was not entirely present with us, and/or that she wasn't hearing much of what was being said. In fact, I had to repeat my question as to whether or not she had anything to ask the witness..

"Can these people talk?" she said, motioning to the three others she had brought with her. I said if she wanted to call them as witnesses in a moment, certainly they could testify, but for now, did she have any questions for Ms. Smith? No, she didn't

So I asked Ms. Jones, "Do you have a defense against the eviction?"

"What?" she said. I couldn't tell if she hadn't heard me, even though I was speaking clearly and firmly and was barely eight feet away from her, or if she didn't understand the question. I decided to rephrase as well as turn up the volume.

"I said, do you have anything you would like to tell me in defense against being evicted?"

"Let them tell you," she said tersely, as if implying she didn't know how to go about giving a defense, or didn't really have any. So far, I didn't know what the other people were here for, including the elderly gentleman who I didn't yet know was her husband. Nevertheless, I looked toward them and the younger man standing behind the table raised his hand as if he would like to be the first.

André Jackson, it turns out, was no relation to Ms. Jones, nor a resident of the apartments. Right off the bat, in fact, he said something I might have taken as good reason to disallow his testimony.

"Your honor, we're actually not witnesses. We're more advocators [sic]. I'm the director of a behavioral health center where Ms. Jones has been receiving services. Now, Ms. Jones has agreed she's guilty, and obviously the lease says if she's arrested, she can be removed. We'd like to see her remain in her place, and we're trying to do all we can to keep her there, for several reasons.

"Number one, she has nowhere else to go. I know that under no grounds does that make her right, but that's what we're here to plead for. She's paid her rent on time and she's never been in any trouble before, okay? But the night her husband came by, she hadn't taken her medication on time. And again, she's a mental health patient who's been diagnosed schizophrenic, bipolar, as well as depression, okay? As we know, in many cases, participants in a program like ours, providing psychotropic therapy and so on, these participants aren't always like we are, especially when under anxiety. And that's what happened to her: she had an anxiety attack and she wrote on her husband's car. [Big breath.]

"Ms. Jones has gone through cardiac arrest; she had a heart attack not long ago. She was just admitted to a psychiatric hospital a few months before she was placed in our program, to get her the help she wants and needs. And that's what we're here for, to advocate on her behalf, okay? because at this point, she doesn't have a place to go. [Big breath.]

"She only pays a hundred bucks a month because she's on low income housing; and every place we've called, fifty or a hundred places between here and the surrounding cities, all of the housing authorities have lists two or three years long. [Quick breath.]

"Our concern is her health. She lives alone, and she's taking several medications, and she can't remember when to take them. We've hired a medication administration coach who will help her to get on schedule."

Jackson had gone on for about five minutes in a fairly rapid delivery. I had not interrupted him because I had determined to allow the "testimony," though it might well have been considered irrelevant. Jackson, however, interrupted himself at this point:

"Your honor, this"—and he gestured to the woman sitting in front of him—"is Tiffany Green, and she has dealt more directly with Ms. Jones and she can tell you what's going on with her on a day-to-day basis outside the program, as well as what treatment she is receiving." Tiffany raised a sheaf of notes to reading position in front of her and opened her mouth to speak, but I held her off with my raised hand.

"If this were a Probate hearing concerning Ms. Jones's commitment to mental health care," I said, "Ms. Green's testimony would be appropriate for me to hear. As it is, I don't believe it would be appropriate or relevant to this hearing. As well, Mr. Jackson, your 'testimony' is more in the way of argument—in the legal sense." Jackson nodded and understood completely. After all, he had begun his spiel by disavowing that he was a really a witness.

"May I assume," I continued, "that you have no further testimony in the way of defense, Ms. Jones?"

Jones just looked at me with that toothless, pinched mouth, as if she were not really in the room. Jackson stepped in.

"This is Ms. Jones's ex-husband, sir. He's the one who was actually involved."

I looked at the ex, looked back at Ms. Jones, and asked her, "Do you want your ex-husband to testify?"

Jones looked at me as if taking a few seconds to register what I had said, then looked at her ex-husband, and back at me. "Yeah, let him talk," she said. I swore in the ex and asked for his name.

"Rev. Jessie Jones," he said. I decided to take the initiative and ask him questions. If I let loose an elderly preacher, he might wax both eloquent and lengthy. I had personal experience to speak from.

"Did you take part in a grievance hearing that Ms. Jones had with Smith Grove Apartments?"

"No," he said. "I tried to go up to the court and dismiss the charges, but they wouldn't let me talk to the judge."

"What judge?" I asked.

"Judge Johnson," said Rev. Jones.

The malicious damage charge was in Johnson's court, not mine. It should have been in mine, but it was just one of hundreds of charges every year that wound up in Johnson's court simply because officers took all traffic cases to him (our county has four regional traffic courts, to consolidate the efforts of the sheriff's department). The deputies took all of their other criminal cases up to Johnson for their own convenience, never mind the rules.

"I see," I said to Jones. "Well, he wasn't being rude to you; ethically he could not give you a hearing by yourself. Both the state and the defendant have to be present for a hearing. If you were acting on the defendant's part, it would have been an *ex parte* hearing of the kind not allowed." Jones nodded.

I turned to Ms. Smith and asked her if Smith Grove was aware of the details of the incident between the divorced spouses. No, she said, they were not; they just knew about the arrest and the damage to Rev. Jones's truck. What I was wondering is if they had enough knowledge about the actual incident that led up to the arrest to have made an informed decision at the grievance hearing as to whether or not to proceed with the eviction.

Thinking that the Apartments might be interested in the background of the original dispute between Jones and Jones, I let Rev. Jones speak a little more. However, he didn't tell me anything about the dispute, only that he wanted to drop the charges against his former wife.

"Rev. Jones," I said, "Dropping the charge is not yours to do, not even the judge's to do, but the deputy's, or the solicitor's. At any rate, that matter is before a different judge, and it really doesn't pertain to this case."

André Jackson wanted to add something to his previous testimony, and I allowed him to do so. He emphasized that Smith Grove didn't know what kind of person they were dealing with in Ms. Smith (and he implied they didn't care), and that he had tried to contact Smith Grove hundreds of times in the past month (—I doubted the accuracy of his count), but he couldn't get through most of the time. When he did, he was given an answer that Smith Grove's policy was not to speak with any advocate for Jones unless it were an attorney. Jackson said he had referred to a release-of-information form that gave him the privilege of speaking on Jones's behalf, but such a release wasn't enough for them. Jackson criticized the corporate rules as insensitive, and he argued that they should have some way of authorizing discussion about people's needs.

I glanced casually about the bench and courtroom and let my eyes take in the Plaintiff briefly. I was looking to see if she were showing any reaction to the direction of the testimony/argument. She appeared completely serene. Meanwhile, Jackson came to a stopping point and I took the opportunity to call an end to the Defense's defense.

"Ms. Smith, do you have any questions of any of these witnesses?" I said.

"No," she said very calmly, "but I do have some rebuttal." I signaled her to continue, and she did.

"As you know, your honor, we have a contract with each of our tenants. It is unfortunate for Ms. Jones, but we can't pick and choose who we evict for criminal activity. If we did, we would expose ourselves to lawsuit. In Ms. Jones's case, it wasn't the first time we had had problems with her. A resident complained about her previously, and in her complaint form she said"—

"Ms. Smith," I interrupted, "I know that you don't have that complainant here, and so I'm going to rule her statement inadmissable."

"All right, your honor," she said, "but as I said, we have had trouble with her before. And she didn't pay her rent last month."

I questioned Smith about the rent, thinking perhaps that if Jones had defaulted on rent, that would be sufficient reason for her being evicted, even without the criminal activity allegation. It turned out that Jones had not paid on time, but that Smith Grove had accepted payment a day late. Under the law, Smith Grove could still evict, but they had made their case on the criminal activity and had not even pled the late payment of rent as a cause of action. I dropped the subject.

I thought we were finished, but the young woman who came with Jackson wanted to speak. After asking Sybil Jones if she wanted the woman to testify, I allowed it.

Tiffany Green was sworn in. Again she raised her sheaf of papers, and she began to read a statement that she had prepared. It sounded like a speech to a community gathering, acquainting them with the behavioral health program. If the speech had continued in that vein, I would have interrupted her, but she shifted to speaking about Sybil Jones, still from her prepared notes, maintaining that Jones was "passionate about her own mental health, and committed to becoming better," etc. etc. "We feel she is a model candidate to continue with our services." She went on, actually reporting on Ms. Jones's blood pressure and other medical information.

I stepped in at a pause. "Ms. Green, I appreciate the spirit of your advocacy for Ms. Jones. However, this material is not going to have any effect on an ejectment hearing, and I really don't believe that additional information about her medical condition is appropriate on the record, since it is not germane to this matter."

I turned to Ms. Smith for the last word. She empathized with Ms. Jones, but reemphasized that Smith Grove couldn't make allowances for Jones's noncompliance with the rental agreement based on her inability (or lack of discipline or unwillingness) to take medication. Smith spoke in gentle, even tones, simply making her case. I had the feeling as I watched her that she knew that I had allowed the "advocators" to speak out of an abundance of fairness. She was confident that Smith Grove had a successful case and that I was fully aware of that fact.

When everyone had his or her say, I gave my decision.

THE JUDGMENT

This is not a criminal hearing where two decisions are in my lap: one to find a person guilty or not guilty, the other to pass sentence. In a criminal case, I must find a person guilty if the facts prove him guilty beyond reasonable doubt. In determining sentence, however, I can factor in many things, including the types of arguments made by Defendant's witnesses here today. I can "go light" on someone if I believe the maximum sentence allowed by law would not be productive or appropriate. If lawmakers have not told the Judge exactly what sentence to meet out and forbidden him to do otherwise, then the Judge has much discretion in saying how the Defendant will be sentenced. But again, that's in a *criminal* case, and this is a *civil* matter.

In the case at the bar today, the decision as to whether to approve the Application for Ejectment is *not* left to the *discretion* of the Judge. Rather, there is a certain set of facts for the Court to find in an ejectment case, and if all the requisite facts are found in favor of the landlord, the Court *must* determine the case in his favor.

A landowner has the right to determine who can have possession of his property. He needs not go through the

Court in order to secure that right; it is his right simply because he owns the property. Instead, he needs to go to the Court only to have his property rights *enforced*. In this case, the Court needs only to find: (1) that the Plaintiff owns or otherwise has legal right of possession of the property; (2) that if permission for another to possess the property has been given previously, it has been lawfully terminated; and (3) that a tenant is in possession of the property without the owner's consent. Once finding these are facts, the Court must *as a matter of law* deliver possession to the landowner.

In the present case, Smith Grove is the owner—fact. A rental agreement existed between Smith Grove and Sybil Jones—fact; Jones breached the agreement materially—fact; and Smith Grove lawfully terminated the agreement—fact. Jones has failed to vacate the property—fact. There is no dispute of these things between the parties. Having found these matters factual, the Court grants the Application for Ejectment *as a matter of law*. The Writ of Ejectment will be issued.

It is imperative that Defendant realize that it is not within the authority of the Court to deny Smith Grove its right to recover possession of its property. I cannot give Ms. Jones more time; that's Smith Grove's right. I cannot give Ms. Jones a second chance; that's Smith Grove's right. I can't simply find for the Defendant out of sympathy, in the face of the facts; if I were to do so, I would be acting with bias toward the Defendant.

In fact, if I were to find for the Defendant in this case, I would be violating my oath of office to be impartial.

Defendant's defense was an argument in favor of the tenant's being allowed to stay because she has nowhere else to go, that her mental condition should justify an exception to the rules, and that if allowed to stay, she will not repeat her behavior. I want you to know, Ms. Jones, that while the Court rules against you today, the Judge is not without compassion for your situation. I don't have the answer to your predicament, and there's nothing the Court can do for you, but your advocates here today have shown themselves concerned with your life situation. I wish them, and you, success and a better future.

The greatest value of what has been said by the Defense here today appears to the Court to be as information for Smith Grove, in the event that it should wish to hear Ms. Jones any further on the matter of the eviction. Whether or not they do is entirely in their discretion.

In order to facilitate any further discussions of the parties, I will hold open this case for Smith Grove to pay for and receive the Writ of Ejectment at any time within the next thirty days. Ms. Jones, you need to realize that Ms. Smith may leave this courtroom and secure the Writ before leaving the building; that's entirely within her power. If there is any last chapter to this matter other than the one I have just set down with my decision, it will be written by discussions between the parties outside my presence, and only with their mutual concurrence.

Smith Grove did not immediately apply for the Writ of Eject-ment. I learned later that Gladys Smith had gone to her corporate board and told them what she had learned of Ms. Jones's situation. I had sized up Ms. Smith as someone who was not without compassion and understanding, even though she was fully capable of making the difficult decisions constantly required of someone in her position. The board, however, was not interested in reopening the matter, and Smith returned to the Court ten days later to pay for the issuance of the Writ. Sybil Jones was set out of her apartment within the following week. Where she went—since she had "nowhere to go"—I never found out. I hope it was someplace where she would be secure and could be helped. The Court's duty is to enforce the right of the prevailing party; sometimes that enforcement is a tough thing to do.

9
SPIN THE TALE

Few of us *never* spin our accounts of our experiences. Usually our selection of facts is designed to avoid inviting criticism, or our verbs and adjectives are carefully picked to create a good impression. We could argue, as academicians frequently do, that history is never a pure recitation of facts but instead the interpretation of those facts by the historian, and that some histories are utterly fraught with political, religious or nationalistic agenda or other advocacy purposes that twist the accounts so much that they are highly suspect as to their truthfulness.

Such spinning of the facts occurs regularly or almost unexceptionally in the courtroom. The judge's continuing challenge is to determine whose spin machine is in a higher gear.

THE PLEADINGS

Gabriela Smith came to the Court to sue her former landlord, Jones Avenue Apartments. Smith filed a Complaint that alleged that Jones had evicted her wrongfully and that events related to the eviction had cost her $7,500.00. She was asking for the jurisdictional limit because an attorney had referred her to the Magistrate since her case would have been too expensive to file in the Circuit Court. Jones Avenue submitted an Answer with numerous documents, and a date was set for the case to be heard.

THE EVIDENCE

Gabriela Smith appeared with her children in tow and a family member, who turned out to be her mother and who minded the children in the courtroom gallery. Smith herself was a forceful looking young woman who exuded a slight air of belligerence in her bearing and facial expression. Amanda Jones for the Plaintiff moved into place as if tired already, weary with her job and its stresses.

Plaintiff

Smith's tale was one of mounting and multiplying woes. She was renting one of Jones Avenue's apartments with part of her monthly rent being paid under Section 8 by the local housing bureau. In August of the previous year she left town to go help her daughters get settled in their apartment in Atlanta and to be with them briefly as they began college there. (She didn't say which college.) She told the Court that the housing authority's portion of her rent was paid on August 2. She said she had asked her neighbor Liz to watch her apartment for her until she returned, and that she asked her mother to check her mail.

Upon returning to town and her apartment on September 15, Smith said she found an eviction notice (which turned out to be merely a photocopy of the Apartments' receipt for filing the Application for Ejectment) on her door and her car was gone. She went to see her neighbor Liz, who told her the apartment manager entered the apartment a few days earlier. Smith said Liz told her the manager appeared to be acting with no reason at all, and Liz described the manager to her as just being "nosy."

Smith went to confront the office manager, Amanda, about the eviction. Smith said Amanda told her she had called the housing authority and told them that Smith had abandoned the unit and that the power was cut off. As a result, the housing authority didn't pay its portion of Smith's rent for September, which resulted in Smith's being in arrears in rent for that month. However, Smith told the Court she had absolutely no knowledge of the housing authority's cutting off her Section 8 rent assistance.

According to Smith's testimony, Amanda then took it upon herself to have Smith's car towed away on September 9, and neither Amanda nor anyone else left any information on Smith's door as to where the car was. Smith said Amanda told her she had the car towed because no one was driving it and she didn't want it there. Smith said that she couldn't afford to get the car back (by paying the towing agency).

Further adding to her troubles, Smith said she was served with the Eviction (this time, the actual Rule to Show Cause — the "ten-day notice"— from the court) on September 16, giving her twenty-four hours to vacate. She observed that at the time her car had been towed, she had not actually been served with the Notice to Vacate or Show Cause. (Apparently, Smith believed that the towing of the car was connected to her being evicted.)

Looking into things, Smith said she concluded that Amanda had not notified her emergency contact, her mother, to tell her that if Smith's power wasn't cut back on, her rent would not be paid under her Section 8 voucher. Further, Smith said her mother was listed on her lease as being a contributor to her finances monthly, which should have enabled her mother to take care of the rent if she had known about the problem. Smith laid the fault squarely at the feet of the Jones Avenue Apartments manager for her being in arrears in rent.

Smith's problems were compounded, she said, by the fact that she never received the notice she should have gotten from the housing authority that her Section 8 benefits were being discontinued. The reason, alleged Smith, was that manager Amanda had her mail delivery stopped. Smith contacted Amanda about this outrageous action. She said Amanda told her by way of explanation that she, Smith, was supposed to inform the office when she was going on vacation. Smith told the Court that by the time she returned from Atlanta in September, the post office had already returned the mail to sender.

Then Smith telephoned the housing authority. She said they told her they sent a notice about the termination of Section 8 benefits and that after ten days with no response from her, they discontinued her assistance. Smith assured the Court that she never got the notice. She said that she still had seven more years to receive assistance, amounting to $48,000.00 over that period of time. In view of this fact, Smith said she was certainly entitled to ask Jones Avenue Apartments for $5,000.00 to help her find another place to live and get on her feet.

At the time of her eviction she and her boys (she motioned behind her) had one week to find someplace to live, and she had no job or income. At present, at the time of the hearing, her sons were living with her mother. According to Smith's testimony, she herself was going back and forth from Atlanta (where she was staying part time with her daughters) to South Carolina (where she was staying the rest of the time with her mother). The one way trip was about $100.00.

Adding even more to her burdens as a direct result of the "wrongful eviction," she had to rent a storage unit she could afford, to store all her belongings, at a cost to her of $75.00 per month. Insult to injury, she told the Court that six weeks later someone cut the locks on her units and stole everything she owned. She felt that if she had been able to afford a storage facility that was gated, the theft wouldn't have taken place. She believed somehow that the Apartments, and Smith in particular, were responsible for this loss, too, because of the "unlawful eviction."

Supporting her testimony, Gabriela Smith submitted several papers from the Court and from the Apartments that merely documented the eviction and Jones Avenue's bills. She also submitted her bill from the storage company for the two months she had rented space there before the theft. The proprietor of the company had refunded her money and had written a note on the receipt expressing his sorrow for her loss and his promise to continue trying to identify the thief.

After this truly depressing litany of cascading, negative events, Gabriela Smith totaled her damages for the Court. In view of what she referred to as the illegal entry to her apartment and the unlawful eviction: she asked for $1,500.00 for the car Jones Avenue Apartments had towed away; she wanted $2,500.00 for the belongings she had to store hastily as she was ousted from the apartment and which were then stolen; she asked for $1,532.00 from the Apartments to cover what they said she owed them, stating that if they hadn't broken their contract with her, she wouldn't have owed them any money; and she asked the Court to award her $1,968.00 for her being homeless, separated from her children, and losing a great deal more money, $48,000.00, in rental assistance from the housing authority. The total she requested in a Judgment was $7,500.00, usually the limit the Magistrate can award.

For all she had been through, the amount hardly would have seemed excessive.

Defendant

Jones Avenue Apartments manager Amanda Jones appeared for the defense. She had a short stack of papers with her, one of which was a time line of events transcribed from the other documents in the stack. As most other apartment managers do, she had written copious notes about her actions and her interactions with residents. This time line was the outline of her testimony.

Amanda Jones started with the fact that Gabriela Smith had been a resident of Jones Avenue Apartments for three years when she was evicted in September of the previous year. During that time she had been late in payments of rent more than ten times.

In August of the previous year, before Gabriela Smith had left for Atlanta, the Apartments sent to her a lease renewal offer. Monthly rent was going up by $50.00 and all residents would have to renew their leases at the new rates as their lease terms were completed during the year. Jones said Smith did *not* return the renewal letter. Although she was sent a reminder that her lease would end on October 31 and that if she wanted to renew she was *required* to accept the renewal offer by September 1, Smith left town for Atlanta in mid August and was still out of town when the renewal deadline passed. By itself, this neglect would have resulted in the termination of her lease at the end of October.

Also before Smith left, she was given notice of a damaged set of blinds in her front window that would have to be replaced within fourteen days. Apartment rules required these cosmetic repairs at the tenant's expense. Smith didn't respond to the notice, and again, she took her trip to Atlanta leaving the blinds as they were.

After giving the appropriate notice, maintenance men entered Smith's apartment August 14 to install new blinds, for which Smith would be billed, and they reported to Amanda that it appeared that Gabriela Smith was moving. A mattress was leaning against the wall in the hall and another one was similarly situated in a bedroom. The couch had been removed. Second notice about the blinds and other notices were still posted on the apartment door.

Two weeks later Jones Apartments sent notice to the housing authority about the rental rate increase, as required by law. Two days later the Apartments hand-delivered a final notice about lease renewal to the door of Smith's unit. Smith was still gone and all the notices were still on the door.

One day after the deadline passed for renewal of Smith's lease, maintenance men working on the adjacent apartment saw that the power company had placed a red disconnect tag on Smith's meter. After announcing themselves without answer, the maintenance men entered Smith's unit to see if Smith had vacated, as they had believed earlier that she was doing, and to check for spoiled food. Everything looked as it had before, and the fridge was empty. Upon hearing this report, Amanda checked with Mary Green at the housing authority to see if Gabriela Smith had spoken with them about her housing assistance. She had not. When Amanda told Green that Smith's power had been cut off, Green contacted the utility company. She learned that power had been disconnected ten days ago for nonpayment of the utility bill.

As a result of these events, the housing authority, under procedures dictated by law, discontinued housing assistance to Gabriela Smith—her Section 8 voucher was cancelled. The cancellation came just before September's rent would have been paid. Since the housing authority did not pay a portion of Gabriela's rent for September, and Gabriela was still out of town and had not paid her rent or arranged for it to be paid in full, she would be in default as of September 6.

Alec White, the resident next door to Smith, had been irritated for weeks by the presence of a Honda Civic taking up a space between his and Smith's unit. The car had a flat tire and had been there for two months. White submitted a complaint about it. He said he believed the car belonged to a boyfriend of Gabriela Smith. Amanda tagged the car with a warning that it would be towed on September 9 because of the flat tire and failure to move it in more than thirty days (also an apartment rule). A photocopy of the Rules and Regulations as signed by Smith three years ago when she first moved in was affixed to the car with the warning.

When September 6 came, the rent had not been paid, the car was still there, and there was no sign of Gabriela Smith. Amanda posted a late rent notice, adding to the other notices languishing on the door. On September 8, Amanda called the telephone number listed for Gabriela Smith on Apartment records. It was disconnected. Amanda then emailed Smith at the email address on her records. There was no response.

The following day, the Honda Civic with its flat tire was towed. Jones entered into evidence a document showing that the car had never been listed as a vehicle belonging to the unit in which Smith lived. Their records showed she owned a Hyundai Accent.

On the morning of September 14, Amanda came to the Court and filed for eviction against Gabriela Smith and several other tenants who were in arrears in rent. That afternoon, however, Smith finally returned to town and the Apartments. A maintenance man nearby told her she should go see the apartment manager. Smith went to speak to Amanda.

Amanda Jones emphatically told the Court that Smith had given no notice to the Apartments of her trip to Atlanta. Jones moved into evidence the section of Smith's lease that made clear her obligation to advise the office of any absence from the rental unit of more than ten days. Amanda testified that she asked where Smith had been. She said Smith said she had been in Atlanta helping her daughters get settled, and she had also been working in Asheville. [Atlanta, Asheville and the city where my court and Smith's apartment are located are on three points of a triangle, with Asheville being an hour away from Smith's apartment but three and a half hours away from Atlanta. Atlanta is two and a half hours from Smith's apartment.] In her testimony, Smith had said nothing about having found work in Asheville. Not only that, but Amanda Jones said Gabriela Smith made some mention of having stayed part of the previous month in Greenville, less than thirty minutes away.

Amanda updated Smith on what had been taking place and her inability to reach Smith. She brought up the fact that the power had been disconnected and that the housing authority had accordingly cancelled her Section 8 assistance. In her answer to Jones at the Apartments office, Smith said she hadn't had the money to pay the power bill and she decided to let power be disconnected since she wouldn't be staying in the apartment right then anyway; however, she had intended to pay and have power reconnected when she returned.

Further, as Jones testified, Smith said she had told Alec White she was "going on vacation," so he should have known and could have told Amanda. Jones said when White complained of the Honda with the flat tire in August, he didn't know where Smith was. (Smith could have objected to hearsay evidence, but didn't know to, and by this time, I was "letting it all in," as often happens under the relaxed rules of Magistrate court. It didn't much matter factually, as neither Smith nor Jones testified that Smith gave any notice to Amanda she would be gone.)

Bottom line, however, Amanda Jones told Gabriela Smith she would have to pay her rent in full to stop the eviction filed that morning. She referred Smith to Mary Green at the housing authority for an explanation of their cancellation of benefits.

The next day, Jones placed yet another reminder notice about the rent on Smith's door. Smith called the office and confirmed that since the housing authority would not be paying most of her rent, she would be moving out. She finished vacating the apartment on September 29 and returned the keys to Amanda at the office.

At this point in her testimony Amanda Jones seemed to be finished, so the Court asked her about the mail. Smith had told the Court during the presentation of her case that she believed the Apartments had "stopped her mail." Jones said she had taken no such action. She said, however, that in her experience as manager, mail carriers have returned mail to the post office when boxes got too full, until mail was picked up and there was space to resume delivery.

The Court remembered Smith's testimony about her giving the Apartments her mother's name and number as an emergency contact and also as someone who contributed to Smith's income. The Court asked Amanda about this testimony. In response, Amanda showed the Court the relevant applications and resident information sheets. Gabriela Smith's mother, Maria Smith, was listed as an emergency contact, but Amanda did not regard the situation as qualifying as an emergency, stating to the Court that per their policies emergencies were accident or injury related events. The Apartments did not use emergency contacts for late rent or abandonment of a unit. Jones also stated without wavering that Smith's mother was nowhere shown in their records as contributing to Smith's finances, and that even if she were, absent specific instructions and permission to do so, the Apartments would probably not have called Maria Smith to ask her to pay Gabriela's rent.

THE JUDGMENT

During deliberation the Court concluded easily that Gabriela Smith had been in full spin mode when she spun her tale of woe. If all of it had been true, it would have merited a stern judgment against the Defendant, Jones Avenue Apartments, which would have been guilty of violating several laws. However, Smith's tale, devoid of any documents to back her up, was full of sound and fury, but not much else. It was also a story chock full of holes and it was missing critical information.

For instance, Smith was on Section 8 and had income of only $700.00 per month, as her apartment application said. She had no job, so the conclusion seemed to be that she received welfare in addition to housing assistance (she never said). Yet, she had not just one but two daughters who had just entered college in Atlanta. Where? At what cost? And where did the money for college come from? Her mother? Her children's father (who was not her husband)?

For another instance, when Smith returned after her extended excursion to Atlanta, Asheville and parts unknown, what vehicle did she drive? How many cars did she *have*? Where did she get the money to buy newer cars (records showed the Hyundai was a 2009 and the Honda was a 2011, which at the time of this writing were five and three years old, respectively), if she didn't have the money to pay her utility bills or her rent?

When Jones Avenue Apartments had begun giving its Answer, the spin on Smith's story was evident, but Amanda Jones had the hard evidence to back her version up. I said in my decision:

> It is apparent to the Court that Jones Avenue Apartments' eviction of Gabriela Smith was lawful, being occasioned by her default in rent, and that Jones Avenue did not contribute at all to the circumstances that resulted in Smith's default. To the contrary:
>
> > Smith left town for an extended time without notifying the Apartments;
> > Smith failed to pay her power bill;
> > which led to the company's disconnection of her utilities;
> > which led maintenance men to make lawful entry after notice;
> > which led to the discovery of Smith's being in the process of vacating the unit;
> > which led to notifying the housing authority;
> > which led to their discontinuing Smith's rent assistance;
> > which led to Smith's default in rent;

which led to Jones Avenue Apartments' application for eviction.

Nor did the Apartments contribute to Smith's losing one of her cars. In fact:

Smith never informed the Apartments of her having a different car;

Smith then failed to fix her flat tire and her car acquired status as an abandoned and inoperable vehicle;

which led to a resident's complaint;

which led to the Apartments' response to the complaint;

which led to the proper notice of towing;

which, when Smith failed to respond, led to the vehicle's being towed.

Nor does Jones Avenue Apartments have liability for the stolen items from Gabriela Smith's storage facility unit. The Court certainly hopes that they are recovered.

Gabriela Smith certainly did experience a cascading set of events, and no one wishes them upon her. However, it is the Judgment of this Court that her losses stem from her own actions, not those of any other party.

THE COMPLAINT OF PLAINTIFF IS THEREFORE DISMISSED ENTIRELY.

A tale may be spun for sympathetic friends, and they may never know the whole truth is otherwise. Not often, however, can someone play "spin the tale" in court and win: adverse parties usually have documentation of their version, and the Court is pretty good at telling which one is the un-spun truth.

10
DOG CUSTODY

Pets become almost as dear to us as children—maybe more, depending how the children turn out. In this day of easy-come, easy-go relationships that are based on little more than sex, and end over even less, pets, like children, are sometimes the ones caught in the middle. That was the little drama provided by two parties who both claimed to own a dog.

THE PLEADINGS

Ryan Smith filed a Claim and Delivery action with the court against Katie Jones, alleging he was the owner of a dog named Jasper Smith, now in the possession of Jones. Said Smith (Ryan, not the dog), Katie was withholding Jasper from him out of retaliation. He valued the dog at $800.00, and a dog carrier at another $100.00. Katie Jones got an attorney and filed an Answer claiming that she, not Ryan, owned the dog, and that Ryan had abandoned the dog carrier in question. If the Court were to find that Ryan owned the dog, Katie wanted Ryan to reimburse her for the care of Jasper for six months.

THE EVIDENCE

Ryan Smith appeared at court alone. An upperclassman at a nearby university, he looked very much the part, and carried an air of casual self confidence. Katie Jones came with her attorney, her parents, and several friends. She was a smartly dressed young woman whom one might easily guess to be headed into a business or professional career. She also wasn't going to give up Jasper without a fight.

Plaintiff

Ryan told the Court he and Katie went together for about a year, while they were freshmen and sophomores at the university. One evening he said they were driving in the country when they saw a puppy in the road. They were a mile away from the nearest house, it was raining, and the puppy appeared to him to be abandoned. They picked up the dog and went to the nearest house intending to see if it might belong to the resident, but they found no one home. Ryan Smith took the lead in making the decision that the dog was abandoned and belonged to no one, and he decided rather unilaterally that they would keep it and share ownership. They took the dog back to school with them. Initially, Ryan took the pup to his apartment.

Ryan introduced pictures of Jasper to the Court. It wasn't an unusual kind of evidence, but it served no real purpose except to give the Court an image to think of when Jasper was spoken of. Jasper was a cute pup—a lab mix, I think—but if Ryan were hoping to stir some sentiment towards him in the Court's heart, he should have asked around beforehand. He might have found that I am a cat lover.

Ryan and Katie named the dog Jasper, after one of Ryan's relatives, which he told the Court further implied his connection to the dog, not Katie's. (He didn't say what his relative by the same name thought of having a dog as a namesake.) Within two weeks, he found out that he couldn't keep a pet in his apartment, and Katie took Jasper instead. In two or three months, however, Ryan broke up with Katie. He also moved into another apartment, for reasons unrelated to having a pet. He couldn't have pets there, either.

After the breakup, Ryan said he and Katie had an arrangement whereby he would come for the dog later. He said there were numerous emails between the two in which she referred to "your dog," or specifically said that she would take care of the dog for him until he could get it. He introduced a few of those emails, and generally they did look like she was granting him "custody" of the dog after their breakup.

Moreover, he said his purchase of the dog carrier and a trip to the vet right after they found the puppy proved that he was the owner.

Katie was very slightly shaking her head in denial of parts of his testimony. When it was the defense's turn to cross examine, Katie's attorney, Belle Johnson, asked Ryan Smith about different portions of the emails in which Ryan had said things like, "I know Jasper means as much to you as he does to me, and I can't keep him where I live now, so I'll be glad for him to stay there." Ms. Johnson asked Ryan what those meant if they didn't mean the dog was hers, not his. Ryan quibbled about the meaning of "stay there," and argued he meant "temporarily." Johnson asked him if he paid for Jasper's veterinary care now and Ryan had to say No. She asked him if he paid anything for the dog's feeding or other necessities, and Ryan had to say No, though he said he had offered but never had the opportunity. Had he followed through on his offer, Johnson asked? Well, No.

"Now, Mr. Smith," said Belle Johnson, "Are you aware that the law requires you to report an estray?"

"Estray?" Ryan said.

"That's what the law calls a stray, an animal straying from the property of its owner.

Ryan gulped almost audibly. "Uh, no," he admitted. "We just tried to find the owners, that's all. It was obvious that no one owned him."

"Are you aware that under §47-7-10 of our laws, you commit a misdemeanor if you fail to report an estray?" (The statute requires the finder of a stray to report it to the nearest magistrate. A court sale would ultimately result if the dog were not claimed by the rightful owner.) She was clearly intimidating him. Ryan admitted he had not been aware of the law.

Johnson sat down, finished with Smith.

Defendant

Katie was eager to be sworn in and testify, and Johnson called her first. Katie didn't go into the reasons she and Ryan broke up, and they weren't relevant. Under questioning by her attorney she quickly told the Court that Ryan moved into an apartment that didn't allow dogs, and she thought I should draw the conclusion that if he didn't care enough about Jasper to move into a place where the dog could be with him, Jasper must not really be his.

At this point, the two were beginning to sound like the two women who appeared before King Solomon to contest which was the mother of a baby. Judges have been known to make Solomonic decisions, "splitting the baby" (though Solomon only threatened to slice the child in half, but didn't do so), and I was thinking to myself that such a solution might be interesting here, but I didn't have the luxury of that option in this kind of case.

Johnson produced still *more* emails (the sheaf of printouts was beginning to get thick) in which Ryan made further comments conceding Katie's being the better person of the two to keep the dog.

In cross examination, however, Ryan wanted Katie to tell the Court why, if she owned Jasper, the dog was actually staying with her parents. (I could see why Johnson hadn't brought that up on direct examination; it tended to confuse the situation.) Katie was quick and undaunted in explaining that it was because her parents' home was her permanent residence after all—the college was in the same town where she lived—and the dog had a yard there to play in, unlike the apartment.

Well, who paid the bills for the dog's food and such—did she, or her parents? Katie showed the first bit of being flustered, but answered honestly, "My parents." Ryan gave the Court a look like the cat that swallowed the canary.

And wasn't it true, he followed up, that Jasper had not been to see the veterinarian on time for required shots this year, but that Katie's parents had taken Jasper for the inoculations only after Katie was served with this lawsuit? (I wondered how Ryan knew this.) Katie said she didn't know. (She probably did, if my reading of body language was accurate. However, I didn't think such a thing mattered.) Again, Ryan looked as if he believed he had sealed the deal.

When both sides had rested, I asked Ryan if he wanted to tell me what he thought the evidence showed me. He took about sixty seconds to argue his case, resting on the emails where Katie referred to Jasper as *his* dog. When I gave the floor to Belle Johnson, she moved for a directed verdict, usually a tactic between the presentations of the Plaintiff's case and the Defendant's. It seemed unnecessary here after both the Plaintiff's and Defendant's cases had been presented, when I would ordinarily step out for a bit to deliberate; however, the motion served mostly as a vehicle for Johnson to argue that Smith hadn't made his case.

She first brought up the contrary emails, although, as both she and I realized, they were not the real determinant. She argued mostly that Katie, not Ryan, paid for the dog's keep while it was in her apartment, that Katie, not Ryan, had kept the dog when Ryan broke up with her and left.

Then attorney Johnson brought out a case in point that seemed perfectly fitted to the situation. In fact, she said that she had just come across the case that very morning. She handed me a decision in *Blanton v. Watson,* a two-year-old case decided in our own circuit. It dealt with a remarkably similar situation, only the dog in question was discovered on the defendants' porch. They took it in, advertised it in the newspaper as lost and found, and were contacted by the owner. When they demanded a little under $500.00 for the care and keeping of the animal, the owner went off in a huff and became a plaintiff, suing for possession by means of a claim and delivery action. On a technicality, the magistrate they went before dismissed the case without prejudice. Plaintiff took the matter before a higher court, adding defendants' failure to comply with the estray statute. (Like Smith, in my case, they hadn't reported the stray to the county, either.) Defendants counterclaimed for now much higher costs, keeping the case in the circuit court.

The judge who decided the case found that since the defendants *did* find out who owned the dog, the facts permitted the case to be decided not by the requirement to report the stray, but by other factors that would determine who was entitled to the dog. The judge pointed to other parts of the same law about strays, which said that the owner is liable to the finder for the cost of maintaining the animal. In order to claim the dog, the owner had to pay the finder's expenses.

Belle Johnson offered the higher court's order for the sole purpose of showing that *that* court had applied standards other than an unsupported claim to ownership, to determine who really should have possession of the dog in this case. Johnson apparently had not had time to study the decision in *Blanton v. Watson* thoroughly, which might have changed her mind about using it in her argument. The judge in *Blanton* actually awarded the dog to the plaintiff as the original owner, *if* he paid the defendants their expenses (the lower, original amount).

In my decision, I sorted it out:

> Plaintiff took the dog from open road in the northern part of this county, presuming it to be a stray. Consequently there is no evidence in the way of documentation of sale, registration, transfer of ownership and so on. Having then failed to comply with State law providing for ownership to be established by a court sale of a stray, Mr. Smith would have to have shown this Court other evidence of his right to possess the dog as opposed to Defendant's right, the dog's having been in her possession for more than a year. Plaintiff Smith did not provide the Court with sufficient testimony that he and Defendant Jones had an agreement stipulating his sole ownership of the dog. Plaintiff spent significant time pointing the Court's attention to verbal concessions by Defendant to his ownership; however, the record displays an ongoing dispute between the parties about ownership. In any event, ownership of the dog is not established by the sheer amplitude of claims by one side versus the other.

Plaintiff Smith did not follow State law requiring him to report his taking possession of a stray, but this statute has little bearing on this civil case since the dispute is not between the Plaintiff and a claimant to the *original* ownership of the dog—a person as yet unknown. Rather, the dispute is between two persons who, upon finding the dog on the road in the rain away from habitations, assumed co-ownership of the animal. Plaintiff's failure to report the seizure to the Magistrate for a court sale resulted in his not having any documentary evidence that the dog is his—no title, as it were, even though dogs are not titled in this state.

In consequence, the Court's province in this case where possession is demanded is to determine first whether Plaintiff Smith is the rightful owner of the dog, not as opposed to any other claimant but the Defendant only, who now has possession. Drawing upon statutes and common law regarding property, a well founded truism is that possession is nine tenths of the law, meaning that in a property dispute, in the absence of clear and compelling testimony or documentation to the contrary, the person in actual, custodial possession of the property is presumed to be the rightful owner. Defendant Jones's now being in possession of the dog in dispute, Plaintiff Smith has the burden of showing the Court clear and compelling evidence that the dog is his. Lacking documentary or other physical evidence, or convincing evidence of a contractual agreement, even oral, between the parties, the Court must look solely at the actions and investment of Defendants.

It appears to the Court that the dog was co-owned to begin with. Smith's own evidence by way of his documents reflects the couple's previous anticipation of sharing ownership. Smith's early discovery that he could not have a dog in his apartment led to Jones's taking care of the dog, a situation that continued to the present. Smith, however, did not seek to terminate his rental agreement and move to a unit where pets were allowed. Later, Smith and Jones ended their romantic relationship. The dispute then arose over possession of Jasper.

Actions demonstrating ownership of the dog are almost all on the side of the Defendant. Notwithstanding Mr. Smith's statement that he offered some repayment, he did not follow through, and his statement that he "never had the opportunity" strikes the Court as disingenuous in light of the availability of the U.S. Mail and a personal check.

As Jones is now in possession of the dog at her permanent residence, and because Jones and her parents have borne the investment of time and money for the care, feeding and other responsibilities of ownership, and in the absence of any clear and compelling evidence to the contrary, the Court determines that the dog is not the property of Plaintiff Smith, and accordingly the Court will not order dispossession of Jasper from Katie Jones.

THE COURT THEREFORE GRANTS THE MOTION FOR DIRECTED VERDICT IN FAVOR OF DEFENDANT, AND DISMISSES THE CLAIM AND DELIVERY ACTION OF THE PLAINTIFF.

It was best for Jasper, too, not to be uprooted after so long with Katie. It's always hard on the children when Mommy and Daddy fight.

11
DOGGONE SHAME

As previously noted, few things invoke passion in their owners like dogs. The only thing that comes close may be motorcycles, and while their owners tend to name them and talk to them as if they were alive, they aren't. Dogs are in a category all to themselves. A dog gets into his owner's heart, and if anything threatens the dog, it threatens the owner. Likewise, anything that threatens the owner's possession of the dog might as well be an invading international army: it will be fought with every resource available.

When two people both believe they own a dog, emotions run high. The Court sometimes finds itself in the middle.

THE PLEADINGS

Gwyn Smith came to the courthouse to file a Claim and Delivery action against Ben and Lucy Jones for possession of Kimba, a three year old Siberian Husky. On the Claim and Delivery form, on the line where Smith told the Court why the defendants are wrongfully withholding the property, she wrote, "They *believe* the dog is theirs."

Ben and Lucy Jones didn't need to file an Answer, since a court date is automatically assigned in this kind of case. A date about two weeks from service was set for trial.

I generally don't study case files until they are about to come to trial. We process some 2,000 cases per year and I sign the filings and summonses on them all, but I won't familiarize myself with the issues until it's time to get "hot prepared" for actually hearing the testimony and then making a decision. Certainly I don't know the names of individual parties right off the top of my head until it's nearly time to go into court.

A week or so after the Smith v. Jones Claim and Delivery case was filed and served, my clerk told me a county investigator was at the window and wanted to speak with me. I had him ushered back into chambers and expected him to have a warrant request or something similar. However, he seemed to be wanting judicial guidance about some breach of trust issue he was dealing with: he had made an arrest of someone on that charge. Since he had not gotten the warrant through me, I assumed his issue was not related to my court.

He began to describe a situation involving a dog and soon told me that there was a Claim and Delivery filed in my court over the issue. That's when I stopped him. I said it sounded like *ex parte* information that would best be left to the courtroom setting. He was apologetic, but I let him off the hook by assuring him that I was sure he hadn't intended to do anything unethical. I suggested that he make himself available to the party or parties for testimony, and they could subpoena him if they wanted to. He left, and in a few days, trial took place on the matter, and he, as well as a half dozen other witnesses, were there.

THE EVIDENCE

Presentation of the evidence in this case was at best convoluted and at worst absolutely confusing. The story, however, was fairly simple, though laden with complexities of human interaction that aren't typically experienced by most people. For the reader's benefit, the Court summarizes the entire matter in simple narrative fashion.

Ben and Lucy Jones acquired Kimba as a puppy at a flea market three years before. They took him to their chosen vet, which happened to be the same vet I use—useful information because I knew the trustworthiness of that particular veterinarian. The vet went through the proper procedures and had the dog chipped, showing Ben and Lucy Jones as the owners.

Skip forward about two and a half years to the spring of the current year when Ben and Lucy were having some renovation done in their house. Concurrently, they were having a problem with the fleas that had made their dwelling on Kimba. They had had him treated for the fleas, but it would be a few days before Kimba would be pest-free. Since Ben and Lucy were currently keeping their grandchildren by one of their three children, they contacted a county animal care center and asked them about temporarily keeping Kimba; between the fleas and the renovation, it was not wise for him to be in the house. The animal care center agreed to take the dog in for five days; after that time, Kimba would have to be reclaimed, or he would be put down. The Joneses understood perfectly, and they assured the center they would get him back within that time.

On the fifth day, since the work inside the house was not quite done, Ben and Lucy asked their daughter Regina, who lived a few miles away, to retrieve Kimba for them and keep him at her house for the time being. She agreed, but the animal care center wouldn't release Kimba to her; they read the dog's chip and saw that Ben and Lucy Jones were the owners, and they either had to have Ben and Lucy come for Kimba, or get their permission to release him to Regina. Regina asked them to call Ben and Lucy. The Jones's gave their permission, and Regina took the dog to her house.

Now, Ben and Lucy, who seemed like nice people to me when I saw them in court, didn't have an especially good relationship with any of their children. They probably got along with Regina best of the three, enough to prevail upon her to keep the dog for a few weeks anyway, but Regina apparently didn't have a wonderful opinion of her parents. After she got the dog, she decided her parents shouldn't get it back. The Court never got to hear the reason, because Regina—though given a summons to appear as a witness—didn't show up.

From the admissible facts available, however, it was evident that Regina assumed ownership of the dog and then transferred ownership to someone else. Interestingly, it had nothing to do with money. In fact, she posted a message on Facebook saying she had

a Siberian Husky to give to a good home. That very day, Gwyn
Smith saw the ad and called Regina. Late that afternoon, Regina
took Kimba to Gwyn Smith and gave him away. No papers were
involved, since there were none to transfer, and no money was
paid.

Gwyn, it turns out, dabbled in pet rescue. It seemed evident that
Regina was saving Kimba from her parents. However, Gwyn
Smith didn't intend to turn around and find Kimba yet another
home; she wanted him for herself.

Regina didn't tell her parents Ben and Lucy what she had done
immediately. They weren't to find that out for another thirty days
or so.

For a month, Gwyn doted on Kimba, taking him to the vet
(another one) and of course feeding and caring for him lovingly.
She had a little boy who became quite attached to Kimba as well.
Gwyn found out that Kimba was chipped, and she tried to get her
vet to have Kimba's chip changed to show her as the owner. The
vet told Gwyn she would have to secure the proper papers of
transfer of ownership from Ben and Lucy Jones and submit those
papers to the chipping company, before she could register Kimba
as hers. Actually, as testified to in court by the witness from the
animal care center, ownership would have to be transferred first to
the person who gave Kimba to Gwyn, which was Regina. That's
where the process broke down. Gwyn contacted Regina, who
stonewalled her, obviously because Regina had now been
discovered to have transferred ownership when she didn't have a
right to do so. Gwyn was stymied for the present. As far as she
knew, however, Kimba was hers—until county deputies showed
up at her door one day.

Regina, as it happens, after something of a row with Ben and
Lucy, had finally told her parents she had appropriated the dog for
herself, telling them it was for the good of the dog, the good of the
grandchildren living with them, and possibly for their own good.
They were outraged. They managed to get out of her the name of
the person to whom she had given Kimba—or she let it slip, one
or the other—and they decided to report their daughter's actions

to the police. A county investigator looked into the matter, questioned people involved and decided to seek a warrant for Regina's arrest on a charge of breach of trust (this was the investigator who came to see me).

Investigator Johnson, along with an animal control officer, took Regina into custody and then went to see Gwyn Smith. They told her the dog was stolen property, and they seized him. Gwyn's little boy cried and urgently begged to know why the police were taking away his dog. After the officers left, Gwyn went into action to find out the back story.

Meanwhile, the Joneses still needed someone else to take care of Kimba temporarily, and Regina's being both untrustworthy and now unavailable anyway, they asked another child of theirs, their son Trent, to take Kimba in for a while. Trent lived with his girlfriend in a mobile home on the other side of town. The Joneses got along with Trent even less wonderfully than with Regina, but they were running out of free options. Trent agreed. His two children would love to have a dog anyway.

Trent didn't have a job at present; he stayed at home with his two children by his girlfriend Carla. Carla was employed someplace about twenty miles away, and every day Trent would get in their ramshackle car, drive her to work, and then go back for her at the end of the day. Shortly after Kimba went to live with Trent and Carla and kids for a while, someone (it was never made clear who) told Ben and Lucy that he or she believed Trent was leaving his children unattended at home when he went to pick up Carla. Ben and Lucy were obviously immediately concerned about their grandchildren, and they investigated. They got in their car and drove over to Trent's neighborhood the next afternoon and waited around the corner to see if he would leave without his children to go pick up Carla. He did.

Ben and Lucy had a key to Trent's trailer for emergencies, and they went in and discovered that Trent had locked his kids in their room from the outside, while he made the round trip of just under an hour to pick up Carla. They freed the children and made the momentous decision on the spot to call the cops on yet another of their children. County officers were on the scene rapidly, and when Trent and Carla returned, deputies were there to welcome them home and to show them the back seat of a cruiser. They took them both into custody on charges of child abandonment. Ben and Lucy took Kimba home with them. Dog and owners now reunited, one daughter out on bond for breach of trust, and a son and daughter/girlfriend-in-law in jail for child abandonment, the Joneses went home frustrated and sorrowful.

Gwyn Smith, however, was just getting started. She filed her Claim and Delivery action against Ben and Lucy, wanting to get Kimba back. She believed she was the rightful owner, on account of her having received him in good faith, having paid some vet bills, and having loved and cared for him. She also believed that the shenanigans that had been going on with police, the animal care center, county animal control, the Joneses children, and the Joneses themselves, cast into serious doubt their right to own poor Kimba, who hadn't offended anyone and probably thought to himself that he wished he could be certain where he would lay his muzzle each night.

When all the facts came out at trial, just as found and summarized above, the decision was not difficult, though getting the facts straight between the disparate witnesses was at times not easy. Early on in the hearing I was mostly convinced that I had enough evidence to decide the case right then and there, but the story was so fascinating that I decided to let it all come out. I had nothing pressing following it, and besides, the saga was beginning to sound like "one for the book."

The Court determined that Gwyn Smith, whose burden was first to prove that she owned or was the rightful possessor of the hapless Kimba, could not meet her burden: the dog belonged to the Joneses. As I delivered the summary judgment off the cuff at the close of the hearing, I thought to myself that Smith might have had a cause of action against Regina, but I was not going to advise her to sue anyone. This case was closed, and the Joneses went home to their innocent Siberian Husky. It was a shame for Kimba that he had been put through all this shuttling back and forth between shelter and several homes, in and out of the arms of loving and then crying children; it was a doggone shame.

12
It's All About the Dress

When I was growing up, the high school promenade—which everyone knows as "the prom"—was certainly a major event in the school year, but never as big as it has gotten during my lifetime. Somewhere along the line people began spending extravagantly on this teenage ritual of near-adulthood, hiring limousines, going to spas and expensive hairdressers, and of course, putting together lavish after-prom parties. The one guiding principle, I am told, however, is that "it's all about the dress." Guys can rent a simple tux, maybe varying the color here and there, but for girls, nearly the entire focus is on that one, special dress that will be completely different from every other girl's, will make every other girl envious, and will turn every guy's head. That means a lot rides on getting the dress just right. Sometimes things go awry.

THE PLEADINGS

Kenisha Smith came to the court to file a Summons and Complaint against Juliana Jones, a dressmaker. Smith had shepherded her daughter Jasmine through the process of having a dress custom made for her prom in May, finding the perfect "pattern," going to fittings, and so on, only to have the dress turn out disappointingly. She wanted all her money back, plus the cost of having someone else fix the dress at the last minute, and $4,000.00 in compensation for "emotional distress." Juliana Jones filed an answer saying she did a good job under difficult circumstances and that Smith was just looking to make money off her. Having picked up on the tone of the writings of each, I anticipated something of a fight.

THE EVIDENCE

Smith came with her daughter Jasmine and the woman who turned out to be the last-minute seamstress. On the plaintiff's table was a large garment bag that appeared to be filled with a fluffy dress. Jones came with several people who stayed in the gallery to observe.

Plaintiff

Kenisha Smith told the Court how she and her daughter had planned the dream dress beginning in December the previous year. They had a Barbie® at home (which from clues here and there I took to be the mother's) and had seen a dress for the doll that they wanted Jasmine's prom dress to look "just like." The doll dress cost $175.00. They didn't buy it, but took a picture of the dress with a cell phone, then started looking for someone to make the full sized version. They were referred to Juliana Jones, a Jamaican by birth who had become successful in her country and then moved to the United States where the market for her talents was broader. Smith was told that Jones could look at a picture and design a dress. That's what she needed.

Smith took the picture to Jones in January. Jones assured Smith she could indeed use the pictures of the Barbie® to create a dress for Jasmine. The two seemed to have gotten on very friendly terms quickly, and when it came time for Jones to give Smith an estimate, she low balled it. She agreed to make the dress for $275.00. They signed a contract that Jones used, briefly laying out the steps—three fittings, a final inspection, etc.—and Smith paid $100.00 down on the contract.

Over the next four months, however, Smith said Ms. Jones dragged her heels on the project. Smith found out from phone calls that Jones had been out of state with sick or bereaved relatives. Smith thought Jones had probably gotten behind on all her work. She made numerous calls to check on progress and try to speed up the process.

The final two fittings were crammed into the last two weeks before the prom, and Jones delivered the dress less than twenty-four hours before the hour the event began. In fact, she called and then showed up at Smith's residence at 10:30 p.m. Kenisha Smith was in bed—she had to go to work early the next morning. Jones handed the dress to Jasmine, who had been given the money for the final payment, Jasmine gave Jones the money, and Jones drove off. Jasmine opened the dress and then got her mother out of bed.

The Smiths, mother and daughter, noticed several defects, photographs of which they put into evidence. There were lone stitches holding up ruffles as if only tacked up, not finish-sewn; there were unfinished edges; the dress dragged the floor where it hadn't at the last fitting; and the lining, upon inspection, turned out to be inside-out.

Ms. Smith called Ms. Jones on her cell phone. Jones was still driving back home, answered the call, and the two got into a conversation that became increasingly heated. Smith angrily demanded that Jones return for the dress and fix everything. Jones said it was finished and she wasn't going to come back. Anyway, she had plans for the next day, and she couldn't give the dress any more attention.

Smith was furious, of course, but even at that late hour she called a few people and came up with the name of a seamstress who would tackle the repairs. The woman dropped over early in the morning, worked til just past noon, and Smith picked up the dress about 2:00 p.m. the day of the prom. She took a picture of Jasmine in the dress, and moved the photo into evidence.

Kenisha seemed finished with testimony, so I asked her to go over the amounts she hoped to recover from Juliana Jones. She wanted the $275.00 repaid in full. She wanted the $100.00 she paid her second seamstress to fix the dress at the last minute. And for the hectic 24-hours before the prom and the emotional upheaval she had been through over the whole thing, she wanted $4,000.00.

On cross examination, Juliana Jones seemed ready to burst with counter attacks and angry rebuttal. I asked her if she had any questions, however, and she really couldn't think of any. She would save it for her defense.

Smith called a second witness, the seamstress, Shirley Jackson. Jackson asked if she could open the dress bag, and of course I welcomed her doing so. She had pulled the zipper no more than halfway when she said, "O Lord, this is the wrong dress."

It appeared, upon some explanation, to have been a simple mistake, not negligence of any kind. Sometimes a person who has been *instructed* in writing to bring all evidence to court with him has come unprepared for inexcusable reasons. Often I will not continue such a case, but in this instance the mistake seemed entirely inadvertent and the evidence was, of course, highly material (pun intended). Since it was near noon, I continued the case until 1:00 p.m. and I took lunch.

When we reconvened, Ms. Jackson pointed out to me the various problems the dress had when it was brought to her, and she explained how she had corrected this and that, all in time for the prom the next day. At one point as she explained a process, I thought she had the tone of a sweet grandmother giving me a little sewing lesson when she asked if I knew what a lock stitch was, and I assured her I knew. In fact, when she approached to show me how the dressmaker had used a gather instead of an overlap technique, I offered, "Yes, I see—the first one looks more like smocking"—which brought a look of surprise to her ancient face. What she didn't know was that I had a wife who used to sew a lot and had broadened my knowledge about the craft.

Juliana Jones didn't have any questions of Ms. Jackson—she seemed content to show respect between persons in the same profession. Besides, she was going to have her turn presently.

Defendant

Ms. Jones was sworn in and began to tell me all about her learning to design and make dresses. She wanted to tell me all about some other dresses she had made and how elaborate and wonderful they were and how her other customers were always satisfied. I had to rein her in and make her focus on the dress in this particular case.

Jones's description of the process of designing this dress, her comparisons of photographs of the dress as it progressed with the photos of the doll's dress, and her discussion of the hours the entire project took, were very revealing. Clearly, she did not do this in lickity-split fashion. Further, her take on some of the "problems" the Smith's had with the dress as delivered made it sound as if they were making mountains out of molehills. She also said they had instructed her to change this and that throughout the process, such that the final result might not have been what she would have done, though she tried to please them. "She wanted too much," said Jones; "I didn't charge her but $275.00—the Barbie® dress cost $175.00!"

Her tone became even more irritated, however, when she began to tell me why she thought Kenisha Smith had sued her. "When she was at my house, she saw how successful I had been in this business, and she thought she would just try to make some money off me. That's why we're here today!"

Smith was letting out sighs of denial over on her side of the aisle. Yet when Jones was through testifying, Smith didn't want to ask her any questions. I think she was afraid of the confrontation. Jones's Jamaican accent and flaring temper were intimidating.

Jones had actually filed a counterclaim for the same amount as the Plaintiff's complaint, obviously in an attempt to retaliate in kind. Her claim was for costs over the $275.00 agreed upon and the balance of about $4,000.00 for the aggravation of working with such a demanding customer. I made certain she had the opportunity to pursue the counterclaim, but she had little else to say that she hadn't already said, and Smith had nothing to offer by way of contradiction.

Both sides now satisfied with what they had told me, and my being uncertain of how I was going to rule, I dismissed the hearing with a promise to weigh everything carefully and rule within the week. In fact, it was within the day, as I looked at everything in chambers and all the evidence came into clear focus.

THE JUDGMENT

"...The evidence shows conclusively that the dress was not acceptable to be worn to the prom without further sewing. The dress did not hang correctly, some stitching was insubstantial, and the lining was inside-out. A contact to Defendant resulted in an argumentative exchange. At both the late date and late hour of the dress's delivery, Plaintiff's mounting concern was whether Defendant could perform the necessary repairs when she had delivered the dress in that condition, apparently thinking that it was acceptable as it was. The Court normally holds that a workman be given the opportunity to cure defects; however, the testimony in this case shows that Plaintiff's choice of another seamstress to repair the defects was justified.

A visual defect in a garment made for show warrants strong complaint. However, Plaintiff asked the Court to award her the entire cost of the dress, as well as the cost of repairing its visual defects. The cost of the dress and the value of the dress are quite different. Defendant gave value far exceeding what she was paid: she did not have a dress pattern to work from; she was asked to create a prom dress from a picture of a foot-tall Barbie® doll dress; she did so with the usual time and expense involved in creating other custom gowns costing much more; and she charged the Plaintiff only $275.00 for her work. In a word, the dress was a steal. Notwithstanding the actual value of the dress, however, the contract was for $275.00. However, Plaintiff's request to be awarded the entire cost because of the defects noted upon delivery would, if granted, constitute unjust enrichment of Plaintiff. The award must have parity with the loss.

As to Plaintiff's loss, then, Plaintiff succeeded in getting another seamstress, Shirley Jackson, to repair the dress, and paid her $100.00 for her work. The Court finds that Plaintiff is entitled to recover this $100.00 from Defendant.

Plaintiff's pictures of her daughter in the dress the day of the prom convince the Court that the dress, once undergoing last minute repairs, was otherwise impressive, and no substantial evidence was presented suggesting otherwise.

Aside from the emotions that attend all human lives when they are ruffled by controversy or disappointment, Plaintiff presented no evidence supporting her claims for emotional distress, and accordingly those claims are denied.

Defendant's counterclaim cannot withstand the Court's findings in favor of Plaintiff, and the counterclaim is therefore dismissed in its entirety.

THE COURT RENDERS JUDGMENT FOR PLAINTIFF AND ORDERS DEFENDANT TO PAY TO PLAINTIFF $100.00 PLUS COURT COSTS.

Since the parties received the Judgment by mail, I had no idea how it was received. Thirty days passed for appeal—I've actually had a few parties, who won in court, appeal the decision because they didn't win *enough*. But nothing more came of the dress case. I assumed that Smith was miffed that she didn't get more but self-satisfied that she had won in principle, and that Jones was miffed that she had lost at all but relieved to be out only $180.00.

I doubted, however, that Juliana Jones would soon be trying to copy any Barbie® doll clothes.

13
HOME INSPECTION BLUES

Magistrate Courts in South Carolina don't hear cases where title to real estate is at issue, but they do occasionally hear a case where title has passed and the new owner is displeased with what he got at closing. Plaintiffs in such cases often start out at a significant disadvantage because of the stringent requirements of real estate closings. While a seller being sued over a home sale may not exactly have the benefit of rebuttable presumption,[1] laws and lawyers generally make sure that all the I's are dotted, the T's crossed, and the loopholes closed, so that the deal, once done, is unassailable.

Occasionally, however, a buyer, while not wanting a do-over, wants a rebate of sorts. Things come to light that weren't apparent before the sale was concluded, and they're significant enough to the buyer that he thinks a lawsuit is in order. Such was the case with a home buyer who had problems underneath his home shortly after taking possession.

THE PLEADINGS

Charlton Smith filed suit against Angela Jones about six months after buying her home. He claimed that Jones's agents had failed properly to complete repairs in the crawl space and that Jones had known there were water problems under the house but had failed to disclose the problems as required by law. Jones's Answer simply denied both allegations.

---

[1]For readers not trained in the law, a rebuttable presumption is a matter assumed to be fact by the court until proven otherwise by a party contesting it.

THE EVIDENCE

Charlton Smith and his wife Judy came to court in their Sunday best and sat unrepresented opposite Angela Jones and her young attorney, Bradley Jackson. Smith's eyes darted nervously toward Jackson, and he seemed worried about Jones's being represented. Frequently people come to court not expecting the adverse party would have gotten a lawyer, and many people resent it deeply, as if it were unfair—though everyone has the same right to seek legal help in conducting his suit.

Plaintiff

In his story about buying Jones's house, Smith told the Court he had a professional inspector perform an inspection and this person had made a list a page and a half long of things Smith then requested that the seller fix. He moved the official Purchaser's Requested Repairs list into evidence. It included a request to reattach fallen insulation and supply additional insulation where missing. At least thirty other requests were itemized, but Smith made no mention of any of them. He also supplied the Court with pictures of the insulation, asking the Court to note that it was tacked up wrong-side-out.

Then Smith testified that after heavy rains in the month or so after the sale, he noticed clogged gutters and down spouts and when he looked under the house, he saw there was a water problem. He said his next witness would describe the situation, but he added to his own testimony that it was clear to him that Jones had known about the water problem—how could she not, he argued—but had failed to disclose it as required by law in the process of negotiating the sale.

Jones's attorney Bradley Jackson had no questions of Smith and Smith called another witness, Joe Miller, a contractor who had replaced the insulation a month or so ago, when Jones declined to be further involved in the house. Miller affirmed Smith's assessment that the insulation was wrongly positioned, and he testified as to how much he had charged Smith to fix things under the house. He also testified that he had noticed dripping pipe fittings while he was deep under the structure, and he said that the situation required repair, which hadn't yet been performed. In fact, he recommended a French drain and wondered why no one had installed one already in the past. It appeared to him that the dripping had been going on a long time. He told the Court how much he would charge to do everything necessary to put the crawl space in the dry.

This time Jackson did have some questions of the witness on cross examination. He wanted to know if Miller could tell when the dripping had started. He couldn't. Where was it? Far back under the house, under the location of a bathroom. Did he know who had installed the insulation in question? He didn't.

After this brief cross examination by Jackson, Smith was finished, and Jackson brought the case for Defendant Jones, who eagerly took the stand.

Defendant

Jones presented the Court with copies of closing statements, complete with all the signatures of the parties. Under her attorney's questioning, Jones reminded the Court that the closing statements marked the point at which the buyer was satisfied with the house and the seller was no longer responsible for its upkeep.

Jones then told the Court that she responded to every item on the list presented for repairs, that a certain Andy Griffin had performed all the repairs, that she was no carpenter and had only briefly looked under the house from the crawlspace doorway before asking Griffin to do the work required. He had, and she didn't question it.

She did show up, however, the day that Charlton Smith came to perform his final inspection after she, Jones, had told him everything on the list was done. Smith didn't bring his original, professional inspector. At some point, however, when the list returned to Smith, he had initialed it. Angela Jones presented her copy of the repair list, with Smith's initials in the "approved" column beside each and every item, including the insulation. She asked the Court to note that nowhere on the list was anything about a water problem underneath the house, either citing a problem or that such a problem had been fixed.

After Jones's attorney, Bradley Jackson, sat down, Smith cross examined, Jones, asking her if it weren't true that the insulation was upside down. She didn't know that to be fact, and it didn't matter what she knew, she said, because she hadn't done the work and after all, he, Smith, had checked off the repair as satisfactory. Smith tried to get her to admit that she had known about a water problem, but she was unblinking, forceful and unmoveable.

The testimony from both sides was relatively brief, taking no more than a half hour. The parties wanted to present final arguments. Smith in particular wanted to argue in his most persuasive manner that it was clear from the evidence that Jones knew she had a water problem, didn't disclose it, and therefore was in violation of state law. What Smith did not do was reference any evidence at all that pointed to Jones's prior knowledge of a water problem.

Bradley Jackson pointed up these deficiencies of Smith's case in his closing, and asserted that the closing documents, as they are designed to do, bring finality to a house sale.

THE JUDGMENT

The Judgment I issued stated in part:

> The evidence is convincing that the repairs attempted by Mr. Griffin did not correct the improperly installed insulation. The evidence is not convincing that any water problem underneath the house pre-existed the sale, and while drains and down spouts may have had some clogs, it is abundantly apparent to the Court that in the process of inspection, no problem with either clogged drains and down spouts or water incursion underneath the house was identified.

Plaintiff faces the plain fact that after requesting repairs and having an opportunity to do a final inspection of the home he was purchasing, he concluded a sale of real estate and accepted the condition of the property "as is." In the matter of the insulation, Plaintiff appears to have failed to inspect adequately, if only to have professionally inspected, the repairs to the insulation that he requested, before accepting the property and going through with his purchase of it.

As to the matter of alleged water problems, to prevail in his Complaint, Plaintiff's burden was to show the Court by the evidence, not merely argue his opinion, that Defendant and seller Angela Jones knew there was such a problem underneath the house but failed to disclose it. Plaintiff Smith did not meet that burden. The failure of Smith's home inspector to reveal a water problem initially speaks either to the absence of any problem or to a lack of thoroughness of the inspector in the performance of his job. In any event, the testimony and other evidence did not in any way suggest that Defendant Jones had knowingly concealed a problem. The real estate closing on the home having concluded any residual matters between the buyer and seller, responsibility for subsequent repairs or remediation became that of the buyer, Mr. Smith.

JUDGMENT IS RENDERED FOR DEFENDANT JONES. THE COMPLAINT OF PLAINTIFF IS DISMISSED.

The Latin motto still applies: *caveat emptor.* And as Ronald Reagan used to say, trust but verify. As nice and as honest as people seem to be when you're buying a home, you're risking trouble if you don't inspect meticulously.

14
COMMON ENEMY

Many suits in Magistrate Court arise over land and buildings. Some of these suits must be transferred to the Court of Common Pleas or the Master in Equity, either because they involve more money than the Magistrate has jurisdiction over, or else because they call into question title to property. The rest tend to be intense squabbles over construction, renovation, plumbing, landscaping, or the subject of this chapter: surface water.

THE PLEADINGS

Nina Smith filed a Summons and Complaint against J. C. Jones alleging as follows (I have not corrected any errors):

> Mr. Jones has been digging a trench on his property along the fence line to divert his storm water drainage onto my property. Since I had a new driveway put in on March 18, he has worked deligently to make the trench deeper & wider. On May 3rd, I asked Mr. Jones to stop diverting his storm water onto my property because it ruined my new driveway and is causing erosion. He swore at me & said, "Where the bleep do you want me to put it?" ...He has placed brush all along his fence line so that he will not receive any of his own storm drainage run off.

There were several interesting things about the Complaint that I'll note for the reader as the account progresses. Mr. Jones filed an Answer that said:

Mrs. Smith filled the drainge ditch whith all Kind of Trash and when she bought the Trailer the ditch was all Ready There (I would like a beanch Trial)

On the surface of things, it sounded like the matter was quite likely to go the defendant's way because of the Common Enemy Rule[2] under the Common Law. I pulled out some notes on the subject and had them in hand for use if necessary when the trial came to a close. As I've often said in these *Smith v. Jones* volumes, I never make a decision in advance, however, even though the pleadings may seem to constitute an open and shut case.

THE EVIDENCE

Mrs. Smith, a woman of about sixty, was flanked at her table by two gentlemen who turned out to be coworkers in a little company that did small paving, gravel and grading jobs. They had put in Smith's driveway a few months ago. I asked Smith (whose real name was something else, of course) how she pronounced her last name, so that I would get it right during the hearing, and she told me. To keep things even, I asked Jones what the J. C. stood for, and he and his wife answered practically in unison, "Jus' J. C. Ain't no name. That's wha's on my birf certifikit. Jus' J. C."

---

[2]For the non-legal reader, the Common Enemy rule can be stated in this way: Regarding diversion of surface waters naturally flowing across land, a landowner has a right to improve land by changing its surface or erecting structures on it, unrestricted by the fact that improvements may cause surface water naturally flowing or accumulating on his land either to stand in unusual quantities on his neighbor's lands, or to pass onto and over them in greater quantities and in other directions than it would otherwise flow. One exception exists to the rule, which is the case in which the diversion is effected in such a way that the surface water is delivered in concentrated form to the destruction of the neighbor's property. If this happens, the Court may find that the diversion caused a nuisance, which is legally described as substantial interference with the right to use and enjoy land, which may be intentional, negligent or ultra-hazardous in origin, and must be a result of defendant's activity.

I said I had been called R. F. by a few people, but they could just call me "Judge," and there was a relaxed chuckle across the aisle.

Thus set at ease, the parties were ready to tell me what the difficulty was between them. I sensed that the Magistrate Court rule about relaxed rules would be especially appropriate at this time.

Plaintiff

Mrs. Smith began her testimony by telling me that about a year ago she had moved here from Michigan—of *course,* she had. I had just returned from a vacation to Michigan a month ago and I recognized her Michigan twang right away. My wife and I had been charmed by the sights of Michigan but had found the Michigan accent a constant source of laughter. Anyway, Smith had moved into a mobile home on property adjacent to Jones's, and pretty much right away she had hired Gravel Guys, the little company represented in court, to put down a gravel driveway where there was only a dirt one at present. The driveway divided Smith's property from J. C. Jones's, and was on her side of the line.

As the Complaint implied, Jones had already been at work on a ditch on the side of his property, and Smith said that once her driveway had been laid down, Jones stepped up his pace to deepen and widen the ditch. Not all of the ditch paralleled the driveway; up the slope it ran alongside Jones's land, beside a road, and it butted into the driveway at one end, where it turned the corner and then ran beside the driveway to the middle and then into a large pipe. Jones was enlarging the ditch and also creating a cinder block wall at the edge of his property in such a way that the water he diverted around his property line would not then pool at the edge and make a lake at the corner of his lot when it rained heavily.

Sure enough, it rained heavily. Spring in our area had been particularly wet. During the first storm after Jones had completed his ditch revision, water rushed down the side of his yard, channeled out the land in the corner where it turned, and rushed alongside the driveway, making a small pond at the pipe opening until it could all go down into the storm drain. Smith's driveway was heavily damaged.

As Smith told her story I was inexorably drawn to thoughts of my own drainage problems, which were remarkably similar. Since we moved into our home five years before, new construction above us on three or four lots resulted in significant silting in our yard, which is only one property from the bottom of a long hill. We had a sink hole ten feet deep and fifteen feet wide, a clogged drain pipe underneath the whole width of the yard, and every time it rained heavily we had a river thirty feet wide, which in the spring had brought down thousands of pounds of large logs from the last construction site up the hill. I felt Mrs. Smith's pain, but I couldn't tell her of my experience, lest I appear either to her or Jones to be leaning her way.

So far, the description sounded as if Jones were merely trying to deal with his own drainage issues so as to minimize the impact of storms on his yard. I asked if Mrs. Smith had anything else to tell or show me.

Nina Smith had photographs. They were not immensely helpful. They were taken when there had been no rain, so I didn't have any view of the effect of heavy rains on Smith's property. They did not depict, and Smith had not described, any destructive effect on her property other than the partly washed out driveway. For the most part, the photos merely showed me how industrious J. C. Jones had been in digging his ditch and making his little walls.

When Smith seemed to have spoken her piece, I asked if J. C. had any questions for her. Immediately he began carping in a deep, backwoods drawl about why Smith wanted him to pay for her problems, and telling me that the ditch was there long before Smith moved in. I cut him off gently, at first, and then firmly when he didn't stop, and I asked him again if he had any *questions,* not testimony. That would come later. As if he hadn't heard or understood me, he began repeating his argument. I managed to get him stopped again, and assured him he would have a chance to speak for himself in a few minutes.

Smith called Scott Brown, the younger of her two witnesses, and he told the Court about putting in the driveway. Mostly I asked him about the monetary damages she was asking for. He verified that the estimate he and his partner had given to Smith was for $5,000.00.

Again I asked Jones if he had questions for the witness. As before, he launched into an argument about his side of the story, and I had to stop him. At least, I tried. After several attempts, raising my voice a little with each successive one, I finally realized he was hard of hearing, and I almost shouted, "Be quiet!" Mrs. Jones reached over and grasped her husband by his arm and said loudly in his ear, "Hush!" and he did. I smiled at them both and turned back to Smith. She now called the older of her witnesses.

Tony Green described the water flow situation a little more, but he seemed to be rather on the fence about whether he thought Jones was doing anything wrong. I decided to probe a bit. After finding out that as part of his business he did some landscaping and water mitigation, I asked him if he had done any kind of impact analysis from what he observed about Jones's property. He had, and he stated carefully that Jones appeared to be simply trying to solve his own water problems.

Then he added, "Ideally Mr. Jones should [do thus and such] and the water would go [here or there]." Green gave details not helpful for my account. What struck me, however, was that Green, or more pertinently Smith, wanted me to make Mr. Jones handle his drainage problem in some other way than how he was.

I recalled that Smith had said, "Jones has put brush and blocks all along his property line so he won't receive any of the storm water on his own property." When she had said that, my first thought was, So? Don't we all try to keep things from damaging us? I would deal with that idea later when it was my turn to talk.

I turned to Mr. Jones and said, "Against my better judgment, Mr. Jones, do you have any questions?" Surprisingly, he understood what I meant by the good natured remark, and he smiled and said No.

I turned back to Smith. I had been thinking about her testimony and about her written Complaint, and I decided I was going to find out something.

"Mrs. Smith," I said, "in reading your Complaint I notice you say, 'Since I had a new driveway put in on March 18, he has worked diligently to make the trench deeper and wider.' The way you worded it, I'm inclined to infer that you believe Mr. Jones widened his ditch *so that* you would have water problems. Is that what you believe?"

Smith fumbled her words a bit and seemed to be about to say Yes, but then said she wasn't sure. I went further, reminding Smith that she had repeated her Complaint statement almost verbatim at the beginning of her testimony, only with even more implication that Jones was trying to harm her by diverting his surface water with the ditch. I decided to find out if there were more:

"Mrs. Smith," I said slowly and carefully, "tell me about your relationship with Mr. Jones prior to your having a driveway laid down." She stared at me a moment, evidently shocked that I had divined the truth.

"Well," she said in a low voice, "I've had a lot of trouble out of him. I've had to call the police out a few times, over him standing over there and looking into my windows. I didn't want to get into that because it seemed like it wasn't related to this."

"And you're right to some extent," I said. "We're not here about your other complaints. But I wanted to know if something preceded this whole matter. In your Complaint were you trying to imply that Mr. Jones did what he did, in improving his ditch, for the sole or even the main purpose of causing destruction to your property?"

Smith wasn't certain she wanted to go that far. She paused and seemed to be thinking about how to respond. Finally she answered carefully. "No, I'm not going to say that. I don't know that. I just know that he could have done something different so water wouldn't flood my driveway."

My respect of Mrs. Smith went up a notch. She had thrown out the words in her complaint so as to leave the impression that in altering his ditch Jones was retaliating against her for something. If I found evidence of that, I could determine that Jones's actions were not merely designed to mitigate water damage to his property, but shrewdly designed to damage his neighbor's. That would be pivotal information. Smith could have doubled down on her implicit accusation in court, but she didn't, because I think she realized she couldn't prove such a thing and that it probably wasn't true. She chose to be honest, and I silently applauded her for it. Besides, I reasoned to myself after having observed Mr. Jones for the first half of the trial that he probably wasn't smart enough to figure out that his ditch work would take out Smith's driveway. Then again, I've underestimated simple people before.

I had a follow-up question, however, somewhat repetitive: "Do you have *any* reason to believe that Mr. Jones did all this work mostly or even in a significant way to harm your property?"

Here's where the answer became most revealing. She said, "I don't guess so. I know he's trying to keep water off his property. My neighbor on the other side complained to me last month about the water that comes across from Mr. Jones's property. I told her I couldn't do anything about it."

"Wait a minute," I said, "Are you saying that the neighbor below you complained about the water that comes off your property and damages hers, the way the water that comes off J. C.'s property damages yours?"

Smith fumbled and never really recovered. It was time to hear from Jones, though I thought to myself I really didn't need to. Once I had an answer to my internal question about whether or not Jones was actually trying to harm Smith, I really didn't need to hear his defense. However, I had promised him three times he would get his chance, and he was going to get it.

Defendant

Jones began by repeating his two previous mantras that he shouldn't have to pay for Smith's water problems and that the ditch in question was there long before Smith moved next door. He pulled up a posterboard from beside his table, on which he had drawn a not-so-bad diagram of his property and the area of Smith's driveway. The magic marker drawing showed his house, the ditch, and his fence, and included arrows to show me how the water naturally flowed. He went into detail about how he had dug here and created a basin there, and all in all he displayed a country boy's acquired knowledge of land and nature.

I found him to be without guile and without any hint of animosity toward Smith—at least for any other reason than that she was suing him for $5,000.00. I got no evidence or feeling that the two had had a year long feud. Because he was a poorly educated, rural Southerner and she was a Yankee-come-lately, I had halfway expected to find that this dynamic played into their dispute, but none of that came to the fore.

Jones ended his story with the repeated insistence that the ditch was there long before Smith moved in, and that every once in a while he had to go clean out brush and debris from it so the water would flow properly.

When Jones paused long enough for me to sense that he was done, I asked if Smith had any questions. She did, but they were largely argumentative, and nothing was helpful.

When everyone was silent, they were finished, and I gave both sides thirty seconds to sum up—setting limits on these folks was an absolute must.

Then I gave Judgment from the notes I had made.

THE JUDGMENT

Mrs. Smith's Complaint is that Mr. Jones's actions in diverting water from his property have damaged her own property. Mrs. Smith may really have intended to complain of what the law calls a tort, a civil wrong where damages can be recovered. I considered that possibility while listening to each party and in asking additional questions of you. To find that a tort was committed, however, I would have to have found that Mr. Jones directed an action toward Mrs. Smith that harmed her. I didn't find any such evidence. Mr. Jones merely attempted to manage the water collecting on his own property, and his efforts had a negative result on Mrs. Smith. (Mrs. Smith was nodding and smiling vaguely.)

Unfortunately for Mrs. Smith, the law favors Mr. Jones. (Smith stopped smiling.) Under the Common law, one of the three sources of law for our state courts, an ancient principle called the Common Enemy rule exists. Under this rule, surface water is identified as a common enemy: (to Jones) it's your enemy, and (to Smith) it's your enemy, too. Both of you have a right under the law to manage your own property with your chosen defense strategy against the common enemy. (At this point, I briefly summarized the Common Enemy rule.)

In *Smith v. Phillips,* a 1995 case in our state, the Circuit Court said that a person may obstruct surface water, change its direction and flow, prevent it from coming in, or build barriers and change the level of the soil to turn the water off on a new course after it has come on his land. It doesn't matter how a landowner does it; it's his right to do it.

There's one exception to this right (Smith brightened), but it doesn't apply under the circumstances (she dimmed again).

Mrs. Smith, there's no basis in law for you to recover against Mr. Jones. Both of you strive against a common enemy. In almost every case, each of us must contend with it in his own way. I found it ironic that you admitted that your neighbor complained of the water coming from your land onto hers. You didn't feel you should be blamed for that. Her complaint should have told you something about your own.

Consider an illustration of the principle. A line of knights fight together against an oncoming enemy. A knight in blue sees an archer firing at him, and raises his shield just in time to deflect the deadly arrow. Unfortunately for the knight in red next to him, the arrow bounces off the blue knight's shield and strikes the red knight and wounds him. The red knight has no right to complain that it is the blue knight's fault he was wounded. The blue knight was merely protecting himself against their common enemy—the archer on the other side.

JUDGMENT IS FOR DEFENDANT.

I don't know if the story helped the way Mrs. Smith felt. She still had to do something about her driveway. She would have to spend some money to handle the flow of water in her own way, and the neighbor below her might not like it.

I do know, however, that I listened to my own Judgment. I had harbored some feeling that somebody up the hill from me ought to feel responsible for the river of mud that carved little canyons in my yard. Truth is, they were just doing with their land what they thought they needed to do, and I was going to have to do with mine what I had to. After all, I didn't have to buy the lot in the first place. I could have asked some expert to tell me if I was in danger of extraordinary attacks by the Common Enemy. I suspect he would have told me Yes.

15
THE VALUE OF THE RECORD

Summary Courts in my state are required to record trial proceedings. Before cassette tapes became commonly used, the requirement was for a written record to be made by someone who had the skills to get most of the testimony down as it whizzed by. When I came on the bench, cassette tapes were the norm. Many magistrates still use cassettes; in my court we've kept up to date. We use a digital system that gathers audio from each party's table, the witness box, the bench, and a movable speaker's stand.

The court has to keep recordings for sixty days in most civil cases before being able to delete them. Rarely is there a need to access the digital recording. An appeal is one of those rare occasions, but other than that, the computer files pretty much just sit there on the hard drive until deleted to make room for more.

Every once in a while, however, especially after a long trial with lots of detailed testimony, the only way for the Judge himself to be entirely certain what was said is to listen to the recording again. In court, I often make notes I can refer to quickly if ruling on the spot, or that I can type into a judgment back in chambers after deliberating. But I can write only so fast, and anyone can miss something in the midst of muddled testimony. In the following case, if I hadn't had the recording I might have decided the matter before me in a different way.

THE PLEADINGS

Wojciech Smith (it was actually a common Polish surname) came to the Court to Complain of Hans Jones (it was actually a German surname related to Jones) that he performed construction services for Jones for which Jones refused to pay him. Jones answered with a flurry of papers saying that Smith was responsible for flooding that took place on his property and damaged items in his basement—actually a ground floor where he had a recreation room. Jones asked for a jury trial. Per the order of our State Supreme Court, a civil suit where a jury trial is demanded goes to mandatory alternate dispute resolution—mediation. After a few months, the matter reached an impasse there and returned to my court for trial.

THE EVIDENCE

The parties appeared with attorneys but without any other witnesses. The attorneys, Mr. Sommers for Smith and Mr. Johnson for Jones, had both appeared in my court before. Wojciech (pronounced **Woh**-chek) Smith was a short, solid, stocky man sporting a bulky moustache that completely obscured his mouth and a thick shock of salt and pepper hair on a quintessentially Slavic face, dressed as if he intended to go to a construction site after leaving the courtroom. Hans Jones was a slender, fair complected, extremely blonde man, wearing slacks and a colorful knit shirt bearing the logo of a local, German company.

Plaintiff and Defendant

Smith took the stand and under questioning by his attorney, Mr. Sommers, began telling the Court his story. The trial would last more than three hours, with re-direct evidence and re-cross questioning in an escalating presentation of the respective cases that muddied the waters of some issues and cleared up others. As I have done in a few previous chapters, I'll summarize the proceedings in narrative fashion for greatest clarity.

Hans Jones, a manager at a local German automotive plant, was building a large home that included a pool. The lot had been graded, and the house had been framed, roofed and bricked. While the house was being finished inside by carpenters, a pool company was installing the pool out back, and Jones also hired Smith, who ran a small landscaping business, to do fine grading, lay sod, install shrubs, and lay drains for water mitigation. Workmen were crisscrossing the yard and furiously trying to meet deadlines. The Court had a copy of the contract between Smith and Jones for his various tasks.

When Smith arrived on scene, the pool people had already dug the hole for the pool and had put the massive, fiberglass pool inside the hole. The hole around the pool had not been filled in and no deck had been poured. The pool was about forty feet from the back of the house and while Jones said it was "level with it," it turned out to be about twelve inches higher than the ground level doors to the house. Jones wanted Smith to install a drain from the middle of the grassy area between house and pool, to the side of the house, underneath a walkway running down the side, and to "daylight"[3] at the edge of his property, near a fence. This was the drain that ultimately became the focus of the parties' dispute.

Smith said that Jones had had a French drain installed under the house and that he wanted it to empty into the drain that Smith was installing, but that he didn't want Smith to connect the two. Jones's plan was to let the French drain company's work be completed, have it inspected, have Smith's drain installed, and Jones would connect the two drains himself. The Court was under the impression that Jones was trying to skirt either some construction standard or some warranty condition and that he didn't want the Court to know the details. When he testified giving his version of things, Jones said, "Nein!" and denied in the crispest German accent that he told Smith not to connect the two drains; Smith, however, was adamant that he did. "Tak," he said in Polish—"Yes," he said it.

Anyway, Smith installed the daylighting drain, laid sod over some 8,000 sq. ft. of yard, installed shrubs around the house and along the side fence where the drain discharged, and, satisfied with his own work, he left the property at the end of February and

---

[3]A drain "daylights" at its end when it comes out of the ground and discharges water.

billed Hans Jones $5,570.00 for the balance of the job: Jones had already paid two installments on the work. The entire job totaled around $12,000.00. Jones paid the invoice for $5,570.00 sometime in March.

About three months later in early June, after the house and pool were completed and Hans Jones was comfortably situated in his new, very nice home, torrential rains came upon the area. (I remember the storm system vividly. It created a river in my own yard and brought down thousands of pounds of logs from a construction site up the hill where trees had been cleared. The logs came to rest all over my property.) Jones's back yard flooded and water stood on his back patio and leaked into his ground floor. Jones took pictures of his side yard, where Smith's drain daylighted. Jones called Smith to come see what could be done. Smith came promptly, and assessing things rather quickly he wanted to dig in the area of part of the underground portion of the drain he had laid, the part coming out of the back yard.

Once Smith had uncovered the drain, the problem became evident. About ten feet of the 12" diameter drain pipe was crushed. Self-evidently it had been crushed since the construction period. Smith told the Court that it was evident to him that after he laid the drain and left the site, someone in the pool construction crew had used a concrete buggy—a motorized cart that carries about a half-yard of concrete from the truck to the site where it is to be poured—and had driven the buggy over an area where the drain underneath was becoming increasingly shallow, crushing it underneath the ground. Smith had seen such a buggy being used just before he left the site in February.

In its crushed condition, the pipe would not conduct water. Light rains would have caused no problem, but the torrents of water that fell in the early June monsoon quickly filled up the first thirty or so feet of pipe from the middle of the yard and overflowed into the porch area. On the side of the house, water flowed toward the house and covered the side patio.

Smith said Jones asked him to fix the problem. Jones also asked Smith to install some additional drains around the pool and have the water from them conducted off in different directions. He came up with a list of projects to augment the drainage system, including splitters on some down spouts, and Smith accepted the project and got to work.

As Smith's men were digging up the rest of the pipe they had previously laid, they found the end of the French drain system. It was not connected to anything; in fact, it was capped on the end. A French drain, if it daylights, may normally have a cap with holes in it, designed to spray out forcefully in a dispersed pattern. This drain was underground and the cap was solid: the drain was not draining anything away from the foundation of the house. Smith took pictures of the drain and cap, which the Court received as evidence.

Smith worked on, completing the job and then billed Jones for the additional work he had performed. This time, Jones didn't pay the bill.

Jones in his defense told the Court he didn't pay because he said he believed the flooding was Smith's fault to begin with and that he regarded the job Smith's crew had just completed as merely "fixing his own mess." Jones claimed two things: first, that Smith had run over his own pipe (though with what, he didn't say, and no evidence indicated that Smith had any heavy equipment at the site); and second, he said that Smith had graded the side yard defectively such that it sloped toward the house instead of away from it, resulting in drainage of heavy rains toward the house. Jones argued that if Smith had not dug up the side yard and found the crushed drain, he (Jones) might have been suing Smith for defective grading. (I wondered why, if Jones was representing himself honestly, he hadn't filed a counterclaim to that effect.)

In fact, in his defense Jones made a big deal of how the grading of the side yard was defective. He said it was fine before Smith did his work. Mr. Sommers wanted to know: if the slope was fine before, why didn't Jones have Smith come out and grade it? There was a lot of back-and-forth questioning and testimony about this grading, who did the initial grading, what Smith did, and so on.

There was no "gotcha" moment at trial, but I felt the truth was in there, somewhere. At any rate, Jones didn't pay the July invoice.

The unpaid bill remained unpaid for another couple of months and then Smith sued.

Attorney Questioning and Closing Statements

The attorneys in this case latched onto some particulars of the matter and tried to hammer home their respective cases. Defendant Jones's attorney, Mr. Johnson, noted repeatedly that the contract between the two, signed in January, stated clearly that change orders were to be in writing, signed by each party. Since the June work requested by Jones had not been in writing, his attorney argued that the work was self-evidently warranty work, and that by virtue of that fact it should not be compensated.

Johnson also used questioning of his own client and of Smith to show that the balance for which Smith billed Jones in February and the amount Smith billed Jones for in July were identical: $5,570.00. Johnson took significant amounts of time questioning Smith about the invoice. How did it happen that the amounts on the February and July invoices were the same, and not an simple figure at that, but an odd one? Why wasn't there any breakdown of labor costs on the July invoice? How did Smith arrive at the figure if he didn't have any record of how many hours were worked? Johnson was implying that the figure was a mistake, and that *even if* his client owed Smith some money, it couldn't be as much as $5,570.00. What's more, the invoices looked similar. Was it possible, he wanted to know (and he argued as much) that Smith had gotten the $5,570.00 figure from the earlier invoice and that it was nowhere near accurate? He left his argument at that point, hoping I think to cast doubt in the Court's mind as to whether Smith's accounting procedures were even remotely reliable.

Johnson also attempted to discredit Smith's testimony in which he concluded the pool crew must have run over his freshly laid drain pipe with a heavy buggy. Johnson had had his client Jones testify that he never saw a buggy in the back yard. Mr. Sommers, however, had been quick and thorough in questioning Jones from multiple angles and uncovering testimony that Jones had been not only away from the construction site, but actually out of the country during significant times during which the pool and the drainage systems were being installed. In other words, there was much he didn't see.

When arguments were completed, I had two stacks of photographs and documents, one for each side, and the clock said well past quittin' time. I promised a decision within the week, and I rapped the gavel with satisfaction.

THE JUDGMENT

After a night to "sleep on it," I still wasn't certain in whose favor I would render Judgment. The figures were uncertain and several issues were still murky. I had four pages, back and front, of scribbled notes; I use my own system of identifying witnesses, direct testimony, cross examination, and the occasional interjection of my observations that might eventually become part of written decisions. After reviewing these notes I still had a couple of major questions.

One thing that troubled me was the confusion over the $5,570.00 that appeared on two invoices six months apart for different work. I believed that Defense attorney Johnson was genuinely confused by the figure and that he really believed it was a gross error on Smith's part. I wasn't convinced that if, indeed, it was an error, it was a gross one: it might have been minor. My own belief was that the facts were to be found in the testimony somewhere. But where? I couldn't find the smoking gun in my notes.

Another lingering question was over whether Smith had actually changed the grade of the side yard such that, where it had sloped away from the house before (of which I wasn't certain), it now sloped toward it.

Analysis of the testimony convinced me fairly quickly that Smith was entitled to Judgment in his favor, because of arguments I'll make below. My challenge at that point, however, was to determine what the damages were. Faced with the odd coincidence of figures from the February and July invoices, I had to make some sense of July's figure, and from what I remembered from the testimony I didn't recall anything that specifically explained the amount of $5,570.00. How had Smith figured his labor charges? I didn't remember anything about how many hours had been worked, and as Johnson had pointed out in his questioning of Smith, there was no breakdown of labor costs on the invoice itself.

Initially dissuaded from listening to the trial recording because of its sheer length, I now decided I needed to do so. In addition to wanting to rehear any explanation of the invoices, I also hoped I would hear something about grading that I missed at trial. Surely something had been said about these two issues. Maybe I missed it due to Smith's Polish accent, Jones's German accent, and the tendency of both parties to speak in low tones and mumble away from the microphone. I made a copy of the courtroom recording and put it on a USB thumb drive.

The recording was frequently not clear or loud. During testimony, Mr. Smith in particular had spoken so softly that I couldn't make out what he was saying—in the courtroom I had asked him to move the microphone closer to himself and to speak up, and even then I missed some of what he said. I didn't realize how important two particular bits of testimony I missed actually were.

In reviewing the recording at home, I used audio editing software to increase the volume of the sound as much as eight times, until I could make out some of the phrases I had never heard in the first place. Suddenly, buried in rapidly spoken testimony by Hans Jones, a segment of the amplified audio clearly revealed, "The side yard was already graded before construction of the house…" and then muffled but barely discernible, "it had a small slope toward the house." There was the answer to my first question.

Another particular phrase kept eluding me until I had both amplified it and also used software to clear up background and baseline noise. After working with the audio for about fifteen minutes, finally I heard Plaintiff Smith saying, "I had a crew back there for more than three days." That was the testimony I needed to complete my deliberations.

Minus the passages that duplicate material summarized above, here's the Judgment:

> The Court's judgment in this matter rests principally on the determination of two questions. First, were the tasks performed by Plaintiff for Defendant in June included under the first contract between the parties entered into in February as work to cure defects under that contract; or did they constitute offers under a separate contractual agreement? Second, did Plaintiff cause the physical damage to the drain pipe that he had installed?
>
> In some measure, the determination of the first question depends upon the determination of the second, and for that reason the Court looks first at culpability for the broken pipe. The Court finds the following facts upon the preponderance of the evidence.
>
> *Liability for Crushed Pipe*
> Plaintiff installed the pipe in question as part of Defendant's requested work under the contract agreed to in February. ...Plaintiff's work was finished prior to March of this year, and he billed Defendant for this work. Defendant paid that bill...
>
> ...From photographs of the area during the period when the pool deck was poured, Plaintiff pointed out that the concrete forms for the walkway alongside the house had been left out of a small area at the corner of the house so that the concrete buggy could go through. This area was precisely where the drain pipe installed by Plaintiff was.
>
> ...Defendant insisted that the pool contractor did not damage the Plaintiff's drain pipe, but the problem with his testimony is that Defendant was not at the construction site constantly and did not witness events that may have damaged

the pipe and doesn't know who did the damage. Plaintiff, on the other hand, spoke from personal knowledge asserting that he and his men did not damage the pipe.

Further, no evidence was presented at trial that supported any theory that Plaintiff himself damaged the pipe. The Court finds that **Plaintiff did not damage the pipe.** Because he did not, the Court finds that *Plaintiff did not perform his subsequent work for Defendant in June to cure alleged defects.* This finding is key, because Plaintiff and Defendant are in conflict over whether Plaintiff's June work was performed under the February contract between the two, or constituted new work under a subsequent agreement, whether a written one or not.

Whoever damaged the pipe, its not having been Plaintiff, and his knowing this, suggests that any work Plaintiff performed for Defendant subsequent to the discovery of the crushed pipe was work under a separate agreement. Further evidence for this conclusion exists:

Grading of Southeast Strip of Yard

Defendant argued at trial that the cause of the flooding at the corner of his house was Plaintiff's allegedly defective grading of the strip of land on the southwest side of the property, alongside the walkway from his driveway to the back of the house. Yet the evidence did not show that Defendant was especially concerned about that grading immediately after Plaintiff's work, or after the landscaping had been finished in the area, or at any time until flooding in the area occurred in June. If he did have such concern, the record does not show that he complained of it to Plaintiff. In fact, Defendant's own testimony suggested that it was when flooding took place that he considered that the slight slope of grass on the side toward his house might be to blame, but once Plaintiff dug and found the crushed pipe, Defendant relaxed his view of the possible fault of the grading. In his testimony, Defendant said that "if [the Plaintiff] hadn't dug up and found the crushed pipe, [he, the Defendant] might have been suing him for bad grading."

Neither was there evidence presented at trial that suggested that during their meetings in June the two parties had any discussion in the context of the idea that Plaintiff would be doing work to cure a defect in his previous job. While Defendant claimed later that Plaintiff was curing a defect, no discussion ever took place to that effect at the time.

Nor does the evidence support a conclusion that the substantial character of the grading was due to Plaintiff's work: credible testimony, in fact, was that prior to Plaintiff's work, the area was *already* roughly graded, and that Plaintiff performed only fine grading. This testimony indicates that the grade or slope of the area was already basically established. To the extent that the area slopes toward the house, it cannot be established by the evidence, either testimonial or documentary, that Plaintiff changed the slope of the strip of land, the initial angle of which he was not responsible for.

[The following evidence the Court gleaned from studying closely the exhibits admitted into evidence, though the parties had not taken much time to analyze what they had given me.] The proposal that became the first contract required Plaintiff to "Level and slope area (the entire yard of approx. 8,000 sq. ft.) for proper drainage." However, where the very edge of Defendant's property meets that of his neighbor on its southeastern side, a fence now stands where at the time of, or immediately prior to Plaintiff's initial work in February, a temporary, safety fence stood. Even if Plaintiff had intended to create a slope away from the house toward the neighboring property, he would not have been able to change the level of the contiguous property: therefore, the fixed level of the edge of the house and the fixed level of the contiguous property determined the basic slope, which was *towards* the house. Other drainage solutions would have to have been employed to mitigate drainage coming toward the house.

Nor, in fact, was it shown to the Court's satisfaction at trial that the slope of the strip of land was the total or even primary cause of the flooding. The Court finds Defendant called Plaintiff after the June flooding because he believed Plaintiff might be culpable. However, water came not simply from that narrow strip of land but also from behind the house: the water from that area certainly contributed substantially to what collected on the side of the house. The whole purpose of Defendant's request for the drainage pipe in question, when the house was being built, was to alleviate rainwater in the area, some of which would flow from the pool deck, and some from the strip of ground between pool and house. Because none of the water that was supposed to drain from the back through Plaintiff's pipe actually did—because the pipe was crushed—the side yard was burdened with water it could not handle.

The Court will add at this point that one of Plaintiff's photographic exhibits shows a plug his men discovered when they dug up the crushed drain pipe. The plug was in the end of the French drain coming from the house. The plug had no holes and the French drain was not connected to the drain pipe Plaintiff had installed. The plug obviously had kept the French drain from working, which allowed water merely seeping under the foundation to gather without being drained off. Plaintiff insisted that Defendant had instructed him to run a drainage pipe but not connect it to the French drain, per the demand of the installers of the French drain, and that Defendant had told him he would connect it himself later, after inspection of the French drain. Defendant contradicted this testimony saying he never gave Plaintiff such instructions, but the Court finds that the discovery of the plug in the French drain supports the Plaintiff's contentions: it had been capped until it could be connected. The defeat of the operation of the French drain further added to the drainage problem on the back and southeast side of the house, and more specifically to the water that gathered in Defendant's basement—the very problem the French drain was design to eliminate.

Torrential Rains

The parties stipulated that heavy rains inundated the region the first of June. The Court was struck with how readily each side found the other party or some third party responsible for Defendant's flooding problem. However, whatever personal culpability was involved, the Court regards with significance the evidence of the occurrence of unusual storms, which defeat some of the best drainage systems. The incidence of two parts of that drainage strategy being totally inoperable only compounded the problem. Whether Plaintiff's minor grading work played any significant part in the June flooding cannot be determined by this Court. Nor does it appear that Defendant was sufficiently convinced of that idea to ask Plaintiff to re-grade the area; he asked him only to fix the crushed pipe and install additional drainage solutions from the down spouts and around the house and pool deck.

Separate Contract

At root, the question of whether this subsequent work—not only fixing the crushed pipe but also installing additional drains—constituted a new offer and acceptance requiring separate consideration, depends on whether Plaintiff accepted responsibility for Defendant's June flooding. The three issues discussed in the above findings answer that question: (1) plaintiff did not crush his own pipe; (2) plaintiff did not concede any culpability of his fine grading work for the flooding; and (3) unusually heavy rains taxed the entire drainage plan now hobbled by disabled parts of it. These findings sufficiently support the Court's determination that the offers of work Plaintiff made to Defendant in June subsequent to flooding marked the inception of a new agreement if accepted. Defendant's acceptance of the proposed work completed the contract, enabling the Court to enforce it. In fact, the offers Plaintiff made were in response to requests Defendant made. Defendant's red herring of the initial contract's bolded demand for "a signed change order" were inapplicable: that contract had been completed. Nor did the first written contract preclude the freedom of the parties to enter into a subsequent, oral one. The new contract, separate from the first, was oral, and it called for Plaintiff to add catch basins to a pool deck area and by the east corner of the house, and to "replace broken smashed pipes and extend/split pipes." Plaintiff itemized these contract obligations in writing when he drew up his July invoice.

In billing Defendant, Plaintiff failed to break down labor costs, and he appears to have mingled an element of his initial contract with the July invoice, a "balance due" figure that is for the same amount as the one on the February bill. At trial, this factor seemed confusing, but it does not alter the fact that there was a second contract.

The Court is concerned to clarify any question about whether a meeting of minds took place concerning the offer and acceptance that occurred in June. While Defendant now holds that he believed the work was to be included under the first contract, he had no reason to believe at the time that Plaintiff had crushed his own pipe or that Plaintiff would install additional drainage solutions for free, and the Court holds that Defendant understood this at the time. The Court noted at trial that Defendant contradicted himself briefly as to the nature of the June agreement. Under cross examination about "the July contract," Defendant corrected counsel and said, "There was no contract," and counsel continued by calling it "the July bill." Yet only twelve minutes earlier under direct questioning by his own counsel, Defendant said of the June arrangement with Plaintiff, "I contracted with them." The Court finds that at the time the work was offered and accepted, there was a meeting of the minds as to the particulars of the offer and the nature of the agreement as a contract.

Consideration

The remaining question concerns the amount of consideration for this contract. No conversation took place between the parties in June about the total amount of consideration that would be due, but at trial Plaintiff pointed to the fact that at the end of his written contract with Defendant from February, he had stated that any further work would be billed at $45.00 per man hour for labor, plus materials. Plaintiff's exhibits show that in the same contract the parties had also agreed to a $100 per-hour equipment time charge.

In his Complaint, Plaintiff asked in two ways for damages: (1) for breach of contract, citing the contract amount as being the bottom line on the July bill, which was $5,570.00; and (2) by *quantum meruit,* stating that the service provided to Defendant had a fair market value of $5,570.00.

Plaintiff testified at trial that his labor charges were the same rate in July as they had been in February. While the July agreement was a separate contract involving separate consideration, the per-hour basis of the consideration is reasonably the information provided in the February Proposal/contract.

Plaintiff's labor charges in the February contract were not pulled from thin air but were the amounts he regularly quoted for labor: $45.00 per man hour. Plaintiff had explained to Defendant in the February Proposal that if Defendant wanted to request additional work he should understand it would be billed at $45.00 per man hour. The Court finds that Defendant understood that if he requested any separate work soon thereafter, he would incur the same or a similar charge. In light of the discovery of the crushed pipe, Defendant reasonably knew he would owe Plaintiff for both materials and labor.

It was reasonable, therefore, the Court finds, for Plaintiff to charge Defendant $45.00 per man hour for the extra work proposed and agreed to in June. However, ascertaining what those exact charges were is a matter laced with some confusion.

Plaintiff billed Defendant for $485.00 in materials (briefly itemized) plus $29.10 in tax, and "Labor at $45 per man hour," after which the bill simply listed four names: "Ever, Jr, Lee, Joe." Underneath the last name listed was, "Balance due $5,570". This figure is identical to the balance-due figure from the February bill. Defendant was adamant in cross examination of Plaintiff that the figure was inexplicable in the July bill. In the Court's view, Plaintiff mistakenly included the February balance in the July bill. The nature of the figure itself proves this finding:

(1) The total of the materials and tax listed is $514.10. If the balance due of $5,570.00 were correct, the labor charge would have been $5,055.90. If the four men listed had all worked the same number of hours as the bill implies, this exact figure would indicate that together they worked 28.088 hours, a odd number of hours and minutes to be recorded for the exact time of labor on the project. Exactly how long the men worked is not in the record, but when questioned by Defendant's counsel about the coincidence of the two "balance due" figures, Plaintiff stated with punctuated remembrance [and here's where the amplified, cleaned up recording came into play], "I had a crew back there for over three days doing the work at $45.00 an hour…" This estimated time lines up with very near precision to the 28.088 hours each of the four men would have worked as calculated from the July bill. If "over three days" were simply 3.5 eight-hour days, that would be 28 hours. The difference is so slight as to defy niggling criticism. Further, Plaintiff's testimony

about the three and a half days stands as conclusive testimony to his claim of damages in *quantum meruit*.

Interestingly, Plaintiff's testimony as to the ballpark figure of hours worked was un-contradicted. Defendant later said he thought the July bill was "extremely excessive," but he offered no testimony contradicting the length of time the men worked or how many of them were on the crew. When questioned as to whether he ever asked for a breakdown of the labor costs, he said No, "because I didn't agree with the bill in the first place." The Court finds that odd; it would seem that Defendant would *want* a full and detailed explanation of a bill he didn't think he owed.

(2) As for the figure of $5,570.00 appearing as the balance due on the February bill, it may have been transferred or retyped into the July bill by mistake, as Plaintiff referred to the February bill for some other purpose. It is worth noting, however, that even if Plaintiff mistakenly put the balance-due figure from February into the July bill, it may not have been to his benefit at all. The figure of $5,570.00, which includes materials, implies a labor time of 28.088 hours. If the crew had worked 29 hours instead, the mistaken balance due would have deprived Plaintiff of more than a hundred and fifty dollars.

The Court cannot determine with painstaking exactitude what precise figure Plaintiff may have meant to put in the July bill for four men working at $45.00 per hour for "more than three days," and Defendant did not offer testimony on that matter either. The Court is satisfied, however, that the total invoiced amount, from which can be calculated the labor charge, is a fair and accurate representation of the labor performed by Plaintiff for Defendant, both from the standpoint of the per-man-hour charge and from the principle of *quantum meruit*.

In sum, the Court finds that an oral contract, agreed to in June, existed: Defendant requested work done, Plaintiff offered to perform what Defendant requested, and

Defendant knew or had reason to know he would be billed for both materials and what Plaintiff's labor was worth. Defendant breached this contract by refusal to pay the amount billed, and Plaintiff has been damaged by $5,570.00 as the reasonable amount of his services.

THE COURT RENDERS JUDGMENT FOR PLAINTIFF AND ORDERS DEFENDANT TO PAY TO PLAINTIFF $5,650.00, WHICH INCLUDES THE COURT COST OF $80.00.

The Judgment in this case was the longest I had written to date. It brought to mind a comment made by the previous judge in my court, when I asked him about the relative wisdom of a magistrate's writing out judgments as opposed to using the simple Summary Court form that just says who won and how much he got. The judge told me, "Sometimes it works in your favor, sometimes not. On the one hand, you get to tell people exactly why you found for or against them, which they probably want to know. On the other hand, you give lawyers a lot of text they can pore over to find grounds to appeal you." Bottom line, you're damned if you do and damned if you don't—or, you manage to make your argument so well that there are no grounds for appeal, as long as you didn't make a legal error at trial.

I've always reasoned that where the issues are complicated, the written Judgment is a service to the parties, and that I'm a public servant, after all. I've also reasoned that *if* I'm appealed, the record that will go up to the circuit court will include a nice, fat written Judgment that will be in the hands of the judge who hears the appeal. He'll read that Judgment. If he had nothing but a terse Summary Judgment in front of him he would know nothing of why I decided what I did, unless I had read the Judgment in open court on the record: the appellate judge will listen to the recording of the trial. When I delay issuing judgment until a day or a week later, however, the decision isn't in the recording. If I don't write out my findings, my basis in law, and my arguments as well as conclusions, the appellate court will have no idea if I made a finding of fact that supported my Judgment. On the whole, I conclude that I will be appealed less often if I write than if I don't.

In this case, I waited out the thirty days and closed the book. Hans said Nein to an appeal and Wojciech said Tak! to his check for services rendered. I was glad, not only because I wouldn't have to go through the drudgery of preparing a return, but because there really was no sense in Germany and Poland getting into it again.

16
DRUNK SPENDING

Numerous people who are well to do and generous of heart spread their money around liberally and never look back. A few, however, regret their actions when they find themselves in a bind. This is never more true than when they parted with their money when they weren't sober.

The Plaintiff in the following case found herself in such a predicament after several years of friendship with the objects of her benevolence, and the situation turned into an adversarial proceeding in my court.

THE PLEADINGS

Jolene Smith filed a Summons and Complaint with the Court against Bill and Lynn Jones alleging a host of debts: principally the balance owed for a motorcycle; then a half dozen small loans totaling $750.00; six months of health insurance payments at $250.00 each; two month's rent and a security deposit; and a sofa valued at $1,000.00. She tacked onto these claims a prayer for the Court to order the return of other furniture valued at $1,100.00— items she claimed Defendants possessed.

The Joneses Answered admitting their debt for the sofa, denying they possessed any other furniture belonging to Smith, denying almost all the claim for the motorcycle, denying the claims for rent and security deposit, and denying they owed any money for loans. In an extended note along with their Answer, the Joneses wanted to inform the Court that Smith was an alcoholic who was rarely sober in the previous two years.

THE EVIDENCE

Plaintiff, a woman of perhaps forty—though she bore some of the physical indications of hard living—appeared for court with a slightly younger man, who turned out to be her live-in boyfriend. Defendants were a couple who looked wiry and fit, both of them. Mr. Jones had a long goatee and moustache, previously blonde but now mostly white. Both were tanned and a little prematurely lined from a lot of time outdoors. No other witnesses were present.

Summary of Proceedings

Before any testimony, I informed Smith that her request for the return of furniture was not something the Magistrate Court would do under a Summons and Complaint: she would have to file a Claim and Delivery action, or she could ask the Court for the monetary value of the furniture if she didn't want the pieces back. If she did that, however, her total suit would be for more than the Magistrate Court's jurisdictional limit, and the case would have to be transferred to the Court of Common Pleas—I wouldn't hear the case. She agreed to drop that part of her claim, wanting the matter to be decided *today!* There was a note in her voice that said she needed money.

Jolene Smith's story was that she and Lynn Jones had been friends in another state from years back. At some point Smith moved to South Carolina. A few years ago Lynn, still living out of state, called to ask if her daughter Kristen could come live with Smith for a few months while Jones was going through a rough period and then a messy divorce. Smith agreed, and subsequently became quite fond of Kristen and thought of her almost as a daughter of her own. Smith was not married but she was living with a man. Eventually Lynn Jones got a divorce decree, found a boyfriend, Bill, and quickly remarried. Kristen moved back to the other state to be with her mother and new hubby but remained in close touch with Smith.

About two years before this court case, Jones and her new mate decided to relocate to make a fresh start. They told Smith about this desire, and Smith said she knew of a rental house, right across from her home in fact. The house seemed perfect to the Joneses, but Bill Jones needed a few months to exit his job smoothly and find another in the new location. It was never made clear to the Court exactly why, but Jolene Smith cosigned with Bill Jones for the lease on the house. One of the major claims in her suit was that the Joneses owed her for the security deposit and two months of rent that she paid on their behalf. She didn't have receipts. However, Bill Jones did. They were made out to both him and Jolene Smith, because her name was on the lease with him. However, he had a fourth, numbered receipt in series with the other three, made out to him alone, for some application he had paid for when he paid the deposit and rent—a background check as he thought he remembered. In rebuttal, Smith claimed she was standing next to Jones at the time and had given Jones the cash to make the payments. Jones indignantly and very credibly denied any such thing.

Smith also said that she paid for the utilities to be connected. She *did* have receipts for these deposits and connection fees, but so did the Joneses! They had recently put the utilities in their names, and the utility companies indicated they would take care of refunding Smith for her previous payments. Jolene Smith sheepishly admitted at this point that she had gotten a refund check from the water company about two weeks ago (so why didn't she tell this to the Court up front before making the claim for repayment?), but she hadn't gotten any money from the power company. The Joneses said energetically, almost in unison, that the power company told them Smith had an outstanding balance on her own power bill, and they would deduct that amount from any refund. (I didn't have a chance to disallow the hearsay before they blurted it out, but it wasn't material to the issue. The Joneses had documentary proof that they had negotiated the refunds for Smith by making their own deposits with the two utility companies. Whether Smith had forfeited getting a refund because she fell behind on her own bill, was not relevant to the case.)

Anyway, the Joneses both said, they didn't ask Jolene to pay the fees for them in the first place. She did, however, and then she waved off their offers to repay her and said, "I got the money, don't worry about it." Smith, it seems, had just received a very, *very* lucrative severance payment from her employer, and she felt generous. She was also a little tipsy at the time.

Lynn Jones and daughter Kristen moved in after the lease was signed, and in a few months Bill joined them. For a year or so things went well between the friends. Then Smith decided to buy a motorcycle for the Joneses. The Joneses had ridden together often in the other state but Bill had sold his motorcycle to help with moving expenses. (Learning of the Joneses' riding together, I could now easily see Bill in the driver's seat, his goatee parting around his face in the wind, and Lynn on the back with her bottle blonde hair braided down her back.) Smith, without being asked by the Joneses to shop around for a bike, had found a nice, used Honda Shadow 750 she thought would be perfect for Bill and Lynn. (The Court's ears pricked up, since I ride a similar bike.) Bill said that Jolene talked him into buying the motorcycle. She sold it to him for what she paid, $2,500.00 (quite a steal for that motorcycle). He bought it in spite of the fact that he considered himself a Harley man, and he made an initial payment to Jolene Smith. *He* said it was a payment of $1,100.00. *Smith* said she had never gotten that payment. She did say he had paid her $800.00 somewhere along the line, and perhaps another $150.00, though she couldn't remember exactly. It was Smith's uncertainty about the payments and their dates, and her inability to produce any receipts or anything written about an agreement to buy a motorcycle, that began to leave the Court dubious of her claim.

Smith also claimed that on numerous occasions she went over to the Joneses or Lynn Jones came over to her house, and that Lynn asked for money—to pay a bill, to buy clothes, or to pay "court bills." During this testimony Jones looked outraged, and when she had the opportunity both to cross examine and to testify, she vigorously denied ever receiving any loans. In fact, she didn't have, and never had had, any "court bills." She had no idea what

Smith was talking about. She said her husband had a very good job and they didn't need anyone to lend them money.

This bit of testimony by Smith then prompted Lynn Jones to tell the Court that in the previous two years, up until about six months ago anyway, Smith had rarely been sober. Her abuse of alcohol coincided with her job loss. Even though she had been given a large severance check, she may have been angry and hurt about the job situation and turned to the bottle. Lynn was happy to say that Jolene had gotten sober a few months back, but she said that for well over a year Smith had spent like a drunken sailor and had given them money indiscriminately. Bill Jones chimed in, confirming that Smith was an alcoholic and was usually at least a little bit drunk.

My initial reaction to this testimony was to squelch it, because it seemed to me it was likely irrelevant—*ad hominem* argument instead of actual evidence. The connection to the case, however, was made apparent by one particular event that Mr. Jones described when telling me about the disputed payment of $1,100.00. Jones said he gave Jolene Smith $1,100.00 as sort of a down payment on the motorcycle, when the two were out in her front yard. He said Smith was visibly drunk when she took the money. Jones handed over cash and didn't get a receipt. A couple of months later, Smith asked when he was going to pay her for the bike, and he said he could give her "another few hundred dollars" in a week or so. Intoxicated on this occasion, too, Smith asked what he meant by "another," since he hadn't paid anything yet. He reminded her of the $1,100.00, and she became irate, cursed at him and told him she didn't have any of his @#$%& money. A few days later, however, mostly sober, she told him she had found the $1,100.00 in her washing machine. At court, however, she didn't remember any of this.

Smith, revealingly, never contradicted this testimony, but she ignored the defense and still maintained the Joneses owed her $2,000.00 for the bike. Noting that the bike was $2,500.00 and she had acknowledged payments of around a thousand, I wanted to know where she got her figure, and she said she had added in miscellaneous loans that offset the Joneses' payments of about $950.00.

The Joneses were willing to admit to owing a little money on the motorcycle: $400.00. They stated they had paid the disputed $1,100.00, $800.00 (stipulated), $200.00 (not $150.00 as Smith said). They told the Court they had promised Smith they would pay her the remaining $400.00 when she produced the title. I asked if that was sort of "the deal" they made with her, and they said it was. However, Smith couldn't find the title, they said. Several times in the previous year they had asked her for the title, and she promised to look for it, but on most of those occasions she had been drinking and seemed morose and distant.

She had been paying the property taxes on the motorcycle and then coming over with updated registration and license plate stickers. The Joneses couldn't put the bike in their names and take over the registration until they got the title, and they were holding out the final payment until Smith located it. Smith never contradicted this testimony about the title and last payment. Nor did she contest the Joneses testimony that Smith's new boyfriend had menacingly told them that if they didn't pay Smith, he would help her get a replacement title on the basis of its being lost, and he personally would come over and take the motorcycle back. (The Court believed he wanted the bike for himself.)

On the other claims, Smith said the Joneses owed her six months' payment for health insurance for Kristen, at $250.00 per month. The Joneses were visibly fuming across the aisle, and Smith reacted by stating that she would take just three months instead of six. However, when Lynn Jones got a chance to counter, she produced a text on her phone from Jolene that read a lot like Jolene had decided all on her own to take out the insurance policy for Kristen (who was in her early twenties and not covered by anyone else). Lynn stated in no uncertain terms that Jolene had never asked her if she and Bill would pay for the policy, and they had never offered to repay her. Lynn's position was that if Jolene wanted to act like a rich godmother and give Kristen things, she would let her.

Finally, Smith said she had bought a sofa for the Joneses when they moved in and that they had agreed to repay her for it. Bill and Lynn across the aisle were reacting visibly, but this time they were nodding enthusiastically and they interjected that they had indeed agreed to repay her: they owed her $1,000.00 for the sofa. They were more than willing to admit to what they *did* owe her, and they did so just as demonstrably as they denied the other claims.

JUDGMENT

I briefly deliberated on the matter and called to mind the numerous things the two parties displayed that pointed me to the truth. Body language, speech patterns and content of testimony were all considered. People often, if not usually, give themselves away when they're lying: wandering sentences, suspicious use of the passive voice in verbs, lack of energy in making claims, fuzzy details, shifting story—all the things that the average person uses to detect dishonesty. There was plenty of that in this hearing. In part, here was my decision:

> Upon the preponderance of the evidence the Court finds as follows:
>
> Plaintiff's claims for a security deposit and rental payments on Defendants' behalf in June and July of the previous year were not substantiated at trial. ...The Court finds Defendant's account to be reliable that he himself made those payments, for which he has receipts. That claim is dismissed in favor of Defendants.
>
> Plaintiff asked for repayment of amounts she paid for electric and water hookups at Defendants' leased property. The evidence is substantial that Defendants do not owe Plaintiff for these amounts. This claim is dismissed in favor of Defendants.
>
> Plaintiff alleged that she lent Defendants at least $750.00 in cash for various reasons, and Defendants strongly denied the claims. The Court has insufficient evidence to find for

Plaintiff in the matter, as there was no writing memorializing such loans. This claim also is dismissed.

Plaintiff alleged that she had purchased health insurance for Defendant's daughter, and she asked the Court to order repayment. The preponderance of evidence, in particular the documentary evidence, persuades the Court that Plaintiff unilaterally purchased insurance coverage without consulting with Defendants and without securing any agreement from them to repay any amount of said premiums, whether in whole or in part. This claim is dismissed.

Plaintiff also alleged to have bought a motorcycle for Defendants for $2,500.00, to which Defendants agreed. Plaintiff alleged that Defendant(s) owed her $2,000.00 for the balance of the motorcycle. Plaintiff stated that she had figured into her claim of $2,000.00 the miscellaneous loans she said she made to Defendants. The Court notes that Plaintiff's accounting for this alleged balance of $2,000.00 was more than fuzzy and was not supported by any documentation.

Defendants, however, testified that they made an initial payment of $1,100.00 which Plaintiff lost and then found in an odd place in her own house; that they made further payments of $800.00 and $200.00; and that they therefore currently owe a balance of $400.00, which they previously proposed to remit to Plaintiff in exchange for the title to the motorcycle. However, Defendants alleged vehemently, in testimony *not contradicted* by Plaintiff, that Plaintiff would not and could not produce the title.

The Court finds Defendants' testimony compelling, and finds that they currently owe $400.00 toward the purchase of the motorcycle.

During the two year period preceding this case, Plaintiff appears to have been engaged in casual largesse in the wake of her having received a generous severance package from her previous employer, but she didn't come to a meeting of the minds with her neighbors about much of her generosity.

Because of its relevance to this case, the Court notes as a matter of law that failure to deliver title within forty-five (45) days of final payment constitutes title fraud under South Carolina law. The Court further notes that it appears that the motorcycle referenced in this suit is not subject to any perfected lien, is therefore not collateral for any loan, and that no written agreement exists by which the motorcycle could be seized whether by private action or through the courts.

Upon the above findings, in which the Court has found a stipulated claim for $1,000.00 and a balance of $400.00 due toward a motorcycle:

THE COURT RENDERS JUDGMENT FOR PLAINTIFF AND ORDERS DEFENDANTS TO PAY TO PLAINTIFF $1,400.00.

A week or so after the trial Defendant Bill Jones wrote the Court a note thanking me for the Judgment against him. He and his wife always paid their bills, he said, and they had already paid Smith the $1,400.00. Now they were just waiting for the title to the bike. The Fall Motorcycle Rally in Daytona was coming up soon, and they wanted no loose ends when they hopped on and took off for the beach.

17
ITEMIZED DEDUCTIONS

Annual tax returns aren't the only place where people become concerned about itemized deductions. In landlord-tenant situations, once a rental period has ended, a landlord typically has a security deposit in trust from which he or she may deduct the cost of repairing physical damage to the rental unit that is beyond normal wear and tear. Quite often, landlords and tenants have significant disagreements about whether or not the deductions are justified. When they can't work it out, I often see them in court.

THE PLEADINGS

Juanita and Javy Smith filed suit just before Thanksgiving against Liza Jones over the amount of their security deposit returned to them after they were evicted from a rental house Jones managed. They claimed Jones had promised them the return of $1,400.00, which represented a security deposit of $900.00 and a last-month's rent payment of $700.00 (required by their lease), minus some agreed-upon amounts. Jones had returned only $387.69 to them. The Smiths wanted the balance up to $1,400.00 and another $2,000.00 for "stress." (I think they needed Christmas spending money; in a decade on the bench I had never awarded money for stress). In her Answer to the Complaint, Liza Jones—who, from the look of the filing, had obviously consulted with an attorney but prepared her own document—took issue with service of the suit and claimed that she was not even the proper defendant. As to the specific issues of money, she simply filed a general denial. The Court set a date for trial during the first week of December.

THE EVIDENCE

Plaintiffs appeared with a group of relatives and friends in support of them. Defendant appeared with her husband. The Court put everyone under oath at one time and then tried first to get to the bottom of Defendant's objections to service and whether or not she had been named properly.

In her Answer, Liza Jones told the Court that her company, RESales, LLC, was the proper Defendant, not she. She claimed to be but a partner in the LLC. Prior to the hearing the Court had consulted the Secretary of State website to see what information was there on the incorporation status. RESales, LLC, was incorporated in good standing, and its agent for service of legal process was a Jane Jackson, who lived locally. The Court's initial thought was that Jackson might be another partner in RESales.

Since Jones had made the nature of her corporation the first and possibly central matter of this case, I wanted to probe the subject through a series of questions. First, I asked Jones to confirm the Secretary of State's information about her corporation.

She said, "Well, it's not a corporation."

I paused, curious about her answer, and then said, "Do you know what "LLC" stands for?"

She answered, "Yes, it's 'Limited Liability… uh, Corporation'—oh, I see, of course; I'm sorry."

I then asked her if I were correct that she was not the agent for service, but rather Jane Jackson, and she said Yes. Was Jackson another partner, I wanted to know. No, she said, Jackson was a CPA who did her books.

Finally, I asked her just how many partners there were in this LLC. She stammered softly and then said, "Uh, just one." She was the *only* partner. RESales, LLC, *was* Liza Jones, sole partner. Her reluctance to divulge this information I believed was due to her intention to leave the impression that her company was more than just a one-woman show. Under the counsel of her shadow lawyer, she was probably trying to delay the suit or get it dismissed on the technical requirement of service so that it would have to be re-filed against RESales and served again, next time to Jane Jackson. All that would take time, and it might get her past the Christmas season, too.

I also confirmed from Jones's answers that the Court's information was correct that Jones had filed for the May eviction against the Smiths in her own name, not the name of her company. Furthermore, the check she had written to the Smiths as a rebate of their security deposit came from her own joint account with her husband, not RESales, LLC. In fact, she admitted, RESales had no bank account. She operated the company out of her family funds.

I asked if Jones had a written lease with the Smiths and she did. I inspected a copy without objection and discovered that the landlord was listed as "RESales, LLC; Liza Jones, Operating Manager." On the signature page Jones had written the same thing. "RESales, LLC; Liza Jones, op. mgr." "RESales, LLC" appeared nowhere else in the document and it showed up nowhere else in the evidence that would be presented presently at trial. This was a show starring Liza Jones.

With this picture of RESales as a bare-bones company operating on a shoe string, I ruled that RESales, LLC, was the proper Defendant but that service upon Liza Jones was proper because she had given the Smiths every reason to believe that she was the landlord and the person they needed to sue. I amended the suit to show RESales as Defendant, however, because any judgment against Defendant would be against the company, not Jones herself: the lease had been with the company, not Jones personally.

Preliminaries having been taken care of, I took testimony from each party about the actual Complaint and Answer. I questioned each party back and forth, and then allowed any additional testimony that either one might think was necessary.

The Facts

When Liza Jones and Juanita and Javy Smith signed the written lease on a house at 101 Wonderful Lane in January of the present year, the agreement required that the Smith's pay a security deposit of $900.00 and the first and last month's rents at $700.00 per month. The Smiths made those payments and took possession of the rental property. Barely four months later, however, after they had been consistently late paying rent, landlord RESales—aka Liza Jones—filed for eviction against the Smiths. The Smiths didn't contest the eviction. The Court issued a Writ of Ejectment on May 21 and the constable posted it on May 22, which was a Friday.

The Smiths moved out over the weekend of the 22nd and met Liza Jones the following Tuesday, May 26, at the house to turn over possession. Javy Smith took a cell phone video as Juanita and Liza stood near the kitchen sink. The video captured Jones's agreement to return the security deposit and the last month's rent. (The Smiths had paid rent for May (late), so the last-month's rent they had prepaid would not be needed to cover unpaid rent upon move-out.) Jones agreed to the amounts upon her brief assessment that there was no damage to the rental unit. She testified that she felt rushed, however, because during the hasty walk-through, the Smiths left their car running at the curb with their little children inside. Moreover, Jones said inside the house the men in the Smith group were standing around in the rooms as if guarding something, and she felt intimidated by them. She was referring to the men who were in the courtroom for the hearing.

In fact, Smith's actual statement, as she gestured across the aisle at the defense table and the friends in the gallery just behind it, was that the men were "intimidating, *as you can see,* your honor." I looked at them and didn't see anything of the sort. What I saw was that the men were all Mexicans. While one of them was rather stocky, all of them were very short; Javy Jones later chuckled and told me he was only 4'11" and didn't intimidate anyone. Jones's remarks were reflective of her vague fear of the ethnic group. Jones was painting an uncomplimentary picture of her prejudices.

Since the Smiths intended to make a point of Jones's taking 31 days instead of 30 to return their deposit and/or accounting, I wanted to know exactly when the Smiths turned the property back over to Jones. That would be the exact day from which to count Jones's 30 days. It turned out that the Smiths surrendered possession of the rental property at the end of the inspection on May 26. Did they give her the keys then, I asked. Yes, Jones said, and they gave her *three* sets of keys, where she had given them only *one* set in January.

That thought prompted Jones to further her theory of the damages inside the house. She told the Court, "Your honor, obviously they made other keys, and I don't think they turned all of them over to me. I think they kept a set." As part of her theory, she needed to assume they had keys with which to re-enter the house to damage it once she left, so she grasped for straws in this detail about the number of keys surrendered. I found her logic entirely flawed, but it was revealing to me that she leapt to such conclusions about these Mexican people.

Jones locked the house as they all left, and on their way out, she noticed a garden hose connected to an outside spigot and she reminded the Smiths to take it with them. Jones left without seeing them disconnect the hose. However, when she returned in a couple of hours after having gone to a hardware store to buy new locks for the house, she found upon further and more extensive inspection inside that there was damage to the floors she had not noticed earlier, and miscellaneous damage to other woodwork and the areas around two ceiling vents. She told me she believed someone had come back in and slashed the floors deliberately.

Further, she discovered that the spigot to which the Smiths' hose had been connected was now broken and cast aside. Jones believed the Smiths had gone back in the house and gouged and slashed the family room floor and cut the tile in the kitchen. Why they would have done that she didn't say. I looked at her photographs. They showed some gouges in a place or two that looked to me to be caused by a heavy piece of furniture without any protection for its feet, being moved slightly over a period of time. I saw no "slashes," and the cuts in the kitchen floor were neat cuts down the exact middle of the faux grout, in two or three places. Nothing about the photos suggested malicious damage. Further, as I looked at and listened to the Smiths, I didn't sense anything about them that supported the idea that they had any retributive, violent, or malicious bones in their bodies. In fact, their demeanor and manner suggested they were being honest and ingenuous with me. Sometimes, the sense impression a judge gets when studying people as they testify under oath is one of the most important indicators of who, between the parties, is actually telling the truth, or just making sense.

Jones repaired the damage to the house and tallied the costs, deducting them from the $1,400.00 she had agreed earlier to return to the Smiths. On June 24 she wrote a check for $387.69 to the Smiths and mailed it that day, along with a copy of an accounting of her deductions from the security deposit, as required by law. In their suit, the Smiths had claimed that they did not receive the check and accounting within 30 days as required by state statutes. The law says that if a landlord doesn't send the money and/or the itemized accounting of deductions within 30 days, he or she is liable for *treble* damages. So if Jones were found to owe the Smiths $1,400.00, they might actually be awarded a judgment for $4,200.00. That would be a nice Christmas shopping sum.

Jones had written the check on the 29th of the 30 days' period, mailing the check and accounting from a local post office in time for the afternoon pickup. Jones had a reasonable expectation that the letter would be delivered the next day, since the post office and the delivery address were not even five miles apart. According to the Smiths, however, the letter did not arrive until the 31st day, which was a Saturday.

When the Smiths got the letter and the check, they took issue seriously with Jones's deductions, wanting to hold her to the $1,400.00 she said she'd return, as memorialized in one of the videos. When she didn't do so, they filed suit.

There was a great deal of testimony about the floors, the photographs, the videos, and the accounting. At one point I held up each of Jones's photos one at a time and showed them to the Smiths. What did they have to say about the damage in this one? And this one? etc. When I was showing them Jones's photo of the kitchen before the Smith's move-in, Javy excitedly pointed at a place in the 4X6 picture and said, "In fact, your honor, you can see the floor peeled up right there." He put his finger on a specific place and I thought I saw what he meant, but I was not wearing strong reading glasses and I made a mental note to look closer later. We looked at the other pictures, and while the Smiths contested the kitchen floor "cuts" in vigorous terms, they made no attempt to contradict the other damage except for the spigot. That, too, they denied having anything to do with. It was in great part their sincerity and candor about the items they *didn't* contest that convinced me they were telling the truth about the issues they *did* contest.

After both parties had parried a bit back and forth and rebutted each other's contentions, I announced I would deliberate and return a verdict within the week. When I had the opportunity to study the evidence even more carefully than in court, I used magnifying lenses to look at fine details. I discovered a few things in the video and photographs that helped me decide the case. In most relevant part, here's the judgment that went out to the parties:

THE JUDGMENT

The Court is always concerned with substantial justice, the guiding principle of all our courts. In the Magistrate court where the rules are relaxed, substantial justice sometimes guides a decision where circumstances make the rigid requirements of a statute seem artificial. Such is the case where Plaintiff wishes to hold Defendant to the letter of the law that requires a landlord to return a security deposit and/or itemized accounting of deductions from that deposit within *thirty days* of surrender of possession of a rental unit. In this case, the accounting arrived one day late.

However, I find that landlord Jones acted in good faith with respect to the requirements of law. She had no control over whether the post office did its job with alacrity. If she had mailed the check on the 29th day and the post office had taken not two days but three months to deliver the letter, certainly the Court would have found that she acted in good faith while the USPS was to blame for tardiness. It is the Court's opinion that the USPS was to blame for tardiness for a single day's delay. This case does not merit finding Jones in violation of the law.

As to damages, the Court finds that, according to the testimony of both parties, the physical damage to the spigot did not take place while the Smiths were in possession of the rental unit. Therefore, that damage cannot be deducted from the tenants' security deposit since they were no longer tenants when the damage took place. While Defendant believes someone connected with the Smiths damaged the spigot, she did not observe such and would have to either file suit against them or prefer charges against them and then prove that a particular person committed an act of malicious damage to property. Defendant did not do this at trial. The Court finds that Defendant's deduction of the cost of repairing the spigot, which was $33.12, was unjustified.

Flooring damages consisted of replacement of numerous tiles of laminate flooring in the family room and a repair to sections of vinyl flooring in the kitchen/laundry area. The Court considered the testimony of both parties and their witnesses, viewed two videos moved into evidence by Plaintiffs, and studied photographs entered into evidence by Defendant. Upon close examination of all the evidence it is clear to the Court that:

> 1. The kitchen vinyl floor was damaged when the Smiths moved in. Jones claimed that the floor was new in January of this year, and perhaps it was, but one of her own photographs *taken in January* reveals, upon close inspection, that at the time tenants took possession of the unit, the damage reflected in a *May* photo was already present. I found Plaintiffs' testimony entirely credible that the damage was due to cutting and/or peeling up portions of the vinyl floor to repair a water line; Defendant failed

to repair the cuts entirely by the time the tenants took possession. I must therefore find that Defendant inappropriately charged Plaintiffs for repairing the cuts to the kitchen vinyl floor.

2. Jones deducted $951.19 for damage to both floors, but broke down the costs further for the Court in an exhibit. She spent $8.62 on flooring glue for the vinyl tile. Her cost for "Labor to repair floor damage" covered the repair of all flooring areas including the kitchen tile. Jones described in testimony how difficult and extensive it was to repair the laminate floor in the family room, but she described the damage to the kitchen floor as requiring only some glue. This description justifies my inference that any labor involved in repairing the kitchen floor was negligible, and no one gave me any reason to believe otherwise. The Court finds that Defendant's deduction of $8.62 from the security deposit for repair of the kitchen floor was unjustified.

3. The labor cost of repairing the family area, however, is entirely justified. The evidence shows damage to the laminate flooring that required replacement of a substantial portion of it. Plaintiffs had no effective response to Defendant's photographs. Just before Jones arrived for the inspection, the Smiths walked through the empty house and took a quick, jumpy, cell phone video in every room. They moved it into evidence as proof of their claim that the house was in great shape. I studied this video, and frankly, it didn't support the Smith's claims. Nor were the Smiths able to contest Jones's evidence of other miscellaneous damage to the rental unit, the costs of which she reasonably deducted from the security deposit.

There were two costs, however, that Jones cannot reasonably deduct: $5.80 for a respirator mask that presumably is reusable; and $373.34 for "lost income," which there was no testimony to substantiate.

Finally, the Court dismisses Plaintiffs' claim for "stress," etc. (They never testified about being under stress.)

The total damages RESales/Liza Jones was justified in deducting is $791.43. Originally she deducted $1,212.31 from the $1,400.00 figure she and the Smiths agreed to. However, of this $1,400.00 figure, only $900.00 was a security deposit. The law lets her deduct repairs *from the security deposit.* However, nothing in the statutes provides for her to deduct repair costs from a prepaid last-month's rent. It is the finding of this Court that the $700.00 Plaintiffs paid Defendant as the last month's rent should have been returned *in its entirety* to Plaintiffs. Defendant was justified in deducting $791.43 *from the security deposit only*.

In consequence, the balance of the security deposit, diminished by the reasonable repairs, should have been $108.57. The entire last month's rent of $700.00 should have been returned as well. Defendant should have written a check to Plaintiffs for $808.57. Her check was for $387.69. The difference is $420.88.

THE COURT ORDERS DEFENDANT RESALES, LLC, TO PAY TO PLAINTIFFS JUANITA AND JAVY SMITH $500.88, WHICH INCLUDES THE COURT COST OF $80.00.

The Smiths came hoping to get a Judgment for around three thousand dollars. They got one for just a little over four hundred bucks. I figured the "stress" claim was calculated to get Jones to settle before court, and it hadn't worked. However, the Smiths prevailed, even if not for as much as they had hoped. Still, if Jones paid them promptly, which was certainly in her best interest, the Smiths would have a little extra Christmas spending money. Feliz Navidad!

18
FAITH HEALER WOUND

My background in Christian ministry made me familiar with charismatic churches, though I had more exposure to charismatic worship through television than live worship events. Like most Americans, I've seen televised services from nationally known charismatic churches, featuring rowdy, noisy gatherings down in front of the platform, dancing to rousing gospel music, shouting, rampant tongues-speaking, and flamboyant gestures intended to impart healing, effect spiritual filling, or accomplish casting out of demons. I suppose a service featuring all these things was probably out of the ordinary.

Anyway, watching televangelists and faith healers was interesting for many reasons, not the least of which was observing the coordinated activities of assistants around them who took care of the necessary details: managing the line of people coming for miracles, leading away people who were healed or who needed to be redirected away from the charismatic preacher, and standing by to catch people who fell over "in the Spirit" when overcome in the moment.

It never occurred to me earlier in my life, when I was in career ministry, that one day I might hear a case where someone got injured in a service otherwise all about healing. Of course, back then I had no idea I would one day be a judge, either. And if preachers see all kinds of interesting people, I think judges see even more.

The Pleadings

Wanda Smith appeared at the courthouse one day to file a Complaint against Quentarious Jones, whom she identified as the pastor of a local church. Smith had been in one of Jones's services, when, according to her Complaint, Smith "was hit for no apparent reason." She said she had fallen on the hard floor and that the incident had left her with permanent spinal injuries. It all took place nearly three years ago, and Smith had had dozens of doctor visits, many prescription medicines, consultations with surgeons, and many chiropractic treatments in that time. She waived the amount of her damages over the limit of the Magistrate Court, $7,500.00, but the total of what she had spent to feel better was much, much higher.

I alerted the Constable of the Court that he would be serving a preacher in a couple of days, and that it might be interesting. I had no idea, of course, how or where he might find the Rev. Jones.

The next day I was on my way to lunch with my wife when the Constable called my cell phone. He told me he had served the preacher, and that, "Boy, he's a piece of work." By that, he explained that he meant the preacher was skimming money off the church and had a huge house, a full sized Hummer, and a gleaming new Cadillac, all of them brilliant white. I had to calm down the Constable somewhat. The pastor—whose actual title was not "the Reverend," but instead, "Bishop Jones"—might not be skimming anything but only be the grateful recipient of a grand salary by his church.

I looked up the church. It turned out that it was occupying the buildings of the former Fuller Street Baptist Church, a few blocks from the courthouse. I knew the facility, and their congregation couldn't be very large, and probably was not very wealthy.

Of course, it could be that Bishop Jones was fully in command of the church and personally handled all its finances, and took his salary off the top before the rest was applied to church expenses. There is an old story among preachers that an evangelist took the offering into a room and threw it in the air and said, "Whatever comes down is mine; whatever stays up is the Lord's." I've seen a film where Marjo Gortner, the child evangelist who made it big for a while and was eventually discredited, did pretty much that very thing with the offering. Maybe Bishop Jones didn't so much "skim" as let the church pay the necessary bills, while he took the larger share left over.

At any rate, I struggled to remain impartial. Yet, over the years, I had seen myself experience responses to human beings that were typical in humanity, and yet rise above those responses— sometimes quite cynical on the surface—to hear a case without prejudice, often finding in favor of a party I didn't at all like. I worked at this kind of impartiality, knowing it was crucial to justice.

The Constable had called to tell me not only that the Defendant was riding in style, but that confrontation had taken place at his door. The Bishop became loud and irate and said he wasn't about to take that paper from the Constable, that he was going to give him the name of his lawyer and the Constable could go give it to him. Bishop Jones went inside and returned with a piece of paper, shoved it at my officer and shut the door.

My Constable told me he would just go over and give it to the attorney. I told him no, he would go back and leave the paper and consider it served. The man knew who he was, what he was there for, and what the paper was. That was good service.

The Constable was in his car driving away as he had called me, and as he turned around and began driving back, he saw the Bishop heading out quickly in his shiny Caddy. But the Constable knew there was someone else at home, and he found the Bishop's wife. She was on her cell phone to her husband in his car, and she was giving him down the country for his attitude. She apologized to the Constable and accepted service of the lawsuit. The Constable sent a phone text to me telling me it was done.

Jones, through his attorney Amy Greene, filed an Answer, in which he thoroughly denied all Wanda Smith's allegations. Jones said not only was the floor carpeted, but that someone caught Smith when she fell. Jones gave a blanket denial of any other allegation and then stated a Counterclaim, that Smith's allegations were frivolous, and that accordingly Jones wanted Smith to pay for his costs in defending himself. Further, Jones demanded a jury trial. That meant that the case would go to one of our courts assigned to do Alternative Dispute Resolution—mediation. I wouldn't decide the case unless the parties reached an impasse.

I expected that Plaintiff Smith would see that Defendant Jones had gotten a lawyer and she would get one for herself. If that happened, I would normally anticipate that some settlement would be reached during mediation. While a Plaintiff who is unrepresented might be intimidated by a defendant's lawyer into dropping his or her suit, two lawyers usually mean a fair fight. And of "win, lose or draw," a draw—a settlement—is more likely.

The case sat in the mediation court for months without anything happening. Its being a case I wanted very much to hear, I had the civil clerk call and inquire about its status. The mediation court said they would move it up in the schedule, which they did, and instead of a settlement, as I thought would happen, the parties were at an impasse. While Plaintiff Smith didn't get a lawyer, she was apparently adamant in her claims and didn't consent to dropping a single allegation. The parties were unable to agree on a settlement and the case came back to me.

Nor did Defendant drop his jury trial demand. By the time all this happened, I was within just four months of retiring, and I very much wanted to hear this case, or at least preside over it so a jury could hear and decide it; so I wanted to set a term of jury trials for this one case only, if necessary. We pulled jurors and set a trial date for barely six weeks before my last day as a magistrate.

Jury Strikes

Selecting a jury isn't usually overly interesting; there's a lot of roll calling, speechifying, and repetition. Plaintiff in this case made it interesting, however.

By the time I entered the courtroom at the precise hour of 9:00 o'clock, as scheduled, the courtroom gallery was peopled with prospective jurors, about seventy-five of them. Then the parties came in from the back, the plaintiff Wanda Smith first. She came with agonizing slowness down the center aisle, leaning on her rollator. Around her neck was a padded brace. And on her forehead was an emergency-room type bandage, sort of a white band-aid, about 2 X 3 inches. She looked for all the world as if she had been in a car accident within the previous hour.

My instant reaction was that Smith was making a gambit to evoke sympathy from the entire jury pool—to prejudice them, in other words. She finally arrived at the front and sat at the plaintiff's table.

Plaintiff was accompanied by her attorney, Sam Lester, acquired not more than a week previous. We learned of his being brought on board on Friday, and this was Tuesday. He couldn't have had much time to get up to speed, though it turned out he had come up with an interesting strategy at the last minute.

Defendant came in with his attorney, Amy Green, whom I had not seen before and who was in her early thirties and a diminutive five feet in height, compared to Quentarious Jones's six feet something and about 300 pounds.

After the roll was called I was in the midst of routine qualifying questions when a juror raised her hand in answer to whether anyone in the pool had already developed an opinion about the case they thought they couldn't lay aside to give unbiased consideration of both parties. I instructed her to come forward and she told me very convincingly that she had already had a strong feeling of empathy for this "poor woman" who had come in bandaged and nearly crippled, and she was certain she was already on her side. The case hadn't been announced, and wouldn't be described even when it was, yet this potential juror was already prejudiced.

We had enough jurors without her, so I dismissed her. Otherwise, selection went more quickly than any I had ever done where two lawyers were involved. Only one objection to a random drawing of a juror was made, and that was by Mr. Lester on the last juror, and then only, I believed, so that his client would be convinced that he was doing his best for her.

We had a jury. They went back to the jury room. I dismissed the rest of the crowd. Only one remained; one of my sons had told me of his plans to come to court for a major case before I retired, and he was there.

I held a brief pre-trial conference at the bench to try to get introduction of exhibits and objections to evidence out of the way, and then the jury was called in and testimony got underway. I'll summarize some of it to avoid repetition.

THE EVIDENCE

Plaintiff and Defendant in Contrast

Wanda Smith reiterated the words of her complaint, using the phrase, "hit me on the head out of nowhere," to represent the "contact" of the minister's hand with her head. Defendant Jones said he "laid hands on her, on her forehead." As a Protestant Christian, I'm familiar with ceremonies such as ordinations where ministers and many other persons in the congregation may "lay hands on" someone else, and generally this action is a gentle touch with an open palm and fingertips, more akin to a caress than anything else. Smith made it out to be a slap, while Jones implied it was a feathery touch.

Smith said the contact knocked her over. Jones said Smith "fell out in the Spirit," which, to anyone familiar with this kind of religious event, means she basically collapsed in religious ecstasy.

Smith said no one caught her. Jones said, au contraire, there was someone there and they did catch her.

During Plaintiff's case in chief, Defendant's cross examination attempted to move Smith away from her depiction of the "contact" with her head as a virtual assault. Attorney Wayne Greene approached the witness.

"Ms. Smith, you watch religious services on TV frequently, don't you?"

"Well, some, yes," she said.

"Now, God of Greatness Full Gospel Holy Ghost Temple isn't on television, right?"

"Right."

"Okay," said Greene, "I'm going to call it 'Rev. Jones's church' from now on, which will mean the God of Greatness Full Gospel Holy Ghost Temple, okay?"

"Fine," said Smith.

"So you've watched services in other churches that are a lot like what you experienced in Rev. Jones's church."

"Yes, I suppose so."

"And when you went to Rev. Jones's church, it was exciting, wasn't it?"

"Yes, it was. I mean, I suppose it was."

"You suppose? But you first said it was."

"Well," Smith said, "when they started the part of the service that I guess you'd call the healing or miracle part, a lot of people were down front and there was a lot going on, and people were speaking in tongues, that sort of thing."

"And you went down because your son went down to the front," asked Greene.

"Yes, and—"

"And when you got down front you sort of got caught up in the motion, or the commotion—some people were sort of dancing, weren't they?"

"Well, sort of, yes."

"That's not easy to resist, is it? You've been with people who were moving rhythmically to music, for instance, and you've found yourself moving with it, haven't you." Greene was asking questions but his intonation made them more like statements.

"Oh, yes," said Smith, "of course."

"Before you went down to the front, did you see anyone walk up to the minister and ask him to lay hands on them?"

"What do you mean?" she said.

"I think I described it as clearly as I could, but I'll rephrase. Was there a line of people going up to the minister, making statements to him, whether on microphone or not, and he responded by laying hands on them—sort of one by one in order as they came?"

Smith was trying to figure out what Greene was getting at, but she had to give an answer, so she said, "No, there was no line. He was just sort of moving around up front, and he would pray a word or two beside someone, and he might lay hands on them."

"Rev. Jones didn't strike you 'for no reason' as you said, did he?" said Greene.

"Yes!" she said, "he did! and he knocked me down!" Smith was back to her original statements. She finally realized Greene was suggesting that she had invited the contact. So she doubled down on characterizing it as assault rather than a healing touch.

The parties were miles apart, in fact diametrically opposed for the most part. The additional testimony clarified some issues.

Witness Dr. Ronald Johnson

It's quite unusual for a magistrate court to have a medical doctor appear to testify if he or she isn't actually one of the parties. In this case, it was evident to me from the statements of doctors filed in pleadings that Plaintiff Smith intended to introduce evidence from doctor's statements, so I made certain she understood in the materials our office sent her prior to trial that she would have to have the doctors themselves appear to testify: I would not accept affidavits from them. I had already read the statements of two doctors because I read all pleadings sent by both parties prior to trial. But if these documents and the testimony they contained were to be disallowed at trial because there was no live witness, I could disregard their content. I had a lot of practice doing so.

Smith had convinced a Dr. Ronald Johnson, a surgeon, to testify, on condition that he could be heard quickly and let go. I took his testimony out of order and I made certain that Defendant was satisfied with his opportunity to cross examine.

Dr. Johnson said he saw Ms. Smith after the incident at the church and he had some tests run. He said he had previously operated on Smith for compression of a cervical disc in her neck. Whatever had happened at church had re-injured her neck and was producing severe radicular pain. He concluded that he believed further surgery would not be effective in improving her situation.

I knew what radicular pain was, though he defined it when he used the term. In the late 1990s I had a herniated disc precisely where Ms. Smith had, compressing and inflaming the nerve root controlling my right arm and hand. The pain felt as if I had been shot. I had no doubt Smith had been experiencing significant discomfort.

However, at the time Smith filed her complaint she said she had to use a wheelchair because of the injury. She appeared at court without it, and I noticed as she entered the court complex that she didn't appear to be impaired.

Dr. Johnson, in describing his interaction with Smith, said that she had told him that during the service she had been "in the Spirit," and had been "slain in the Spirit." That testimony was extremely telling.

On cross examination Johnson said that any impaired walking was not caused by the injury Smith complained of. In fact, Attorney Wayne Greene asked Dr. Johnson if Smith hadn't told him specifically that "no one *was there* to catch me." Johnson said Yes, that was the sense of what she said. "So," said Greene, "you got the sense that she had *expected* someone to be there, but no one was. Is that it?"

Johnson paused before answering. I expected an objection on grounds of speculation, but Sam Lester remained mute, so no objection was raised. I didn't see the problem, anyway, with a human being testifying to how he interpreted the obvious language of another human being.

Dr. Johnson said, "Yes, I had no doubt that's what she meant."

I released Dr. Johnson and he left the court.

There were no more witnesses and I invited the attorneys to make closing arguments.

Arguments

Sam Lester had obviously not had long to work on his closing statement. He thanked me for listening and giving the case fair consideration. Then he basically repeated the statements of the Complaint, repeating the language about Smith's being "struck for no reason."

Amy Green reargued her client's Answer, summarizing the evidence as showing that Bishop Jones had merely touched Smith on the head and that she fell out in the Spirit and was caught before being laid on the carpeted floor.

I gave the jury the standard charge with no frills and sent them out to deliberate.

If I had been the finder of fact, I would have come to my own conclusions, but I didn't know—for certain, anyway—how the jury would see things. But from all the testimony and exhibits in evidence, the Court was able to reconstruct the scene:

Smith and her son, Anthony, attended a service at the God of Greatness Full Gospel Holy Ghost Temple during a spring revival, and as things began to heat up about midway through, the pastor, Bishop Jones gestured grandly for people to flock to the front, where several other pastors were waiting. Ms. Smith's son, Anthony, was not suffering from anything, but he was eager to take part in the holy commotion, and he headed to the front of the auditorium, followed by his mother, our Plaintiff Wanda Smith.

While Smith wanted to leave the impression that she had gone forward only to give support to her son, she was actually equally interested in receiving some sort of blessing out of the overflow of spiritual celebration going on. While her son was talking with a pastor and engaging in noisy prayer, Wanda was nearby, twirling slowly with her hands raised, eyes closed, praising the Lord. After a brief exchange of holy words and smiles with one of the roving pastors, the minister reached toward Wanda Smith and contacted her on her forehead. She had her eyes mostly closed, but she was not really surprised by the contact.

The contact was what might be referred to in its Pentecostal context as anointing or applying a healing touch. It was evidently more, but probably not sufficient in itself to harm her, not as forceful as a slap, but enough to prompt her to enter a stage of spiritual excitement commonly called "being slain in the Spirit." Typically, a person in a Pentecostal or healing service who is touched in this way will become faint, or feign it anyway, and may crumple or fall over backwards. Here's where the minister's team of able assistants steps in with practiced precision and catches the falling worshiper. Smith was familiar with what others had done, and though she had never herself been slain in the Spirit, she went along with the flow and responded as expected. She fell backward, in ecstasy and spiritual blessing.

However, not as expected, no one was quite directly behind her. A snappily dressed assistant saw her begin to collapse and took a step toward her, his hands outstretched. He was able only to slow her rate of descent, not stop it. Smith, a substantially sized woman, landed with a powerful thud, first on her posterior, but her body continued to go backwards unimpeded. Her cranium sounded the auditorium floor like an orchestral tympani. The carpet Defendant Jones spoke of in his Answer to the suit was the well worn, old floor covering that had been in the church building for years, long before it changed ecclesiastical hands. The padding was likely entirely disintegrated. Carpeted or not, the floor was hard enough to give Smith a good lick.

The question, however, was whether Jones was negligent and therefore liable for Smith's injury.

Did Bishop Jones have a duty to have people catch Smith if she fell—even if it was up to Smith whether she fell or not? If so, and Jones had not directed men to position themselves behind Smith, perhaps Jones would be liable for Smith's injury.

Or did Bishop Jones strike Smith hard enough to upset her balance, causing her to fall, in which case he would be liable for her injury irrespective of the presence of catchers?

Or, to get more theological about things, was Smith responsible for falling, even if the Bishop's touch was of negligible force? In other words, was the touch responsible for communicating some spiritual event that rendered Smith unconscious or sent her into a swoon? Or did Smith simply expect Bishop Jones to "lay hands on" her, and did she have a preconceived notion as to what this meant and how she should respond, namely by "falling out" and collapsing? Further, however, is this even a question that the jury could—or was willing to—determine?

The jury was not out long. In fact, it was out less than ten minutes. It returned with the jury verdict form filled out and signed by the foreman. I read it to the gathered crowd, which included a dozen or so people in addition to the parties and their attorneys.

WE THE JURY IN THE ABOVE TITLED ACTION FIND THE DEFENDANT, QUENTARIOUS JONES, NOT LIABLE.

Smith was quietly fuming, and as I dismissed the jury with my thanks, I could hear her expelling indignant breaths, muttering something undecipherable. When the last of the jurors was out the back door, Smith's utterances became more audible. I addressed the court by repeating the jury verdict and stating that the Court accepted the verdict and that the matter was concluded. I rose to go.

In the back hall, the jurors were in the jury room turning in their badges and signing forms for reimbursement for travel. Just before I exited to the judicial offices hall, one of the jurors came out, headed the opposite direction, but caught my eye.

She said, "Judge?" I gave her my attention, and she asked me if judges ever wanted to know why jurors had decided as they did. I said usually if anyone asked them, it was prosecutors, not civil litigants. But yes, they were free to talk to anyone after the case was concluded. She then volunteered this information.

"I just thought you might like to know that everybody on the jury agreed right away that the Plaintiff was faking it. I mean, she wouldn't have an emergency room bandage from three years ago still on her head. We thought it was pretty obvious she was putting on a show."

I thanked her for the information, and she left. This rousing drama was to be the last such event before my last day in court. I considered it a fitting conclusion and punctuation of my career as a magistrate.

19
CONCRETE PROOF

People who spend serious time and money on their lawns rarely brook poor or even mediocre quality service to their grounds. I don't spend much money on the curtilage to my property—I've frequently said that I would even love to install AstroTurf instead of grass—but when I do employ some service, I certainly want workers to do a good job. Complaints that come into the court over claims of defective workmanship on a landscape often seem cut and dried on their face; however, they aren't always as simple as they seem.

THE PLEADINGS

Cooper Smith filed a Summons and Complaint with the Court against Mot Jones, d/b/a Color Curbs, alleging that the colored curbing Jones installed was the wrong color and that it developed light and dark spots that defaced it. He further alleged that Jones refused to honor his warranty. Jones submitted an Answer documenting his correspondence with Plaintiff Smith about the color, pointing to disclaimers on the contract about spots, and he admitted to denying Smith further service on the curbing after ten months had elapsed.

THE EVIDENCE

The parties appeared for trial without any witnesses besides themselves. I found this curious since Plaintiff had included in his supporting documents copies of color samples along with statements from a local paint store saying that the color samples provided by Color Curbs were not a match for the color of the curb itself. It was unclear to me from the papers Plaintiff filed whether the paint company had actually seen the curb or only pictures of it, which would make a great deal of difference, especially since one or two of the pictures had a decided color cast to them. Defendant had argued in his answer that the opinions of a paint company were irrelevant since the curb was not painted but rather colored with dyes mixed in with the concrete. I had expected a lively debate over this point but I was prepared to disallow any testimony about what the paint company had said to Plaintiff, since he didn't have any live witnesses who could be cross examined.

As it turned out, Plaintiff had decided, obviously after reading Defendant's Answer, that he would not pursue the matter of the basic color of the curbing, but rather focus on the spots and the issue of Defendant's warranty service.

Plaintiff

Cooper Smith testified that he hired Mot Jones to install colored curbing in his yard, around natural areas and gardens and along his driveway. Jones performed on the contract in June of the previous year and Smith paid him. Smith introduced the contract, which included a disclaimer about light spots appearing as the concrete cured and an assurance that these would go away in time. Smith said after thirty days or so the spots were not going away and he emailed Jones about the matter. A sheaf of emails back and forth between the parties came into evidence. They included comments by Smith about the color, but Smith now said he was not going to pursue his case about the color, and Jones did not object to the evidence.

Smith said Jones came out to his house in September, about ninety days after installation of the curbing, to remove sealant, clean, and then re-seal various portions of it that had spots. Smith moved into evidence several photos printed out on regular paper, showing a few sections of curb that had small light spots. I was waiting for something more substantial; the spots didn't seem to be significant to me. However, more pictures weren't offered, and I wondered what all the fuss was about. Smith then said he tried to get Jones to return to his house later to fix more spots gratis. He was unsuccessful in convincing Jones to come back. In April, ten months after the installation, he decided to send Jones a check for $180.00, the cost of re-sealing the curb. He explained to the Court that he wanted to make certain his warranty would not run out.

What warranty, I wondered? The ninety day warranty had run out in September, as Jones stated and Smith had not contested. I didn't ask Smith this, only thought it, but he produced a photocopy of a Ten Year Warranty, a briefly stated document saying that the curbing would be covered for defects for ten years as long as the customer purchased yearly re-sealing services from Color Curbs at the price of $180.00. The purchase would have to take place before the anniversary of the installation of the curbing. At the bottom of the document were the signatures of Mot Jones, on the left, and Cooper Smith, on the right, with the same date, June 6, for both.

Smith said Jones returned his check and refused to come re-seal the curb. Smith's case therefore focused on Jones's refusal to honor the warranty to correct defects. The damages he had sought in his Complaint were for removal and reinstallation of curbing by another company. Since he reasoned he could not get only portions removed and reinstalled with a satisfactory match, he wanted the entire job redone by someone else.

At trial I had yet to hear any testimony about what Plaintiff Smith wanted in the way of money to replace the curbing. Instead, Smith simply asked for the entire cost of Jones's work refunded. Smith rested his case.

Defendant

Jones, a low key guy, made a few brief statements about the nature of white and dark spots that appear on concrete as it cures. He stated, as Smith had, that he went to Smith's home in September, about ninety days after the installation of the curbing, to clean and re-seal portions of it. Jones said ninety days was the limit of the warranty included in the price of the curbing. On cross, Smith didn't address the point and never contradicted the testimony in any way. Jones said his cleaning and re-sealing solved the problem. On cross, Smith didn't exactly contradict him, which I took to be his concession to the point. He seemed a bit flustered by Defendant's testimony, but he did ask Jones why, if the September treatment worked, he then called (or emailed) Jones in March the following year that spots were back, and asked him to come fix them. Jones said he hadn't heard from Smith between the September re-sealing work and March, a period of six months, and he reasonably assumed Smith was satisfied.

Jones then addressed the matter of the check. He said that after about two months of emails between the two men, during late March and early April, in which Smith tried to get him to come back and treat spots without charge, he finally stopped responding to Smith's requests. Jones said Smith threatened to take him to court and that his last email to Smith said simply, "Do what you have to do."

Then Jones produced his bombshell. He pulled out a yellow sheet of paper, presented it to the Court as the original second sheet to the Extended Warranty he had offered Mr. Smith at the time of the installation of the curbing. When it was shown across the aisle before being admitted into evidence, Smith looked more than flustered: he looked downright nervous. I took the exhibit and inspected it while Jones calmly testified about it.

"You will see, your honor, that my signature is on the bottom left." I looked at the signature and compared it to the photocopy submitted into evidence by Smith. The signature and date by Mot Smith were identical. Smith's signature on the yellow sheet, a carbonless under-copy, had been produced when he signed the original white sheet on top of the form. The white sheet would normally have been retained by the customer. "Your honor," continued Jones, "Mr. Smith's signature is not on my copy of the Extended Warranty." I had already seen that, but I looked at the right side of the sheet and then looked up at Smith. He was trying to look nonchalant, but his body language suggested he had been caught.

"Mr. Smith didn't accept the Extended Warranty," said Jones. "I offered it to him with other papers when we signed the contract. I signed my side. He would have given it back to me with his signature when he paid me after the installation. But he didn't sign it at that time. He was never covered for the Extended Warranty. When his ninety-day warranty ran out, he wasn't covered anymore."

Mr. Smith was still motionless. I took him to be thinking of a way out of this.

Smith continued, "Obviously, your honor, he signed his copy sometime after it was initially offered—sometime long after, I think." I waved off his conjecture, even though Smith hadn't objected on the record. Jones rested.

Smith attempted a few lame questions on cross examination, avoiding the matter of his acceptance of the warranty. He went back to the issue of spots, and again argued that Jones had sent back the check for $180.00. He restated that he sent the check to keep his warranty valid.

Jones sat calmly, reflecting confidence in his defense, and he had no further questions of Plaintiff Smith. I asked Jones if there were any initial payment required to get the Extended Warranty, and he said no, just a signature. He emphasized "signature" ever so slightly to make his point.

I went out to deliberate and returned in a few minutes with my decision. The key portion follows.

THE JUDGMENT

Quite aside from any question of whether spots reappearing on color curbing installed by Defendant Jones were a defect, the controlling issue in this case, which did not come up until this trial, is whether or not Plaintiff Smith ever accepted the Extended Warranty proffered by Defendant Jones at the point of sale. A comparison of the two versions of the Extended Warranty entered into evidence by the parties convinces me that Defendant's signature was the same on the original yellow sheet and the Plaintiff's photocopy, but that Plaintiff had signed and dated his side of the Warrantee at some subsequent time, and had not signed the original top copy, which would have been his. Plaintiff's exhibit is not the original top copy, but a photocopy of it. The absence of his signature, however, is sufficient proof to the Court that at the time of sale, he did not accept the Extended Warranty. If he had signed the original when offered, Jones's yellow second sheet would have contained Smith's signature, and it does not.

In consequence, the Court finds that after the ninety day warranty Plaintiff was no longer covered under any warranty for the concrete. Defendant Jones performed all his obligations under the contract including re-sealing portions of the curbing within the ninety day warranty. Plaintiff's proffered check for $180.00 was not a renewal of anything since he did not have an extended warranty with Defendant, and Defendant was well within his right to refuse the check and refuse to provide further services to Plaintiff.

BASED ON THESE FINDINGS, WHICH THE COURT MAKES ON THE PREPONDERANCE OF THE EVIDENCE, THE COURT RENDERS JUDGMENT FOR THE DEFENDANT AND DISMISSES THE COMPLAINT OF PLAINTIFF IN ITS ENTIRETY.

EPILOGUE

Although sometimes I can predict when an appeal is coming, in this case I was a bit surprised when Smith's wife came by about two weeks later and got a copy of the case file, saying that Smith planned to appeal. I began counting off the days til the thirty day window was closed for filing and serving notice of an appeal upon me. I thought I had seen the slightest hesitation on Mrs. Smith's face when my clerk told her the Circuit Court would charge her $150.00 to file an appeal. I hoped it would serve as just enough disincentive against stringing this case out further. There was nothing on which to lodge an appeal legitimately, since the appellate court would not try the case *de novo*. I had allowed all admissible evidence, nothing had been objected to, and there were no other rulings during trial. As well, the written Judgment certainly had adequate evidence on which to make the findings I made.

On the thirtieth day, Mrs. Smith appeared at the courthouse window and served a copy of the notice of appeal, though not the appeal itself. This was inadequate under law. I made a memo for the file indicating such and intended to include it in the return I would give the Appellate Court when I prepared it. Since a copy of the appeal was supposed to be included in the return, a memo showing that my court never received such from the appellant might be enough for the appellate judge to dismiss the appeal out of hand. I hoped so, anyway.

Unfortunately, Smith appeared later the same day and gave us a copy of the Appeal itself. For the Appellate Court she had written in the line for "appellant's exceptions of the judgment of the magistrate" the following argumentative statements:

> The defendant acknolewdged [sic] the impairment of workmanship by attempting to correct it the first time, then when the same issue arose, he refused repair again. Both under the warranty given for the first year.

Exceptions to the judgment of the magistrate are properly to be the appellant's claim of errors the magistrate made in matters of law, or a finding he made for which there was no supporting evidence. Appellant Smith instead had simply repeated his testimony concerning his side of the story.

I realized I should be able to trust the Circuit Court judge who would be assigned to this appeal to see it for what it was and uphold my judgment. I felt the Appellate Judge should do so even without a hearing, since on its face the appeal was defective and therefore without merit. However, the last appeal to one of my judgments (I had had fewer than one per year) had gone to a hearing even though it was a case of the same sort; that appeal had been dismissed and I had been upheld. I had long believed that my use of thoroughly developed, written judgments had been to my benefit, since they became part of the case file and would be read by the Appellate Court. Especially if a case was intricate and contentious, I made certain to write the Judgment, including my own reasons for finding the facts I did, and my arguments for rendering judgment as I did. While it would be inappropriate for me to write anything specifically addressed to the Appellate Court in defense of my Judgment in a case, the Judgment itself, addressed to the parties before any appeal might be made, would be a convenient way for me to make my argument for being upheld.

In this case, in my written judgment I had specifically shown why the Plaintiff did *not* have more than a ninety day warranty and certainly did *not* have a fifteen year limited warranty. The other issue raised by Appellant Smith I also dealt with by finding that Defendant Jones had successfully corrected the defects Plaintiff Smith had requested that he address in the first ninety days.

Nevertheless, in my return to the Circuit Court concerning the Appeal, at the end of the Summary of the Case, one of the required forms, I included this simple statement: "Appeal: Plaintiff filed notice of appeal without exceptions of law or objections to rulings. Plaintiff reargued the facts of the case."

I couldn't help myself.

It took six months to hear the results of the Appeal—*pro se* appeals, in particular, burden the Court with a backlog—but word finally came through that the Defendant was right, and that I was, too. At last, there was concrete proof.

20
HARD BARGAIN

People who believe they have been wronged sometimes come to the court flinging around terms that mean one thing in their own experience and quite another in the law. A debtor may say she is being *harassed* by a creditor, when in fact the creditor has stayed within the law while trying to collect a debt—the debtor simply resents not being left alone about the money she owes. A man may complain that another person *threatened* him, when what the other fellow did was merely to demand payment or else he would take him to court—the firm promise to have a judge decide a case is not a threat.

In this chapter's case at the bar the complainant believed he had been *coerced* into a deal whereby he suffered financial loss. But was there really coercion involved?

THE PLEADINGS

Tommy Smith filed suit against Debby Jones, his former wife, for financial losses sustained in the sale of their marital home. He claimed that Debby had coerced him into selling the house for a too low a price, and also into paying the lion's share of closing costs. Debby Jones, now living in Florida, submitted an Answer denying coercion and blaming Smith's losses on himself.

THE EVIDENCE

Plaintiff

Appearing wan and harried at trial, Mr. Smith testified that he and Debby Jones had owned a town house at 13 Stormy Lane during the last few years of their marriage and that when they divorced the previous year the Family Court ordered the property sold and the proceeds divided equally. The home was titled in both their names. In the meantime, the Family Court had also ordered him to continue making mortgage payments on the marital home. He moved into evidence a sheaf of email correspondence between him and his wife, in which Smith insisted on the sale of their house to a buyer who had submitted an offer somewhat less than the asking price. While he had originally fended off low offers, several months had gone by and he believed they would have to take less in order to sell the house anytime soon. Jones, however, would not consent to sale at the lower offer. Smith pleaded with her, since he was paying the mortgage on the house and he was basically losing that money every month they didn't sell. Jones was unreasonable, Smith said.

Further, Jones insisted that she would pay only $1,000.00 of closing costs. She wouldn't budge on this condition, either, though Smith told her that closing costs were going to be more than double that amount. His argument to the Court was that his wife *coerced* him into the sale of the house at the lower price, by stubbornly refusing to consent to the sale on anything but her terms. In consenting to hold out for the originally agreed price (which someone did offer them in another two months), Smith wrote to Jones insisting that he was doing so under protest and accusing her of coercing him because he was losing money thereby. He warned her he would be taking her to court afterward. Debby Jones appeared for the closing, where Tommy Smith tried one more time to get her to pay at least half the closing costs, though the sale price of the house was now fixed. Jones refused.

Smith filed his suit against Jones six months after she moved to Florida, which was immediately after the divorce and the order of the Family Court to sell the house. Since an offer had been made on the house in the first month it was up for sale, Smith was asking for five months worth of mortgage payments and for another two thousand dollars to make up for closing costs that fell on his side of the deal—inequitably as he believed.

Jones didn't have any questions for her ex husband, but was sworn in and told me her side of things very simply.

Defendant

Debby Jones, well on the way to being bronzed by Florida sunshine, said she and her husband had agreed on the asking price once they had been ordered to sell the house and she simply wished to hold firm. She said she had also told him at the very first she would agree to paying $1,000.00 of closing costs, a fact established by the email exchanges, and that she had held firm on that point as well. She went through the email correspondence and showed the Court that her husband had tried to argue her out of her terms from day one, but that she had told him she wasn't going to change her mind under any circumstances.

She offered the reason for her intransigence, though it was not necessary for me to know. She told her ex husband that he had cheated her several times before on two real estate sales and the sale of a vehicle, and that she wasn't trusting him to make a deal other than on the terms she dictated, at least with respect to her side of the sale. It was no more complicated than that.

THE JUDGMENT

The Judgment in this case almost took more time to read than the trial had taken to hear. Perhaps it was overkill for a summary court, but no one has ever accused me of being terse. The core of the Judgment follows.

Law

"Duress exists when one, by an unlawful act of another, is induced to make a contract or perform some act under circumstances which deprive him of the exercise of his free will" (Knight v. Brown, 137 Mich. 396, 100 N.W. 602, 603, and other authorities from many states.)

"...Duress may sometimes be implied when a payment is made or an act performed to prevent great property loss or heavy penalties when there seems no adequate remedy except to submit to an unjust or illegal demand and then seek redress in the courts" (Minneapolis, St. P. S.S.M. Ry. Co. v. Railroad Commission, 183 Wis. 47, 197 N.W. 352, 355).

An agreement between two parties may be nullified because of duress on the part of one.

FINDINGS

Upon the preponderance of the evidence, the Court makes the following findings of fact:

Plaintiff and Defendant were co-sellers of their townhouse; no written contract exists between them concerning terms of that sale. The two principal issues for the Court are: whether in fact there was an oral contract between Defendant and Plaintiff regarding their sale of their townhouse; and whether Defendant placed Plaintiff under duress or coerced him such that he agreed to sell the property under Defendant's terms.

Contract. The evidence shows dramatically that Plaintiff and Defendant argued about both the offer made on the townhouse and what portion of the closing costs on the townhouse each one would pay. Defendant resisted the sale to the final, potential buyer on the basis of a low offer. Yet, a trail of email messages reveals indicia of contract negotiations between Plaintiff and Defendant that did not involve the buyer. Defendant was unwilling to agree to the sale at the price offered under the terms Plaintiff proposed for shared liability of closing costs and other expenses. Plaintiff was motivated to sell quickly because he was losing money every day he did not complete the sale. Finally, Plaintiff gave into Defendant's terms, wrote out a statement of his agreement with Defendant on the terms of closing, and closed on the house under those terms.

The Court finds that Plaintiff and Defendant had an oral contract ancillary to the contract for sale, namely an agreement between the two on the terms whereby they would co-sell their mutual property: Defendant's offer was to sell under specific terms; Plaintiff's acceptance was evidenced by his signed statement; and the consideration was Plaintiff's payment of the difference between $1,000.00 plus one half the attorney's and realtor's fees, and the actual costs of closing—which may be seen as his payment of that balance on Defendant's behalf.

Duress. Clearly Plaintiff was not under duress in the classic sense emanating from the Common Law: Defendant did not threaten or enact physical violence, and there is no evidence that she threatened any other illegal act, such as extortion or blackmail. The question for the Court is whether to follow the trend reflected in *Minneapolis, St. P. S.S.M. Ry. Co. v. Railroad Commission,* in deciding whether Defendant placed Plaintiff under duress. The standard being applied in the courts is to find that 1) threatened acts are technically legal, yet 2) wrongful in a moral or equitable sense, and 3) complainant was constrained to do what he otherwise would not have done.

The Court is inclined to adjudge whether there was duress on the basis of three questions: 1) Was there a threat by Defendant to do something either unlawful or merely ethically wrong in order to secure Plaintiff's agreement to her terms of sale; 2) If not, did Defendant lack a legal right to demand that her terms be met before agreeing to the sale herself; and 3) If not, did Defendant hold out for her terms merely or almost entirely to harm Plaintiff? Taken in order, if the answer to any of these three questions is yes, the Court would find for Plaintiff that his contractual agreement with Defendant to sell the townhouse at Defendant's terms was made under duress.

As to the first question, the Court must quickly find that Defendant did not do anything illegal or unethical in holding out for her demands regarding the sale, and Plaintiff has not alleged that she did. As to the second question, the Court also quickly finds that Defendant did not lack a right to hold out for sale terms favorable to her.

The third question requires the Court to look not at the black and white of the law but rather at the mind and intentions of Defendant herself. The Court's review of the email exchanges of Plaintiff, Defendant, and their realtor show Defendant's determination to hold to three conditions: to pay no more herself than a fixed portion of $1,000.00 of the closing costs, whatever balance of said costs Plaintiff might have to pay; to pay no more than one half the realtor's and attorney's fees; and to pay none of the other expenses Plaintiff was incurring while negotiating the sale of the townhouse. The 50-50 split of the sale proceeds themselves was a given.

As to her defense of her position, Defendant was adamant that her stance was predicated on experience with Plaintiff. She stated that he had taken unfair advantage of her on two previous real property sales and the sale of a vehicle, as well as other things. Whether her claims are entirely justified is *not at issue* in this Court; Defendant's plainly expressed opinion, resulting feelings, and motivation are the relevant facts. She felt that the buyer's offers were "ridiculously low and insulting;" she also believed that if she were to agree to pay more than the fixed figure of $1,000.00 in closing costs—say, one half of them, for instance—the costs would eat into her share of the proceeds unreasonably. Patently, Defendant's principal motivation was to protect her assets, irrespective of how Plaintiff felt about it.

Further, Defendant had made her conditions of sale clear at the start, and in spite of Plaintiff's multiple ways of reconfiguring counteroffers and closing cost splits, Defendant held her ground. If she was intractable, at least she made forcefully obvious to Plaintiff that she was not going to change her mind. If Plaintiff lost income because of delay in the sale, it was in large part because he lost time in attempting to make her surrender to his view. A disinterested reader's casual review of their email exchange leads to the conclusion that such surrender would not take place.

At bottom, the Court finds that in Plaintiff's and Defendant's coming to an agreement on the co-sale of their townhouse, Defendant drove a hard bargain and nothing more. She insisted on her terms to protect her bottom line, not to harm Plaintiff. While she no doubt realized Plaintiff would resent her being hard nosed, she did not stand her ground to inflict injury, but only to secure her own profits. Her actions therefore do not constitute duress under law.

THE COURT RENDERS JUDGMENT FOR DEFENDANT AND DISMISSES PLAINTIFF'S COMPLAINT, MAKING NO AWARD.

Tommy Smith left the courtroom in a huff. Debby Jones strode out a few minutes later to avoid any further contact with her ex. She returned to Florida to continue working on her tan.

21
Auto Renew or Not

Interesting trials are not necessarily the most interesting cases on paper. Many times a case may be a fairly routine civil complaint but it becomes fascinating because of the people involved. A suit for the return of a security deposit started out as a predictable matter, and after reviewing the unremarkable pleadings I entered the courtroom to hear Smith v. Jones and be done with it in what I predicted to be fifteen minutes. A little part of me reminded myself that I was often surprised by what developed at trial, however, and I was intrigued by the depth and interest of the facts that emerged.

The Pleadings

Stephanie Smith filed suit against Farhad Jones for $1,400.00, the amount of her security deposit on a rental home she had lived in for slightly less than two years. The Complaint was simple: Smith said the defendant kept her deposit after completing a final inspection, stating he was doing so because she didn't fulfill the lease agreement. Farhad Jones submitted an Answer with a number of pages of neatly detailed and meticulously kept records, along with a few photographs. He also filed a Counterclaim, asking for another month's rent and damages for some landscaping items. It looked like a fairly simple he said/she said that frankly appeared to go the defendant's way. I knew, of course, that often things were not as they seemed, and so I remained, as always, unprejudiced before trial.

THE EVIDENCE

Both parties came unrepresented; Plaintiff was accompanied by one witness and Defendant came alone. Both had numerous documents and stacks of papers surrounding them on their respective tables. Plaintiff Smith was a slender, striking blonde of about thirty-five or six, in a suit that looked like those I frequently see on women attorneys who practice in my court. Her handwritten pleadings indicated she wasn't a lawyer, but her appearance certainly said she knew the best image to present in court. Smith had a confident expression on her face with a slight and pleasant smile.

Defendant Jones was a Middle-Eastern man—his real last name was Iranian, I'm certain—of short stature, dressed in slacks and sport coat, also making a good visual presentation of himself. Jones looked equally confident, but his expression was inscrutable. Throughout the hearing, his face remained virtually unchanged.

Plaintiff

Stephanie Smith stood and addressed the Court with a lawyer-ly, "If it please the Court," and proceeded to tell me her side of the case, in a highly organized way. She had rented the property at 1000 Stately Lane in April two years previous, signing a lease for a year. She presented the lease to the Court, pointing out the date of signing, the $1,400.00 monthly rent (which had been negotiated down from $1,450.00), the amount of the security deposit of $1,400.00, and the amount of a non-refundable pet deposit—$350.00. The pet deposit, however, she said she discussed with Farhad Jones, who allowed her to pay only half that amount, as a concession to her plans to do some yard work that was above and beyond the expected tenant's duties. The lease already called for her to cut the grass and trim bushes, etc., and also "prune trees." Smith said she mentioned to Jones she wanted as well to do something about ivy at the back door, among other things.

Over the course of the next year Smith said she removed the ivy, not only because it was getting out of control but also because she knew it to be home to at least two snakes, one of which she knowledgeably identified as a copperhead. Smith had small children and the snakes obviously posed a danger to them as well as to her. She tore out the ivy, and the area, roughly an isosceles triangle of ten feet on two sides, remained unplanted most of the time.

In addition to the ivy, Smith severely cut back a bush at the front curb beside the driveway, a gangly and wandering bush that spread out into the road. She showed before and after pictures. The pruning had taken place in winter, so there were no leaves or blooms on the bush, but it looked to me like forsythia. I have had such plants in my own yard to become enormous. Smith said she cut the bush back because she couldn't see to get out of the driveway safely, and cars coming along the street couldn't see her, either. I could see the point right away.

Finally, Smith lopped off a small tree on the side of the house because it was dead. The tree, the trunk of which was about five inches in diameter, was no more than about eighteen inches from the edge of the house, and it was certainly conceivable that if it had been alive and had continued to grow, it would have caused damage to the foundation. Smith had cut it off about a foot above the ground.

Smith said that in February of the previous year, as they approached the end of the year's lease, she and Mr. Jones began having some text message exchanges about another year in the home. (Most of their communication was by way of phone texting, and both sides introduced sheaves of print-outs of these exchanges.) Smith actually first brought up the subject of renewing, saying that she wanted to talk about "signing another year's lease." She also wanted to talk about the planned increase in rent. The lease called for a $90.00 increase per month if it were renewed. Since she and Jones had negotiated the rent down from $1,450.00 to $1,400.00 per month, she wanted to verify that the rent for the next year would be only $1,490.00. They agreed on those terms, but there were a couple of other issues they didn't come to firm agreement on. One was the eventual purchase of the house, which in separate discussions Mr. Jones had set at a little higher price than Smith wanted to pay. If Smith could not get Jones to lower his asking price, she would want to look for another house to rent or buy. The other issues remained unsettled, and when April came, no signatures were applied to another year's lease.

Smith testified that she had been in a month-to-month rental arrangement since April of the previous year, when in late August she and her husband took out a contract on another home. On September 1, she gave Mr. Jones a forty-five day notice of vacating, just to be on the safe side. She interjected that she had learned from an attorney friend that she would need to give at least a thirty-day notice, and he had advised making it forty-five.

In her phone text evidence, she pointed to a dispute that arose with Mr. Jones over just what the nature of their rental agreement was. In August, she had referred to their month-to-month arrangement, and Jones had responded tersely that it was not month-to-month, but rather that the lease had auto-renewed on May 1 since Smith had not given him a thirty day notice that she would *not* be renewing the lease. There were a couple of text exchanges about the dispute, and Smith went silent for about two weeks while, as she said, she conferred with her attorney friend, who had told her—and at this point, although Jones had not objected and may not have known to, I interrupted to tell her that what her attorney friend said could not be admitted as evidence in support of a material fact. Smith said she knew this, but also knew, from her time as a police officer in a nearby city, that she could introduce what would normally be hearsay evidence when it went to the matter of her motive for doing what she did. (Ah! So there was the explanation of Smith's professional, lawyer-ly skills: she had prosecuted traffic and misdemeanor cases for the city.) I allowed her to tell me what he had said as an explanation only of her doing what she did. The attorney friend told her that unless the contract said the lease automatically renewed, it didn't, and she would be on a month-to-month basis.

Smith pointed to the relevant clause in the lease, titled "Lease Renewal." It said:

> A. At the end of this Lease Agreement, Tenant shall have the option to renew the Lease for an additional term that is equal to the initial term of this lease with an increase in the Rent by $90.00 per month.
> B. If Tenant or Landlord does not wish to renew the Lease, written notice must be given to the other party at least 30 days before the end of the term to terminate the Lease (including any exercised renewal or extension thereof).

On its face, the section could have been read as an auto-renewal, and Jones took that position. However, Smith said the fact that the section didn't actually say the lease automatically renewed, and since she and Jones had had discussions about another year's lease that began more than thirty days prior to the end of the first year, without coming to an agreement, she was justified in believing that the lease did not and had not auto-renewed, and that since Jones had accepted more monthly rent, she was in a month-to-month tenancy from May 1 until she surrendered possession of the property on October 15 of that same year. Further evidence for her assumption, she said, was the fact that she operated on her belief for six months before conflict arose over the point.

Working on the belief that she was month-to-month, she had given notice forty-five days in advance of leaving, had paid the full rent for September, and then had paid pro-rated rent for October 1-15. That's where the relationship between the two went south.

Smith said Jones and she went through the house on October 15 and that everything was ship shape or even better than when she took occupancy, but that at the end of the walk-through inspection, Jones said he would be keeping her deposit against the rest of October's rent and over some issues with the yard. If she didn't object to that, he told her, he would forget about the rest of the rent that would have been due for November through April, the remainder of the second year's lease term. After a brief dispute, obviously blindsided by Jones's take on the rental situation, Smith left upset. After one or two more text message exchanges in which they didn't see eye to eye, Smith filed suit for the deposit.

Smith had brought one of her former neighbors as a witness, who testified briefly that during her tenancy Smith had maintained the yard nicely, and that she, the neighbor, had helped Smith with the tree cutting and removal of trimmings. She said the tree had in fact been dead.

Jones's cross examination revealed him to be an pretty good *pro se* litigator, though it also showed him to be a dogged and argumentative authoritarian. He asked terse questions designed to pick apart Smith's testimony. He pointed her to the text exchanges where in February of the previous year he had told her that the lease would automatically renew if she didn't do anything—i.e. give a thirty-day written notice. Did she understand that, he asked? She said she differed with him on the interpretation of the lease, and that the lease didn't say it automatically renewed. Jones asked if Smith didn't understand that after *he* said the lease had auto renewed, she should have *known* that was the case. Smith paused (considering, I think, rebuking him for his male chauvinism and then deciding not to), finally saying she didn't agree.

Moving on to other subjects that he would address in his own testimony, Jones asked Smith if she had asked for permission to cut down a tree, to cut back a bush to nearly nothing, or to remove the ivy. Smith had prepared for these questions, and she answered repeatedly, "I already had written permission in the lease." She pointed to the section that said, "Tenant shall maintain the lawn and landscaping by cutting grass, removing weeds and pruning trees." She also referred Jones to their agreement that she would do more extensive landscape work in exchange for a lower pet deposit. Jones broke from his meticulous questioning to argue with her, saying simply that they had no agreement. Smith didn't respond—she knew not to argue with him. I reminded Jones gently not to argue with the witness and not to give testimony while cross examining, and he apologized and continued, to the point of beating a dead horse.

Jones grilled Smith repeatedly about the tree, asking if Smith were trained as an arborist. No. How did she know it was dead? It was spring and there were no leaves on it and branches were crisp and breaking off. Did she know what kind of tree it was? No. He did the same sort of detailed questioning about the bush and ivy. Did she see a bush at all in this photo? Hadn't she removed it entirely? What was that red dot in a picture of the place the ivy used to be—wasn't it a tomato? Hadn't she in fact removed the ivy in order to plant a garden? He covered the matter from all sides and began to repeat himself, at which time I instructed him to move on. He was getting the same answers anyway, from a woman who knew how to give tight testimony and not to be lured into a trap. Jones asked Smith if she realized she owed the entire month's rent for October, not pro-rated rent, because there was nothing in the lease about pro-rating rent. Smith's answer was that Jones had broken his own lease, then, because he had pro-rated her rent for the first month, two years ago. I knew this was a fallacious argument, but she held her ground with him.

There was a brief issue about Defendant Jones's daughter, who came into the picture in August, when Smith gave her forty-five day notice. Jones's daughter's lease in a nearby apartment building was ending at the end of September and Jones told Smith he might be able to get his daughter into the house on October 1 so that she could take up the lease without interruption. As it worked out, that didn't happen, but Jones brought up the matter in a question to Smith. He asked her if she hadn't understood that his suggestion about his daughter, again by a text message in evidence, indicated that the second year's lease was in force, simply by implications of the language—"take up the lease," etc. Smith answered that she didn't agree. The back-and-forth went on for another ten minutes while Jones ground away at his points through questions and Smith resolutely and tersely denied him any ground.

Finally, Jones asked Smith about a statement she made in one of her texts in August. She had said, "I won't default in rent." Didn't that mean that she knew she was in a second year's lease?" No, said Smith, it didn't. It simply meant that she wasn't going to fail to pay him month-to-month as she moved out.

The cross was over and Plaintiff rested.

Defendant

Mr. Jones began his case by giving the Court his authoritative interpretation of the lease at the section that discussed renewal. He stated that the lease had auto renewed (and that was that). After he had talked about this matter for a few minutes, I asked him some questions.

I wanted to know the source of the lease contract. The papers in evidence included a lease and several addenda that had fancy headings. A section called Regulations included twenty-nine prohibitions many of which I imagined didn't apply to this particular house because they referred to things that weren't included with it—a deck, a hot tub, an in-ground pool, etc. Jones appeared to have taken a boilerplate lease and pressed it into service. As I thought, Jones had bought the lease as part of a pack of documents from an online service. I asked if he had done any editing of the lease, which I had already concluded to be the case, and he admitted that he had. He had not only filled in necessary blanks but also changed some wording here and there. In particular, he had added the part about rent increase of $90.00

after the first year if the lease were renewed. Looking at the section, I was curious.

"Mr. Jones," I said, "the lease says if it is renewed, rent will increase by $90.00 for the next year. Would that mean that if the lease were renewed repeatedly for ten successive years, by the end of that time Ms. Smith would be paying $900.00 more in rent than the first year?"

"Uh," Jones faltered, "Well, it would be—no, it would not—that's a mistake. When I changed this section, I didn't—it isn't clear."

I allowed him to continue with his story, and he dealt briefly with the fact that after October's half month when Smith was no longer there, the house was not rented until December 1. In his Counterclaim he wanted the Court to order Smith to award him November's rent as well as the balance of October, or whatever was still owing after his deducting costs from the security deposit.

Jones then moved on to the matter of the landscape. He showed pictures of the yard as it appeared the day Smith left. His version of things was that the bush was all but removed, the tree had not been dead, and the ivy had been torn out against his wishes in order to plant tomatoes. He said the tree was twenty-five feet tall. He repeated this testimony several times. I asked him how he knew the height of the tree. He wasn't prepared for the question but he finally said it could be deduced from the size of the trunk. In other words, he hadn't ever measured it but was only estimating it. It wasn't important. He went on.

He returned to the lease and pointed out a section that required the tenant to request permission in writing if something other than specified yard maintenance were to be done. He said Smith had not requested permission in writing to cut down the tree, remove the ivy or cut back the bush.

After really belaboring his points further, Jones was finished and ready for cross examination.

Smith herself returned to the yard matters and asked Jones if it weren't true that they had an agreement about her doing more extensive landscaping work. No, he said. Why, then, she countered, had he accepted half the pet deposit, as she had testified? Jones didn't have an immediate answer to that, but merely repeated his denial that he had agreed from the first that she could do anything to the yard without asking permission in writing. What then, she said, did the lease mean when it referred to "pruning trees?" Again, the silent pause was revealing. He repeated that she didn't ask permission in writing.

When was the last time he had inspected the tree in question? He said he had seen it before she moved in. He denied it was dead.

Didn't he remember she had mentioned "doing something about the ivy" when they first went through the house and yard before she began the first year's lease? No, he didn't remember that. Why did he give her a significant break on the pet deposit? No answer; he just denied he had any agreement about landscaping. The cross examination continued, barely avoiding my saying, "Asked and answered: move on."

Finally, the ground had been covered fully, and as they realized it, they gave up the struggle.

THE JUDGMENT

I deliberated at length for a day before issuing Judgment in the case. There were several cases I wished to study and I needed to pore over the lease in evidence. It was even likely that I would need to review the four hours of recorded testimony to make sure of several things I had heard. I really didn't know who was going to prevail when the hearing ended. By sometime the next day, however, the picture had clarified and over the next two days I crafted the written Judgment, which follows in part (without the lengthy quotations of case law included in the full text).

1. No written lease or lease extension existed between the parties for the year between April 30 [last year] and April 30 [of the previous year].

The main dispute between the parties in pleadings and at trial was over whether the lease signed by both of them on March 28, [one year before the previous year] had been renewed. Plaintiff contended that the lease had *not* been renewed, that instead she had been in a month-to-month rental arrangement ever since April 30 last year. Defendant took the position that the lease *had* been renewed and that Plaintiff's leaving in the middle of the lease year resulted in his brief loss of rent before being able to lease the Property again.

Plaintiff testified that it was her understanding that in order to automatically renew the Lease, a written contract must explicitly state that it automatically renews if not otherwise cancelled, and that since the contract does not contain that statement, she assumed her tenancy from April 30 until the date she surrendered possession she was in a month-to-month tenancy. Defendant's interpretation of the Lease was that their "contract was written to renew for another term" and that "unless either one of us are [sic] not renewing, nothing needs to be done."

A cursory reading of Section 22 may lead the casual reader to the inference that renewal is automatic; however, the language lacks specificity. Further, Paragraph B of that section refers to "exercised renewal or extension," implying a positive action instead of the absence of an action, and there is no other paragraph that specifically outlines the exercise of renewal or extension.

Additionally, one of the terms in that section introduces further ambiguity: If the parties had had no dispute and Smith, with the assent of Jones, had, by whatever method was necessary, renewed the lease for another year, would her rent have increased again by $90.00 for the following year, and the year after that as well, *ad infinitum?* The $90.00 per-year increase certainly makes the Lease look as though it would need to be amended and a written modification resigned before any sensible tenant would continue renting the Property. The Court's questioning of Defendant at this point yielded the information that he had amended the language of the Lease, which he had purchased from an online service. The $90.00 provision was due to initial negotiations in which Jones had accepted terms of lower rent for Smith's first year. In editing the downloaded lease, Jones had not included language eliminating the requirement of $90.00 additional rent after the first year.

The Court has no way of knowing what other edits Jones performed to the document, if any, or if the document as constructed by 'do-it-yourself-landlord.com' was capable of sustaining court challenges in this section or any other; however, this Court finds the Lease to be ambiguous as to renewal.

Clearly the parties did not interpret Section 22 in the same way and their diametrically opposite interpretations indicate the ambiguity. The trail of text messages beginning in March of last year illustrates the differences in interpretation:

On March 12, Smith referred to the possibility that she could "sign another year lease" and "keep rent at $1400." Jones replied, as above quoted, that unless either of them was "not renewing, nothing needs to be done." But he added that "this correspondence text should serve as the conformation [sic]." At trial, Jones argued that once he said this, his interpretation was authoritative. Smith did not argue with him in March, but she continued to act in the belief that she was in a month-to-month tenancy.

In another exchange the same day, Smith expressed concern about the $90.00 increase, asking that it be increased by only $50.00. Jones agreed, and Smith asked if the increase would start "this month or does that start next month?" [this was still in March]. Jones argued at trial that the exchange constituted contract negotiations which proved that Smith understood they were negotiating the terms of a renewal. Smith argued that the exchange only suggested that they were talking about the amount of monthly rent, not the larger question of renewal.

The next exchange was August 20, when Smith texted Jones that she was beginning to look at options for buying a house, and the parties had already discussed the possibility of her buying the one she was renting. She said, "[A]fter our first year are we now month to month, how much notice do you need and I can't remember what we put down for our deposit."

Writing in general makes the determination of tone difficult, email writing even more difficult, and cell phone texting still more so. From the testimony of the Plaintiff, the Court is convinced that Smith was not questioning out of the blue the status of the lease between the two but quizzing Defendant out of the slight ambiguity that had existed since the earlier exchanges in March. She had operated for four months on the assumption that the written Lease expired and that she was on a month-to-month lease. In this August exchange, Jones was quick to hand down his view of things: "We are not month to month. Our contract automatically renewed…" (The authoritarian tone of this and others of Jones's texts was easily discernible). Smith then asked if there were "a way we can work with you on looking for someone to take over our lease?" and Jones seized on that message at trial to show that Smith knew she was in a year's lease. Smith argued she meant nothing of the kind but only that she would help find someone who could move right in as she moved out (when she bought a house) so that Jones would not lose any month's rent if the house were unoccupied. Similarly, later Smith said "we would not default," and Jones insisted at trial that she meant 'on the renewed lease,' but Smith said she meant only on the monthly rent, as in a month-to-month tenancy.

The final exchange of significance to this question was September 12, when Smith told Jones that she had delayed in writing back to him because "I wanted to make sure I was correct when it came to our lease." She insisted that she had it upon legal authority that "in order for our lease to be any longer than the first year it needed to say on it, 'automatic renewal of lease,' without that it's month to month after the first year with a 30-day notice." The Court considered the evidence of this exchange only for the purpose of showing that Smith's position on interpretation was, as it had been since March, that her first year's lease had not renewed automatically and that she had, in her informed conviction, been on a month-to-month lease ever since April 30 [of last year].

Under *Hawkins v. Greenwood Dev. Corp.,* 328 S.C. 585, 493 S.E.2d 875, 878 (S.C.Ct.App.1997), "A contract is ambiguous when it is capable of more than one meaning when viewed objectively by a reasonably intelligent person who has examined the context of the entire integrated agreement and who is cognizant of the customs, practices, usages and terminology as generally understood in the particular trade or business." This Court as a matter of law determines that Section 22 of the Lease gives rise to ambiguity because of deficient language. Under *Columbia East Assocs. v. Bi-Lo, Inc.,* the Court holds that the Lease is "capable of being understood in more ways than just one," and the Court consequently "allowed parol evidence to supply the deficiency." Also under *Columbia East Assocs.*, as an expression of contract law in general, this Court holds that "Where the contract is susceptible of more than one interpretation, the ambiguity will be resolved against the party who prepared the contract" (Id. at 520, 386 S.E.2d at 262).

Accordingly, the Court finds that the original written lease expired on April 30 [the year before last], as stated in its Section 4, and that Defendant's acceptance of rent thereafter established a month-to-month rental.

2. Plaintiff owed Defendant rent for the entire month of October [of the previous year].

Plaintiff asked the Court to award her $1,400.00, the entire amount of her security deposit for the rental property. However, Plaintiff was under a month-to-month rental agreement after April, and at the time of her surrender of the rental property in October. Despite her having given to Defendant on September 1 a 45-day notice of vacating the Property, Plaintiff's being in a month-to-month rental meant that she owed each month's rent as a separate, month by month agreement; consequently, she owed Defendant rent of $1,450.00 for October, due on October 1. Plaintiff argued that she surrendered possession on October 15 and should not have to pay for the rest of the month. She contended that her rent for April the year before, when she moved in, had been prorated for the period of April 12 to April 30, since she had taken possession on the 12th, and that by the same token she should not have to pay for that portion of October, of the following year, during which she no longer resided in the Property.

Plaintiff's argument is defective, however, since Defendant Jones and Plaintiff Smith had a bilateral agreement about her move-in date, but Plaintiff determined unilaterally that she would abate rent for October of the year she moved out: Jones never agreed to prorated rent for October. In a month-to-month tenancy, a tenant may not abate rent for a portion of a month when she surrenders possession of the property before the month's end. Smith paid Jones $701.55 for October. Jones was fully justified in deducting the balance of $748.45 from her security deposit, as well as the late fee of $300.00 for the month of October, since she had not paid the entire rent due by October 5.

3. An ancillary oral agreement existed between the parties for care of landscape on the Property beyond what was described and anticipated in the Lease.

The Court found entirely credible that Plaintiff and Defendant had reached an ancillary agreement whereby Plaintiff would undertake pruning or more substantial attention to the landscape than what was described in the Lease, which already itemized "cutting grass, removing weeds and pruning trees." The evidence for this agreement exists first in the testimony by Plaintiff that it existed, and also in sworn testimony that the amount of a non-refundable pet deposit, which was $350.00, had been reduced by half, in consideration for the extra work. Plaintiff testified that she paid the security deposit and half the pet deposit, not the full $350.00, and the Court finds her testimony on the matter credible.

A full list of the supplemental tasks was not presented by either party, but inasmuch as the Lease itself called for "pruning trees," it is apparent to the Court that landlord Jones anticipated Smith's being in the Property for a substantial length of time: most renters never take responsibility for tree pruning. Plaintiff's testimony did specifically identify her intention to do something to the ivy at the back door.

The Court finds that Plaintiff's severe pruning of a large, unshapely bush at the front corner of the property was necessitated by the safety hazard it posed to driving. The bush overhung the curb and blocked vision both for Smith and also for other drivers. Its near-removal was justified under the ancillary agreement as well as the Lease. Likewise the pruning of a small tree on the side of the Property was justified by its having mostly dead branches, as the Court finds, and the removal of the ivy on the back of the property appears to have been discussed briefly before the Lease was signed, as Plaintiff testified. The removal of ivy was made necessary by its being home to snakes which endangered Plaintiff's children. Plaintiff's having used this area to plant a few tomatoes appears to the Court to have been simply an alternate use that did not provide a home to the serpents. The ivy removal was reasonably included under the ancillary agreement for extra landscaping work.

Defendant improperly deducted $900.00 for loss of the ivy, the tree and the bush.

4. Plaintiff was damaged by $315.55 for unjustified deductions, and under State Law she may recover treble damages for the amount wrongfully withheld.

Defendant's deductions exhausted the security deposit and claimed an additional amount owed, upon which Defendant brought his Counterclaim in this case. In fact, Defendant should have refunded Plaintiff $315.55. The Court finds under the law that treble damages are appropriate.

5. On Defendant's Counterclaim, the Court finds no merit.

Defendant Jones's allegations on the Counterclaim, with one exception, are based on the amount he deducted from Plaintiff Smith's security deposit and which he claimed were still owed. The Court's having found in Plaintiff's favor on those items—the landscaping issues—those claims are dismissed.

On the remaining allegation in the Counterclaim, Defendant asks the Court for rent for November, a period during which Plaintiff was not in possession, and when, this Court has found, there had been no existing, renewed Lease, and when there was no longer any month-to-month rental agreement. Plaintiff did not owe any rent after October. Consequently, Defendant's request for late fees for November is dismissed as well.

UPON THE FINDINGS ABOVE, THE COURT DISMISSES THE COUNTERCLAIM AND ON THE COMPLAINT THE COURT RENDERS JUDGMENT FOR THE PLAINTIFF AND ORDERS DEFENDANT TO PAY TO PLAINTIFF $1,026.65, WHICH INCLUDES THE COURT COST OF $80.00.

Stephanie Smith and Farhad Jones received their copies of the Judgment by mail about a week after the hearing. Barely ten days after that, Smith filed a motion with the Court to amend the Judgment to require Jones to pay her back the $300.00 he had charged her for a late fee in October, since he had now gotten my Judgment and he hadn't yet paid her the thousand or so dollars I ordered him to pay. She figured she was due a "late fee" of her own.

She was pushing it. Motion denied. Case closed.

22
WHAT DID THE DOG DO?

If dogs knew what headaches they brought to landlord-tenant matters, they might put their tails between their legs in shame. Some landlords, of course, put their foot down from the very first and prohibit any pets. Others include a pet addendum and require a deposit, often non-refundable. Even then, dogs wind up being key suspects in disputes, and they are blissfully unaware of the fact. When the dispute winds up in court, the central question is often, What did the dog do?

THE PLEADINGS

Dorene Smith and her son-in-law Brad Schmidt filed a Complaint against their former landlord, Jones Southern Housing, for withholding most of their security deposit on property they had rented for two years. Smith also asked the Court for $345.98 for lost wages from prosecuting the case, and for an odd figure of $2,654.02 for "other relief as the Court may grant." Jones Southern Housing, which kept Chase Johnson, attorney, on retainer for its regular court visits, filed an Answer giving a general denial.

THE EVIDENCE

Dorene Smith, her daughter Mattie and Mattie's husband Brad Schmidt sat at the plaintiff's table with eager looks, ready to make their case. Smith, as would become evident from her first words, was not a native Southerner. She hailed from Brooklyn, NY. With her daughter and son-in-law she had moved down south a little more than two years ago, having rented a home from Jones Southern Housing without having seen it. Smith had a background in nursing and had found a position at a local hospital, moving with Mattie and Brad in order to take advantage of the lower cost of living in South Carolina. Smith was rapid of speech as many Northerners are, with a kind of intonation and inflection that suggested irritation and obstreperousness to the Southern ear, though probably people where she grew up thought nothing of it.

My observations about Plaintiffs' regional background and characteristics merely serve the purpose of helping to explain some of the dynamics of the parties' interactions. For Virginia Jones, owner of Jones Southern Housing, was a Southerner through and through. Herself the daughter of leading aristocratic Southern ladies of former generations, Virginia Jones was a notable Southern belle in her own right, and a successful businesswoman. As she was to tell the Court several times, she managed 434 rental homes. She employed two other people merely as office assistants.

Jones, however, struck me as up-tight (a delightfully descriptive term originating with my own generation). She had appeared now and again in court when an eviction was contested, and of course she filed numerous evictions regularly. Small and compact, with rich brown hair by choice, she gave the impression of someone who could hold her own, but there was also a pervasive sense of her being overly proper, to the point of repressive tendencies. Her tightly pursed mouth was that of an angry schoolmarm, and when she spoke she reinforced the impression.

What was evident to me from the beginning was the steel-and-flint nature of Smith's and Jones's personal interaction.

Plaintiff

Dorene Smith took the stand first and began telling rapidly her story of beginning to rent the house at 777 Perfect Place. She, her daughter and her son-in-law and their two small children moved in on October 1, two and a half years before, after picking out the house from some pictures sent to them by Jones. One of Jones's office assistants ran the company website, which did a good job of promoting their properties to anyone on the internet, which is everywhere. Smith and crew drove down from Brooklyn with their dog Ruff, cruised past the home they had selected, went to the offices of Jones Southern Housing, and signed a one year lease. They paid a security deposit, which was equal to one month's rent of $1,050.00 plus a pet deposit of $250.00. Smith moved into evidence the Lease, which showed the total deposit but no breakdown of what it represented. There was never any mention of a pet deposit in the Lease, though it did lay down extensive rules for pets and provided that tenants were liable for pet damage.

After the paperwork was done, the Smith party went to the house and walked in. While the configuration of the home was exactly what they had expected, they immediately noticed stains on several carpets, notably the master bedroom and the smallest bedroom of the three, which would be the couple's children's bedroom. The stains were, shall we say, dog related, and they were not only visible but olfactible—they smelled. Mattie took out her iPhone and began taking pictures. Ruff was still in the car and no furniture had yet been moved in. The house was empty.

A few days after they had moved in and gotten wireless connectivity, Mattie sent the pictures of the carpet from her phone to her mother's email account, and Dorene composed a couple of emails to Jones Southern Housing. She had the contact email of one of the assistants, and she sent him a message with a picture, informing him of the stained carpet and making sure she had documented the fact right at the first of their tenancy, so as not to be held responsible for this damage when they eventually moved out. Smith moved into evidence a sheaf of emails, which contained the pictures and also Jones Southern Housing's response, to the effect that the damage was noted and the information would go in Smith's file.

Smith showed the court the photographs that Mattie had taken, which were the same ones that were reproduced in the emails. The photos had better color and contrast, and they showed a distinct, large, and very objectionable area of darkly stained carpet near the center of the master bedroom, and similar stains in the small bedroom. Smith had written in one of the emails that she would forego having something done about the master bedroom carpet since she planned to put her bed over the stained area, but that the small bedroom carpet simply must be replaced. She said Jones had the carpet in that bedroom replaced within two weeks.

After a year's time was up, Smith said she and Brad Schmidt signed a lease for a second year, recently completed. When she did, she said she wrote a note at the bottom of that lease before signing it, and then had Brad take the lease to the company office, which he did. She showed the Court the Lease. A handwritten note was below the signatures on the last page, and was highlighted. Defendant's attorney Chase Johnson objected, politely of course, because he said his client—and he fumbled a bit as he sorted through papers and found the Lease—had the original, signed Lease, Your Honor—and he said this somewhat hesitantly, as if not quite certain of it himself. What he had didn't have on his client's copy was a note at the bottom. I asked him if he intended to place that document into evidence, and he said he would. Actually, he said, he would not object to Plaintiff's version if the Court wanted to receive both copies into evidence. I said I would very much like to compare the documents. On his assurance that he would introduce his client's version, I received Plaintiff's Lease into evidence, looking forward to comparing them. While things got underway again I noted by inspecting Plaintiff's lease exhibit that it was a photocopy and that the handwriting was part of the photocopy.

Continuing with her testimony, Dorene Smith said at the end of the second year's lease she and her extended family acquired other lodgings and moved out, giving the required notice. On the day the final inspection and surrender of the property took place, Dorene Smith was at work and asked her daughter, who was not actually a signator to the lease, to take her place at the home. Mattie would later testify to what took place. As a result of the inspection, however, Smith said Jones, citing the pet stains in the master bedroom as the chief problem, kept all of the security deposit. Smith contacted Jones thereafter and the exchanges became so heated that finally Smith told Jones she would take her to court. Smith said Virginia Jones, prim and proper Southern lady, told her if she did that, she would countersue for everything she could find wrong. Smith took one more step, making a Better Business Bureau complaint, which she entered into evidence along with the BBB's response, which suggested a mediator. After the BBB contacted Jones, Jones sent Smith a check for $300.00 as proffered settlement. Smith showed the check to the Court; she had not cashed it.

Smith was finished with her testimony and Chase Johnson rose to cross examine. I had always thought Mr. Johnson looked like Phillip Seymour Hoffman, the late actor. Johnson was short and stocky with a tousled blond head and a ruddy complexion. Where he differed most from Hoffman was in his dapper, collegiate dress. He always wore a bow tie with his khakis and blazer, but if he had worn a seersucker suit he could have been dropped into "Driving Miss Daisy" and been the perfect picture of a Southern family lawyer. He was equally as casual and friendly. I liked him.

Johnson approached and began recalling parts of Smith's testimony. He tried to identify little inconsistencies and to set up the Defendant's case. Mostly, however, he wanted to bring in the role that he believed Ruff had played.

"You had a dog, I believe; correct?"

"Yes, a Maltese," said Smith. "His name is Ruff."

"And dogs aren't perfect, are they?" asked Johnson. "They have accidents sometimes, don't they?"

"Yes. But we always cleaned up after Ruff."

Johnson went on trying to establish that it was likely that Ruff had accidents and that sometimes, when no one was around, Ruff may have had an accident and no one cleaned it up right away. Smith countered that they were careful to put Ruff in the bathroom when no one was at home: he didn't have the run of the house. Johnson tried another tack.

"And dogs mark their territory, don't they," Johnson said, more of a statement than a question. Smith said she supposed so, though she hadn't ever observed Ruff doing so.

Johnson moved on, asking about the pictures. He asked her to repeat where it was she had gotten the pictures printed, and she said Walgreens, where she always has her photographs done. Johnson was looking at the backs of the photos and remarked, for the Court's benefit, I'm sure, that he didn't see any dates printed there. He said offhandedly that in his experience Walgreens pictures always had dates on the back. Johnson, of course, was the attorney, not the witness, and his comments were not to be taken as testimony. Having never had photos printed at Walgreens (I print my own at home) I didn't know for a fact that they always had dates. Johnson was trying to cast doubt upon the authenticity of the prints, or at least to place some doubt in the Court's mind that Smith had not done any editing of the photos. It wasn't working, but I gave him an A for effort.

Mostly, Chase Johnson tried to establish through cross examination that Smith had received the accounting and itemized deductions from Jones as required by law, which she had, and that Smith had been told by Jones that the master bedroom carpet had been replaced before Smith took occupancy. Yes, Jones had told her that, said Smith, but the pictures showed otherwise. Johnson withdrew politely, and Smith called her next witness.

Brad Schmidt testified to the same things as Dorene Smith, verifying her statements about the day they walked in and saw the master bedroom carpet, echoing the testimony about the dog, etc. On cross, Johnson went again to the subject of the dog, little Ruff, an eleven pound ball of silky fur.

"Dogs aren't perfect, are they? They have accidents, right?" Johnson suggested, and Brad gave the same answers as his mother-in-law. They always cleaned up after Ruff, but Brad gave the impression that Ruff was very good.

Mattie Smith Schmidt was up next and was a little feisty as she said what her mother had said, and she emphasized that it was she who insisted on taking the pictures with her iPhone. She didn't have that phone anymore and she didn't have the original pictures on her newer phone, but she was unbending about her having photographed the stains and about the smell that all could detect.

Mattie had done the walk through with Virginia Jones. She said Jones made comments about the master bedroom in particular, and that Mattie reminded her that they had sent Jones Southern Housing some pictures and descriptions two years ago, for the very purpose of making sure that they were not penalized for the previous tenant's damages due to their dogs. Mattie said Jones was irritable, brusk, and rude, and that she left in a huff.

Johnson asked if on the walk-through Jones had discovered dog mess in the garage. Mattie Schmidt said she didn't see it and Jones didn't comment on it. Was the garage door open when Jones arrived? Yes, it had been.

"Was the master bedroom carpet new when you moved in?" Johnson asked. Perhaps he hoped to catch Mattie in a sudden admission contradictory to what she had said. She wasn't going for it. No, she said, and only the kids' bedroom was replaced after they moved in. And during their tenancy, the kitchen linoleum was replaced as well. (The Court wondered why. The house was barely five years old when the linoleum was replaced. Had the previous tenant damaged it to the extent that with only one more year's use, it was already in bad shape?)

Then Johnson softly grilled Mattie with the same set of questions about imperfect pets, implying that little Ruff had probably "messed" in the corner somewhere or "peed in the floor." Mattie insisted that Ruff may have had an accident or two, but one of the family would always clean up after him right away.

Johnson was finished with the witness and Plaintiff rested.

Defendant

Before presenting Defendant's case, Chase Johnson deftly moved that the Court direct a verdict in the matter of the day's wages part of the Complaint, as well as the "other relief" portion that totaled $2,654.02. No evidence had been given supporting either of these claims. The Court granted the motion as to the missed work claim, and for the specific figure of $2,654.02, though I would not rule out "other relief" if I found for Plaintiff and saw fit. Johnson was satisfied with the ruling. It was clear to me from early in the hour that he thought it probable that his client would go away owing *something,* but he was trying to minimize the damage.

While Johnson was preparing to question his witness, I added up the figures for wages and "other relief." The total was $3,000.00 even. Smith had just wanted to pad her judgment, if she won, by three grand. New home expenses, perhaps?

Johnson called his client, Virginia Jones. She was the sole owner and, I gathered, the only person actually managing 434 homes (a fact and figure she repeated several times). She said on the day of the final walk through as she approached the house she noted that all the doors and windows were open, as well as the garage, which she took to be a "bad sign." Tenants, she said, often attempt a last minute airing out of the house to mask pet urine smells, smoke, etc. Jones said the first thing she noticed when she went into the house through the open garage was a fresh dollop of dog feces (she said poop) in the middle of the garage floor. She took a picture, which showed a very fuzzy image that really couldn't be identified. Jones said she had the garage floor pressure washed. (For that single spot? It fit with Jones's personality.)

Jones then tried to sort out for the Court how and when the master bedroom carpet had been replaced. First she said it had been replaced between tenants. She didn't say which ones. No testimony had established that there had been only one tenant previous to Smith and her family. I began thinking that perhaps there were at least two since the house had been built. Then Jones said she had had the carpet replaced "before the Smiths moved in." Actually she said "during the previous tenant." It was a slip, on her part, I think, and perhaps a critical one. If she meant to leave the impression that the carpet had been brand new just before Smith moved in, she muddied the waters with her varied descriptions.

Jones went on to introduce the bill for changing carpet in the whole house after Smith and family left, then introduced an estimate prepared by her carpet supplier, who had broken down the cost into what just the master bedroom would have cost if done separately. This was what she deducted from the deposit, along with (attempted) cleaning costs. To emphasize the purpose for this, her attorney asked her why she did the break-down of costs. It was because she wasn't going to charge them for everything, only what she could prove, and of course, because she was trying to be fair.

In fact, Jones said, she could have charged the Smiths for replacing the small bedroom carpet. She meant that the carpet replaced at the Smiths' request two years ago already needed replacing. Under questioning by Johnson, Jones gave the Court a long list of things she *didn't* charge Smith and Schmidt for, to make the point of how good she was being to them. Maybe she and her attorney thought that would make me sympathetic to her.

Under cross examination by a surprisingly capable sounding Dorene Smith, Virginia Jones said she thought it was entirely possible that Ruff had soiled the carpets in a few days. "Dogs can pee the day they move in," she said. "The mark their territory." She then said that "the master bedroom carpet may have been a little worn, but not stained." So there was the admission that the carpet in that bedroom was not brand new.

Dorene Smith asked Virginia Jones about the photos in the emails two years before Jones answered curtly, "I didn't see any pictures. There weren't any pictures in the emails I saw." When Smith pressed her to remember what she, Smith, had told her about the carpet when they moved in, Jones said, as she did two other times to excuse non-responsive answers, "I don't know. I don't remember. I've got 434 homes to manage; I can't be expected to remember every conversation I have." She was becoming impatient with this whole matter. She had gotten her lawyer to come to this trial, for heaven sakes, and she was supposed to be going home a winner by now, and here was this, this *woman* (this *Yankee,* I believe she was saying to herself), complaining about a deposit. After all, as she had testified, she had an MBA in accounting from a nearby university.

Smith then asked her a few questions about the walk through, and Virginia Jones barked back that Smith had sent her daughter, who, every time Jones would say something about an issue, would say, "You'll have to call my mother." Jones said she didn't know until those exchanges that Mattie was not the tenant herself.

Jones said, "I didn't have the lease with me that day. I didn't know what your name was. I thought she was you." In other words, Jones didn't know her tenant. What else had she not kept track of?

Smith was satisfied she had elicited enough damaging testimony from Virginia Jones and she sat down. Chase Johnson next called Thomas Green, a man of about sixty-five who owned the flooring company that had provided Jones Southern Housing with carpet for years. He didn't lay any of it himself, these days, he said, because of his knees.

Johnson wanted to know if Green had provided the carpet for the replacement last year, just after Smith, Schmidt and company had moved out. Yes, he had. He had a bag with him that contained samples cut from the carpets in the various rooms. One square was from the master bedroom, and it matched the square from the children's bedroom, the one room nobody questioned had been re-carpeted since the building of the home. The rest of the carpet was the original builder-grade variety. The difference proved that the carpet in the master bedroom had been changed—at some point, anyway.

The square from the small bedroom had red stains, which Green said from his experience typically came from Kool-Aid or juice boxes. He showed how the stain had penetrated to the underside, the primary backing.

Now Chase Johnson wanted to know about pet stains. Green began to show multiple samples from the master bedroom carpet in particular where there were pet stains. He knew them from experience. They weren't produced by a cat, in his opinion, but by a dog. He described, in rather unnecessary detail, how dogs would enter a new home, go into a corner, and urinate to mark their territory. All dogs do, he said.

The squares also had a good bit of odor, a combination of things that was disagreeable, not all of which was pet urine, but there was some of that. He showed the backings of several squares, pointing out urine and other stains, along with more Kool-Aid. Dogs in particular would mark their territory by urinating, and the urine would soak through and stain the underside. He had seen a lot of it.

Poor Ruff was not even present and couldn't defend himself. He would have to count on his owner, Dorene Smith, to protect his interests. She cross examined Green, asking him how long it would take for pet urine to stain the primary backing. She may have been expecting an answer in weeks, but Green said a few days at the most.

Smith switched to the matter of when the carpet had been changed. Green couldn't remember exactly when.

"Could it have been during the previous tenant?" asked Smith.

"I don't know."

"Do you have a bill or an order or something to show when it was installed?"

"Well," he said, "I didn't know I'd need that. I probably have it somewhere. It would be in my files." His tone was filled with uncertainty. He certainly didn't have any bill or order or any other document with him to pinpoint the time.

"Don't you think that would have been a pretty good piece of evidence to bring to court today, since this was about whether a carpet had been changed?" said Smith, sounding very much like an attorney.

Green just stared at her, assuming the question was rhetorical, I supposed.

On redirect, Chase Johnson asked if Green had known before coming to court that he needed to have proof of the carpet's being changed in 2013. Green said no. In my opinion, Mr. Johnson should have thought of that himself and told Green what to bring.

That was all for both parties. I promised a decision within the week. As I studied on the evidence and replayed portions of the electronic record, I reaffirmed what I thought I had heard and then evaluated all of it.

Virginia Jones had never lost a case before, in my recollection anyway. She usually had all her ducks in a row. But Dorene Smith appeared from the very first to be a smart cookie about renting, gathering her information from the start to protect herself from liability later. Who was telling the truth? More correctly, I really didn't think anyone was lying: someone simply didn't have a very good memory of the matter.

I decided to make a two column document in my word processor, label the left side Smith and the right side Jones, and then put down the pluses and minuses of each side's case in the matter of the master bedroom carpet. After all, that was the sum of the matter. Everything depended on my finding of fact in that particular.

After I had spent a half hour or so whittling down testimony to simple propositions, I had no question about who would prevail.

JUDGMENT

The sole issue around which the Complaint revolves is whether or not the master bedroom carpet in the rental home at 777 Perfect Place had been replaced *immediately* before Plaintiff/Tenant took possession of the property. Plaintiff also asked for damages for lost wages and other such relief as the Court would grant, but the Court dismissed both complaints for lack of evidence.

Plaintiff Smith alleged the master bedroom carpet was stained from pets and needed replacing upon her first moving in. Defendant claimed the master bedroom carpet was replaced "between tenants" and was not stained.

Solely on the testimony of the two parties Plaintiff would lack a preponderance of evidence to substantiate her claim—it was a she said/she said. However, Plaintiff produced photographs of the master bedroom carpet taken the day she moved in, when there was no furniture and Ruff, the family Maltese, had not set paw in the place. Despite the absence of dates on the backs of the photographs, the same pictures appeared also in emails sent to Defendant within two weeks of move-in. The emails described the stains, and Defendant Jones Southern Housing, by way of one of its assistants, acknowledged receipt.

Samples of the carpet removed after Smith's surrender of the property showed conclusively that the master bedroom carpet had been replaced since the house was built, but Smith's witness could not remember when that was, and he had no documents to give the Court a clue.

The Court was also satisfied from the carpet squares that a pet or pets, almost certainly canine, had done significant damage to the carpeting here and there, but the question not answered was which pet or pets? Ms. Jones was certain that it must have been Ruff, the canine friend of Smith, Schmidt and Schmidt and kids. Smith *et al* were adamant that it had to have been the pets that belonged to the previous tenants, and they were absolutely certain of this because they documented the stains to two bedrooms when they first walked into the house. Their note to Jones Southern Housing on the second year's lease is further writing that underscores their insistence from the first that the carpet needed replacing from the day they moved in.

Even without making a finding as to when the carpet was replaced, the Court has a snapshot in time convincing it that the master bedroom carpet was stained and in need of replacement when Plaintiffs moved in, two and a half years ago now.

Defendant Jones, because of mistaken memory or inadequate records of the initial complaint made by Smith, improperly deducted from Smith's security deposit the amount spent on trying to clean the carpets and then the amount spent on replacing all the carpet when cleaning was unsuccessful. Further, since it had been six years since the five-year builder-grade carpet had been installed, Jones would have had to replace it anyway, and cannot charge it against Smith as being somehow above normal wear and tear.

State law does provide that a tenant "may" recover treble damages for a security deposit or portion thereof "wrongfully withheld," however, the language of the law implies that such damages must be affirmatively pled, and Smith did not ask for treble damages. Indeed, as she summed up, "I just want my security deposit back. We did everything we were supposed to do."

Indeed she did, and so she shall have it.

THE COURT ORDERS DEFENDANT JONES SOUTHERN HOUSING TO PAY TO PLAINTIFFS DORENE SMITH AND BRAD SCHMIDT $1,300.00, PLUS $80.00 IN FILING COSTS. IF JONES'S CHECK FOR $300.00 BEING HELD BY SMITH IS STILL NEGOTIABLE, THE PARTIES MAY AGREE AS TO ITS BEING PART OF THE SETTLEMENT OF THE JUDGMENT DEBT.

EPILOGUE

I suspected that the fiery Virginia Jones might be so upset at losing the case that she might try to take her eviction cases to another court in the future. When I didn't see any applications for ejectment from Jones Southern Homes come across my desk in the next two months, I figured I had been correct. However, she brought a batch of applications in three months later. Whether she had tried taking them to another court and had been told they were in my venue I don't know. I did notice, however, that her standard contract changed somewhat. She decided to set the amount of the pet deposit—fairly high, too—and to make it non-refundable. If there were ever another question of what a dog did or didn't do, she was going to make sure that she had money in reserve to cover it.

23
WHOSE STUFF?

Breakups between romantic partners usually cause problems. Sometimes the magistrate sees a restraining order case come out of a breakup; sometimes assaults take place and charges are made; other times, as chronicled in this book, pets are the victims of ownership squabbles. In the instant case, a storage unit full of property was in dispute. Two lawyers and a third party defendant became involved and the Court had a lovely afternoon hearing about who had the right to the unit and how much it would cost to be allowed to get in it. Along the way, the parties felt it necessary to divulge personal details.

THE PLEADINGS

Tori Smith, through her attorney Armstrong Wilson, filed a suit against Forest Road Storage alleging that they had denied her access to her property in a storage unit she rented in May almost three years ago. She alleged not only that Forest Road had locked her out, but that in collusion with Shamesha Jones they had removed and disposed of her property. Since Smith believed Forest Road and Jones had acted together, she actually charged them with conspiracy. (No doubt this was under the suggestion of her attorney.)

Forest Road retained the legal bulldog of the county, Rodney Johnson, to handle its case, and Rodney, upon hearing the facts as Forest Road recited them, filed an Answer and Counterclaim and named as a third party Defendant the aforementioned Shemesha Jones. Forest Road's Answer and additional Complaint said that

Smith and Jones "were engaged in a relationship as significant others," and that when they broke up, the storage facility came into dispute.

THE EVIDENCE

Armstrong Wilson and Rodney Johnson represented pretty much the ends of the spectrum of legal eagles when it came to personality. I had seen each of them in my court numerous times and Johnson, in particular, in the Circuit Court for preliminary hearings. Johnson was a lean, wiry guy with a sinewy, rough look, who was like a pit bull in some ways: when he got hold of something, he didn't let go of it until the Court saw it his way (he hoped), and if he did let go, he did it with a visible disgust that left the impression that the judge was blind and deaf. He was intimidating, in other words. By contrast, Armstrong Wilson was an affable, easygoing guy with a fluid, friendly manner of speech who smiled a lot and never seemed ruffled. He represented his clients well, but he did it without making a scene or getting angry.

At the Plaintiff's table was Armstrong Wilson. Two people were in the gallery behind them, one a young woman of noticeably voluptuous proportions and the other of somewhat ambiguous gender. I assumed one of these was Tori. Why she didn't sit at the Plaintiff's table, I never found out.

Forest Road's attorney, Rodney Johnson, was accompanied by a woman at his table who turned out to be the manager of Forest Road Storage. Behind the defendant's table were two or three more people, one of whom was another employee of Forest Road and the other of whom was Shemesha Jones.

Plaintiff

After brief opening statements, which merely reviewed the Complaint and Answer/Counterclaim/Third Party Complaint, Mr. Wilson called Shemesha Jones to the stand. Wilson didn't ask the

Court to declare Shemesha a hostile witness, though at this point the term certainly might have described her in the common sense.[4] But Wilson simply wanted some information that he believed he could get out of her without any prejudice to his client.

Wilson asked Shemesha to tell the Court a little about herself and Tori Smith. Given that general question, Shemesha Jones said she met Tori Smith at work. The two young women were attracted to each other from the first, and they began sleeping together three and a half years ago. Before Wilson could interrupt her, Jones went on to say that she and Smith had sex nearly every night at one or the other of their two apartments. Both women lived at the Crooked Creek Apartments, which coincidentally happened to be right across the street from Forest Road Storage.

"Well, tell us what happened between the two of you during the spring about three years ago," Wilson asked her. Shemesha said the two broke up. Shemesha had been planning a trip to the beach in the late spring, and she said Tori had suspected that she was going with, or going to meet, someone else there—someone Tori thought Shemesha was planning to have sex with— Tori thought Shemesha was going to cheat on her. In fact, Tori thought Shemesha already was cheating on her. Shemesha didn't tell the Court that she wasn't; she simply said she had made her reservations and paid for the trip and she wasn't going to change her plans.

The information was relevant because about that time Crooked Creek filed for eviction against Shemesha Jones. She didn't say why she was being evicted, only that she was. At the point of Jones's beach trip, Smith hadn't actually accused her of cheating;

[4]For non-legal readers, a hostile witness is one who is called by and testifies for the opposing party, who may be asked leading questions, to which the answer typically must be either Yes or No. Such a witness might otherwise be expected to offer prejudicial evidence. Having the Court declare someone as a hostile witness enables attorneys to frame questions in such a way as to elicit testimony helpful to their case, in spite of the witness's inclination to do otherwise.

she had only insinuated it. The two were still "together." In fact, they were still on good enough terms that Jones felt comfortable asking Smith to do her the big favor of moving her things out of her apartment (apparently she didn't have much) to a storage unit, while Jones was at the beach for about ten days. As an aside, Jones told the Court it was "Bike Week" at the beach. Due to the date she mentioned to the Court, evidently she meant Myrtle Beach Motorcycle Rally, a/k/a Bike Week.

Jones said Smith agreed to get some friends help her, and she also agreed to rent a storage unit in her own name and to turn it over to Shemesha when she got back. During that week, Smith rented the unit and told Danielle Brown of Forest Road Storage that in a week or two Tori Smith would be taking over the contract and paying the rent thereafter. She moved all Jones's property into unit 69 at Forest Road Storage. As most storage facilities do, Forest Road had a gate where customers could input codes to gain access to the storage buildings. Each unit then had hasps for the customers' own locks.

When Jones came back from the beach, the breakup began. She didn't have her old apartment to go back to, and apparently she didn't need one. The evening of the day she returned from Myrtle Beach, she went to stay with "a friend." Perhaps the friend was a bit more than just a friend. That's apparently what Smith thought, in fact, because that night Smith went to the friend's house near midnight and demanded to see Jones. The friend didn't allow Smith into the house, and Smith wound up breaking out a window in an attempt to get in, or just because she was angry. The friend called the police, and the upshot of it all was that Jones and her friend both gave statements that resulted in Smith's being arrested and charged with various misdemeanors.

Tori was transported to the county jail and given a bond hearing within twenty-four hours, but she couldn't make bail and she stayed in jail for five days. She got out when the charges were dismissed due to Shemesha's friend's not being willing to testify against Smith, but the damage to the "significant other" relationship was permanent.

While Tori was in jail, Shemesha called Danielle Brown at Forest Road Storage and told her she was ready to take over the storage unit in her name according to the agreement she and Tori Smith had. Danielle complied, having spoken twice with Tori about the plan while Shemesha was at the beach.

Tori Smith then got out of jail and went to Forest Road and attempted to get into the storage area. From later testimony by Smith herself, I learned what happened before Shemesha arrived on the scene. Tori's access code for the gate wouldn't work. She went to the office and told the attendant on duty, Charlie White, that her code wouldn't work. He tried looking up her name but she was not listed as a renter. Tori gave him Shemesha's name, and White found the record, but he wouldn't give her access because Tori's name wasn't on the approved access list. Tori began to make a scene and demanded that White call Danielle Brown, which he did. On the phone, Brown explained to White that the unit had been transferred from Smith to Jones, with Smith's full consent. Further, she asked White to describe the woman claiming to be Smith. Specifically, Brown wanted to know if Smith were bald. White asked Smith to take off a ball cap she was wearing, she did, and she was bald. White relayed this information to Brown on the phone and Brown confirmed from the entire description that the woman was Tori Smith.

Told again that she would not be allowed into the storage area, Tori went into a full blown rage. She insisted that the unit was hers, that she had things in the unit, that Forest Road didn't have the right to keep her out, that Shemesha was trying to steal from her, etc. Shemesha denied there was anything of Tori's in the unit, referred to the agreement that she and Tori had about who would take over the unit, etc. There was much shouting and threatening gesticulation.

Danielle called the police. A unit came quickly and a county deputy tried to sort things out. He wanted to know what was in the unit. Both Smith and Jones claimed to have property inside. Shemesha told the police it was mostly clothes.

Attorney Wilson asked Shemesha, "If it were only clothes, wasn't it possible some of them were Tori's?"

"No," Shemesha said. "They were girl's stuff. Nothing belonged to Tori. Like y'all can see, she dress like a dude." She pointed toward one of the persons in the gallery behind Armstrong's table. The voluptuous girl was 100% girl, but the other person's gender was unmasked by the testimony.

When the deputy couldn't make an obvious determination about the storage unit, he told Danielle to lock both Tori and Shemesha out of it until the matter could be decided by a magistrate or else the two came to some agreeable terms. Forest Road did just that, and neither Shemesha nor Tori had had access to the unit for almost three years, until the matter landed in my court. (Testimony revealed that the two had been scrapping over the unit for all this time, neither of them having filed an action with a magistrate for possession of the storage unit.)

Armstrong Wilson had been asking mere, informational questions to this point but now he began attempting to get from this hostile witness some ammunition for his own side, his client Tori Smith.

He first presented a copy of the storage unit contract for Shemesha's inspection and asked her about it. She said it was a contract between Forest Road and Tori Smith—the name was in the first paragraph and Tori's signature was on the last page. Then Wilson showed Jones another contract, and she said that it was a contract between Forest Road Storage and *her*. It was dated the day after she had returned from Myrtle Beach. Wilson also showed her a copy of a change-of-address form for the Storage company, showing that Shemesha changed both the address of the renter as well as the name, to her own. He asked Shemesha if it weren't true that she intended to disallow access to Tori to her (Tori's) own unit. No, said Shemesha, that was never the plan. There was nothing of hers in it anyway. Why would she want access? Wilson asked if it weren't true that Shemesha wanted Tori to *pay* for the unit. No, and why would I, she said, when "it's not her stuff." Shemesha was adamant that after she came back from Myrtle Beach, the arrangement was that she was to take over the unit. Wilson didn't get any admissions out of Jones that were useful, and he concluded his questioning.

Rodney Johnson now cross examined Shemesha, who must by now have been aware that neither lawyer was her friend. No doubt without planning it, Wilson and Johnson were good cop, bad cop, only lawyers. Rodney was the bad cop. He came in firing both guns.

"You lived with Tori before spring of last year, didn't you?" asked Johnson.

"No! I had my own apartment. I never moved in with Tori."

"You never cohabited with Tori?" Rodney said, as if it were a different question.

"No," said Shemesha.

"And Tori rented the unit for your benefit, didn't she?"

"Yes."

"And after your, er, problems with Tori, you two agreed she would to transfer the unit to her, isn't that correct?"

"Yes," said Shemesha.

"And Forest Road Storage didn't contact you about this arrangement; you contacted them, right?" said Johnson.

"Correct," she said.

Johnson didn't need anything else from Jones and I dismissed her. Johnson sat down, too, and I asked Armstrong Wilson for his next witness.

Wilson called Johnson's client, Danielle Brown, Forest Road's manager. Brown was a bright, blue-eyed blonde of about forty-five who was plain spoken and not at all timid about testifying. She smiled broadly and looked thoroughly comfortable on the witness stand. I know flirting when I see it, for the most part, and in addition to her being outgoing and helpful to her attorney as he questioned her, she was also flirting with the judge. It had to do entirely with her hopes for prevailing in court, I'm certain.

Danielle Brown said she had been the manager of Forest Road Storage for thirteen years and was the manager three years ago when all these things took place. She was the person who executed the contract in spring three years ago with Tori Smith. Wilson showed her the second contract in evidence, the one with Shemesha Jones, not Tori Smith, as the renter. Why, he asked her, is the date on the signature line (which was in mid summer) not the same as the one on page one of the contract (which was in the spring), he wanted to know.

Brown looked at the judge with a brilliant smile. "The software puts in the date when the contract was first generated. That was the spring date. The date on the signature page was when we converted it to Shemesha Jones."

Brown's testimony was that she had talked with Tori Smith at least twice about the transfer to Jones, that Smith agreed to it, and that on the phone Smith had referred to Jones as her roommate. Jones had come and executed the change when she returned from the beach. Brown changed the codes and the contract at that point.

Brown had been the one called to the storage facility when the fracas between Smith and Jones took place. She denied access to Smith because of the agreement that had now been finalized. In fact, Brown told the Court that Smith "admitted in front of the police that she did ask Forest Road Storage to transfer the unit to Shemesha." This testimony certainly didn't fit Wilson's plan, and I wondered if he ran afoul of that cardinal rule of trial lawyer-ing: never ask a question to which you do not already know the answer.

The instructions for the change, however, were all oral. There was nothing in writing where Tori signed over the unit to Shemesha. The manager simply said she had spoken to Tori at least twice and confirmed the agreement, then changed the contract into Shemesha's name. She said that at present about $2,000.00 was owed on the storage unit, which had been secured against any access for almost three years, now.

During those years—particularly early on, said Brown—she had talked with both Tori and Shemesha about settling the issue. Both indicated that Shemesha would get the unit, and Brown said Tori told her she would come up and sign a release, but she never did. Things had stood that way since mid summer the previous year. She had not taken any action against either woman so she could free up the unit, because she thought she had to wait for a court order.

Wilson sat down and Johnson got up to cross examine Danielle Brown.

"Does Forest Road have access to storage unit 69?" said Johnson. He knew they didn't.

"No. We placed one of our own locks on the unit, but the renter's lock is still on it, and that would prevent us from accessing it unless the lock were cut off."

"On my instruction in July three years ago, you locked the unit and cancelled codes, didn't you?" asked Johnson. Danielle said yes. I wondered how that fit with previous testimony that the sheriff's deputy had issued this instruction.

"And I prepared a document for Tori to sign about ownership, didn't I." Brown said yes and that Shemesha came and signed the release but Tori didn't.

Johnson continued: "And Ms. Jones made some payments on the unit, correct?" She had, said Brown; she paid four months worth, almost to the end of the calendar year. The payment record came in as evidence.

Johnson also showed Brown another document, a print out of access to unit 69 during the time in question, in the summer three years ago. Brown said the computer makes a record of the access code used at the gate, the person the code belongs to, and the time it is used. Johnson asked if the document showed that Tori Smith had accessed the unit on a certain date, which, I noted, corresponded to one of the days Tori was in jail. Brown said yes. At the very least this information was curious.

With Johnson's cross examination completed, Wilson had no re-direct and I dismissed the witness.

Wilson now called his client, Tori Smith, finally. The person of ambiguous gender rose and took the stand. Indeed, she dressed "like a dude." Her hair was very short, she wore men's slacks and a polo shirt and she had sizeable athletic shoes. Her proportions fit those of a male her size, which was husky.

Armstrong Wilson jumped about from subject to subject, certainly by design. He first asked her about the contract. She said, "They let my contract be overwritten by her [pointing to Shemesha Jones] without my permission. I moved stuff into the unit while Shemesha was at the beach."

Wilson asked if she and Shemesha had cohabited. Tori said, "We cohabited together six or seven months. I *did* live at Crooked Creek with her. I paid half her rent. When she went to the beach, I moved *all* the stuff in Crooked Creek to the storage unit. Some was hers, some mine."

"Did you ever execute a writing transferring the unit to Shemesha?" asked Wilson.

"No. I didn't."

"Now, tell us about the altercation in July," said Wilson.

Tori Smith said that she was arrested after the fracas at the storage lot. She said when she got out she tried to go get a shirt out of the unit and found out the access code was changed. She denied she had ever called Forest Road Storage to tell them to transfer the unit to Shemesha. She said some cousin of Shemesha's called to urge her to sign over the unit to Shemesha, but she said no. Wilson wanted to know if there was anything in the unit that belonged to her now. She said she didn't know if anything of hers was still there. She implied it might have been removed before the lockout by either Shemesha or Forest Road.

Wilson showed his client a list of things she had made for the Court's inspection. He hurriedly summarized the items as shirts and electronics, and asked her to tell him about the list. She said it was things of hers she had put in the storage unit. The list was entered as an exhibit for Plaintiff. I scanned it while Tori was still testifying. About half the list consisted of briefly described polo shirts, specific brands, with values. The other half was video games and controllers. The lone item that stuck out, so to speak, was a vibrating, strapless, G-spot dildo.

Finished with his questions, Wilson sat down and Johnson stood up.

On cross examination, Rodney Johnson first asked Tori, "It was a bad breakup, wasn't it?"

"Yeah, it was pretty bad," she said.

"But there was no issue about the storage unit until July, after the June breakup, right?"

"Right," she said.

"Now, access to the storage area is just a pass code, correct?" asked Johnson.

"Yes. It's a number. The gate only. You got a lock on the unit after that."

"So you gave Shemesha the code number, didn't you?" said Johnson, hoping to solve the mystery about who accessed the unit while Smith was in jail.

"No. I never gave her that. She was at the beach when I rented it, and then we broke up. I never gave it to her.

"So the only person prior to the altercation at the storage unit who had the access code to the gate was you, right?" asked Johnson.

"Yes," said Smith, with a slightly faltering voice.

Johnson showed Tori the access log from Forest Road Storage. He wanted to know if that was her code showing for an access to the unit during the week before the altercation. It was, she said, but she was in jail so it couldn't have been she.

> Parenthetically, it was evident, in light of the undisputed evidence of Tori's arrest and incarceration for five days, that someone other than Tori used her access code to enter the storage area. I wanted to know who, but no one ever asked the question. Was it an agent of Tori's? A friend, perhaps, who would secretly put stuff in or take stuff out? To what end?

"Have you ever been bald?" asked Johnson.

"No, I never been bald," said Smith. It's been short, but not bald. Privately, I wondered at the difference. I've seen some "short" cuts on women I would describe as being bald. When you expect significant length hair on a woman and see next to nothing, the description begs itself.

Tori Smith stepped down and Armstrong Wilson was through with his case.

Defendant

Rodney Johnson now began his case for his client, Forest Road Storage, and against the third party defendant, Shemesha Jones. He combined the issues to simplify the procedure in court. For his first witness he recalled Jones to the stand.

"I show you the list of items Ms. Smith says are hers. Her attorney placed it in evidence," he said. "Is any of that property in the storage unit?"

"No. Never was," said Shemesha Jones.

"You've heard the Plaintiff testify that you and she lived together," said Johnson. "You did, didn't you? And she paid part of your rent, didn't she?"

"No!" said Jones adamantly, "I didn't need anybody to pay half my rent because I was on Section 8!" In other words, the government paid her rent. Jones then recounted what had been said before, that she went to the beach, that when she came back she spent the first night at her friend's house, and that Tori Smith came over, got mad, and broke a window.

"Did you have the access code to the storage unit?" said Johnson.

"Yeah, I had it," she said quickly and forcefully. "She gave it to me over the phone after she rented it, while I was still at the beach. In fact, it was the last few numbers of her cell phone; that's how I remembered it," she added. Johnson sat down.

Wilson had a few questions in cross. "My client, Tori Smith, paid for the unit in May, right?" Jones said yes. "And you repaid her, didn't you?" asked Wilson, to which Jones said yes. "Did you ever access the unit in June," Wilson wanted to know? Jones didn't remember. But when she went to the unit in July, while Smith was in jail, she saw that some TVs of hers, which she presumed Tori had moved into the unit while she was at the beach, were not there. She believed Tori had stolen them.

Rodney Johnson now had two questions in redirect. "Why would Tori have pursued this matter without resolution for three years?"

"Because it was a bad breakup. She wanted to get back at me," said Jones. It made sense to me. I see it all the time.

"And are you willing to pay Forest Road Storage to get your property back?" asked Johnson. "That's about two thousand dollars."

"If that's what it takes, yes," said Jones.

Johnson sat down. Both sides were finished. With two lawyers, I expected closing statements, and they both offered brief summations but mostly asked the Court, for the sake of all involved, to issue an order deciding who had a right to what and who owed whom how much. After nearly three years it was time to settle this matter.

THE JUDGMENT

Upon the preponderance of the evidence, the Court makes the following findings:

1. Forest Road Storage had an initial contract ("the Rental Agreement") with Tori Smith for unit 69. Plaintiff Smith, Defendant Forest Road Storage and third party Defendant Shemesha Jones subsequently agreed that Jones would take over possession of the storage unit, releasing Smith from her contractual relationship. Smith gave permission by phone to Forest Road, and Forest Road executed a valid agreement with Jones. Although the foregoing facts were contested, testimony to these facts was presented not only by Jones but also by Forest Road Storage, a disinterested party as to the ownership or possession of any of the personal property stored in unit 69: Forest Road Storage had no knowledge in the first place of what that property might be.

2. Forest Road Storage acted in faithful observance of section 9 of its contract with Smith, by which the renting party (Tori) could terminate the agreement "at any time by giving two days oral or written notice to Owner (Forest Road Storage)."

3. Under State law, Forest Road has an implied lien on the contents of the storage unit. Ownership of the actual items of personal property in storage is quite a separate matter, but as found previously by the Court, responsibility for payment of storage rent became that of Defendant Shemesha Jones in July three years ago, and that obligation still is hers. The unpaid storage unit rent and fees at the date of the Judgment is $2,110.00

4. The Court issues the Orders below on a conclusion, drawn from the facts found, that no property in the storage unit belongs to any party other than Smith or Jones. While the

parties allege the presence or absence of personal property belonging to Plaintiff in unit 69, the Court has insufficient evidence to make a finding as to whether such property is there. However, the Court does determine that third party Defendant Shemesha Jones is solely authorized to access the unit once rent and fees due and owing are paid.

5. The Court finds that the items listed in Plaintiff's exhibit of personal property belong to her, Tori Smith.

JUDGMENT IS FOR DEFENDANT FOREST ROAD ON THE COMPLAINT. ON THE COUNTERCLAIM, THE COURT RENDERS JUDGMENT ALSO FOR FOREST ROAD AND FINDS THAT DEFENDANT SHEMESHA JONES OWES FOREST ROAD $2,110.00 IN FEES IN ORDER TO ACCESS UNIT 69.

I then issued orders for my constable to go to Forest Road Storage with Defendant Jones only, to access the storage unit, and to identify any property of Plaintiff Tori Smith if it were there. I ordered Forest Road to keep any such property for ten days, notify Smith of that fact, and give the property to Smith if she came for it, after which they could dispose of it if she didn't. After thirty days, if Jones had not paid what she owed, Forest Road could exercise its lien without involving the Court, which is what the law provides.

EPILOGUE

The Constable found a box with about a dozen men's-type polo shirts, a box full of video games, and a third box that contained three video controllers and, in a plastic bag, a purple contraption corresponding to the sex toy described in Plaintiff's exhibit of personal property. He sealed the boxes and turned them over to Forest Road Storage to be put somewhere secure until Tori could claim them. He then witnessed Shemesha write a check to Forest

Road for $2,110.00, whereupon he concluded his business and returned to the Court with his report.

Unfortunately for Forest Road, when they deposited the check, it bounced, and Shemesha Jones had already removed all her possessions from the unit. I suspected I would see Forest Road again, this time seeking a judgment against Jones. Or, they might turn the check over to the worthless check unit of the Solicitor's Office, and I might eventually sign a warrant for Jones's arrest. Then again, they had probably had all the drama they wanted over the whole thing.

24
WHAT BUGS ME

Truth is stranger than fiction, they say. The earliest attribution for this quote is Lord Byron, in his 1823 poem "Don Juan:" 'Tis strange,-but true; for truth is always strange; Stranger than fiction: if it could be told…" In 1858 Josiah Henson used the line in his autobiography titled *Truth Stranger than Fiction.* More famously still, Mark Twain, the well-read American humorist and writer, with an implied credit to Byron, said, "Truth is stranger than fiction, but it is because Fiction is obliged to stick to possibilities; Truth isn't."

The Court hears many strange stories, told for the truth, and the continuing challenge of the Judge is to decide what to believe. Just because the story is strange doesn't mean it's fiction, but neither does it mean it's the truth. A very strange story came through the court in the form of an Summons and Complaint.

THE PLEADINGS

Few pleadings were ever more plaintively pled than the plaintiff's plight filed with the Court one spring by Rochelle Smith against Jones Grove Apartments. She asked the Court for a Judgment for her first and last month's rent and her security deposit, her pet deposit, and the balance of the Court's monetary jurisdictional limit for "anguish and pain." The letter she wrote to explain these damages was echoed later in testimony:

> I have lived at Jones Grove Apartments for thirteen years. I am completely mortified by the way they have treated me lately. I have been living in torture for the last four months.

My little dog Penny and I have been bitten alive by *micro* brownish red ants.

I got rid of my new mattress and box springs since Jones Grove said I must have bed bugs. Two exterminators came out and said there were no bed bugs or anything else. I thought then that maybe this was bird mites (I found information on the Internet) since whatever was biting us couldn't be seen. Birds made a hole in the building where they could have their babies. The mites came from the birds.

I tried sleeping on my couch and love seat but they were both infested with these insects, too. I had no place to sleep.

Last week as I was tying my shoe, I saw near my foot a pile of very tiny, brownish red ants - *micro!* It looked like a patch of the carpet was moving. I ran for my spray and then ran to the office. An employee named Ashley was there, thankfully. The office manager and maintenance men had laughed off my complaint as if it was no big deal. *They* weren't the ones being bitten. Ashley gave me a key to the guest apartment so I could stay there temporarily.

I appreciated the place to stay, but then the manager told me the apartment had been treated for pests before and she couldn't do anything else to help me. She said I would have to move back into my apartment because the guest apartment was needed for someone else. Jones Grove isn't taking my complaints seriously. I will have to move because they aren't taking care of their responsibilities. They should pay me for my trouble as well.

With the letter was a CD and a note saying that it contained pictures. While I usually read the verbal Complaint, I do not usually access CDs, audio tapes, and USB flash drives when they're offered into pleadings with a lawsuit. I set the CD aside.

When I first read the Complaint Ms. Smith's description sounded a bit like fire ants, except that those pesky critters aren't exactly "micro" sized as she had described. But when they are disturbed they do move aggressively in great numbers, which might have looked like a patch of carpet moving across the floor. Still, the description was odd.

Jones Grove Apartments submitted an Answer through its attorney, Trey Jennings. It was the usual recitation—general denial, failure to state a claim upon which relief can be granted, waiver, estoppel, accord and satisfaction, etc. Clearly, Jennings wanted to get specific only once the matter came to trial.

THE EVIDENCE

Rochelle Smith, a woman who looked considerably older than the sixty-five years she said she was, came by herself to court the day of trial, while Jones Grove came with Mr. Jennings and several other persons, who never testified. Whether they were slated to do so I never found out.

Plaintiff

Smith recounted to the Court the story of her increasing troubles with pests in her apartment at Jones Grove, the story broadening from the brief explanation she had provided in her Complaint. She said problems actually started some time back.

In the summer two years ago, Ms. Smith requested that Smith Grove send an exterminator due to a problem with what she believed to be mites, specifically bird mites. She had been itching from bug bites and had been worried about what might be causing them. While looking out her window one day she noticed birds flying to and from the building, carrying twigs and then bugs and worms, activities associated with building a nest. She went outside and watched until more birds came, and she saw they were going to a hole in an outside wall of the apartment complex corresponding to her unit.

Smith looked on the Internet and finally found information that led her to reason that the birds in her wall carried bird mites. She concluded that the mites had gotten into the ventilation system and that they had infested her apartment. She thought probably that she had a problem with dust mites as well, and that together these microscopic creatures had proliferated to the point that everything in her apartment was covered or saturated with them.

Smith said that when the problem began to be serious, she started to feel very ill, between not sleeping and all the biting on the upper part of her body, not to mention bug poison. (She seemed to be implying that the bug bites transmitted some toxin). Smith related a little of what she had found out on the Internet about bird mites. I didn't interrupt her because Jones Grove was represented; it was Trey Jennings's responsibility to object to hearsay, and he didn't. At one point when she began to relate what she had been reading, I glanced at Jennings in anticipation of an objection. He lowered his eyelids, shook his head ever so slightly, and almost imperceptibly waved off the idea. As Smith continued she said that her research showed that bird mites carry diseases that can make people seriously ill and even cause death.

Meanwhile, maintenance men didn't patch the holes, according to Smith, and they were getting worse. Smith showed some pictures to the Court, which without objection I received into evidence. Most of them were photos of all Smith's bedding after it had been moved out of the apartment, but one photo was of an outside wall and a darkened porch area belonging to her unit. She said I could see a hole, but I didn't. The porch area was very dim because the photo had been exposed for the brilliantly lit wall. Perhaps the hole was in a shadow area where no detail could be made out.

Smith requested that her air ducts be cleaned out. According to her, Smith Grove did not comply. She said they seemed not to care. As the problem got worse, she said sometimes she was bit so hard it felt more like her skin was being pulled off rather than just bitten.

She went to a local pest control company, Bug Assassins, and they recommended and then sold her some do-it-yourself spray supposed to be much, much better than what you would buy at the box stores. She went home and used it liberally. Because she had to use so much bug spray, her couch and love seat began to stink of it. She had given up sleeping in the bed because of the infestation. She got rid of the bedding, though it was only five months old. It was ruined. After another call to management, someone from maintenance again responded to her apartment, but no one saw any mites, she said. What she had learned, however, was that mites bite but they can't be seen.

As Smith continued testifying I remembered seeing scanning electron microscope pictures of mites on human skin. They like to cling to the bases of hairs, such as on the human arm. Most people aren't aware that they themselves are host to millions of such microscopic creatures, chiefly because these mites don't bite. In fact, they consume dead skin flakes. It's what biologists call symbiosis—we need them and they need us. Smith's testimony, however, was that her particular infestation was feasting on *her*. Strange indeed.

The mite problem didn't end at soft materials, either. Smith said that one night a mirror on a wardrobe door suddenly fell off, shattering "to smithereens" in the floor. She said that if she had been under the mirror on her air mattress (which she had taken to sleeping on), she might have been killed.

"Ms. Smith," I asked, "what is the connection to the insects you allege were infesting your apartment?"

"They ate the glue on the back of the mirror, your honor! And it just fell off," she said.

Months later, after more bites, more lost furniture and much more complaining, Smith said Jones Grove repaired the holes in the exterior apartment wall. She was waiting on exterminators again, too, but while she was she also did what she could to mitigate the problem. She rented a steam carpet cleaner and treated her couch and love seat. She couldn't tell any difference afterwards. Finally she saw Ashley in the office and, as she had described in her letter filed with the Complaint, Ashley offered her the guest apartment, for sleeping anyway, while Jones Grove attempted to treat her apartment. They were going to steam clean everything inside.

While she was staying in the guest apartment she would go into her own apartment now and then to get clothes out of her closet or to use her phone and computer. One day she saw to her horror that her clothes had large holes in them, some a half inch or more in diameter. And on black clothes on the right side of the closet she saw several red threads from clothes on the left side, and black threads on the red clothes as well. Her sweaters especially were affected. She could only conclude that the bugs had both eaten the holes and transported threads across the top of the clothes and deposited them there.

At this point I interrupted. "Ms. Smith, do you mean you saw something like *moth* holes?" I had had several sweaters ruined by moths over the years, and if she had moths, that might explain at least some of her problems. But Smith said she never saw any moths in the closets. The mites, however, had destroyed her clothes. ($1,700.00 of her written claim against Jones Grove was for her ruined clothing, but at trial she didn't present any photographs of the clothing, or any bills for new clothes, either.)

Smith said on another trip back to her apartment she saw some folded paper on the living room and bedroom carpets; the paper had some kind of liquid in it. She said no one explained what was being done in her unit. She wrote little notes to various office employees but never got responses. One day she was in the apartment working on the computer when she heard a voice in the front room and went out to find Ashley, carrying Smith's food back in from the guest apartment. Ashley said they were moving

Smith's things back into her unit because they needed the guest apartment; it had been previously rented for the coming week.

Smith said she begged them to tell her where she should go because she couldn't come back to sleep there until it was free of mites or red ants or whatever was biting her and her dog Penny. She said she mentioned red ants in her testimony because there were holes in the ground around the complex that hadn't been there before, and that she had seen "red ant piles that looked like little blood blisters." (At some point, the maintenance men had suggested that her problem might be from fleas on Penny. Smith said Penny didn't have fleas.) Reluctantly and fearfully, Smith began sleeping in her own unit again, and she said the biting resumed. One night, exasperated, Smith called the police.

At this point in her testimony Smith offered into evidence a written record of what had been going on at the time. My clerk showed the document to Mr. Jennings across the aisle.

"Judge," he said, "I don't object to most of the document; it looks like what Ms. Smith has just testified to. But I do object to some of the things she says other people told her, such as the police officers. There are no police officers here to testify and I believe those statements would be inadmissible hearsay."

"Ms. Smith," I said, "Do you understand that I can't admit testimony of what persons who are not here said out of court, if it's offered to prove some material fact?" She nodded. "Then do you object to Mr. Jennings penciling out the statements of the police?" I asked her. She said she didn't.

Jennings worked over the document and then handed it to me. I laid it aside without looking at it because it was what Ms. Smith had just put on the record orally. Only later, after the case was done and the Judgment issued, did I review the document when writing up notes for this book. Jennings had drawn a pencil line through various statements of police, but they were still legible. While I hadn't considered what Smith *said* the police said to her, her report was interesting additional information for this chapter.

According to Smith's written record, a municipal police officer responded to her apartment and listened to her complaint, but Rochelle Smith said that "of course he wasn't on my side. He was just another young, twenty-four year old with a power syndrome. He made me feel like I was senile, talking down to me. He made fun of ants that can't be seen. It was age discrimination. I was so upset an ambulance was called because I started hyperventilating." She said the officer asked her who the President was and what year it was. The next day, Smith said she reported the officer to his superiors. Smith said the woman who was the officer's supervisor commiserated with her, promising also to reprimand the officer for his conduct.

(Reading this exchange with police long after the fact, I found it not entirely credible, especially the part about what the officer's supervisor had reportedly said. I know a lot about the municipal police department in question and I know that complaints are not met with promises to discipline officers. The standard answer is thanks for the report and something to the effect that the matter will be looked into.)

As the situation continued to worsen, Smith said she had scars on her chest from bites, but still had no satisfactory replies to her numerous complaints, and no solution was reached. Finally, Smith sent a certified letter detailing her history of complaints and her frustration with Jones Grove's not solving her mounting bug problems.

Two days later and just before her annual lease term was to expire, Smith received a letter from Jones Grove. For the past thirteen years Smith and Jones Grove had renewed her lease every year. However, the relationship was coming to an end. Smith entered Jones Grove's letter into evidence:

Dear Ms. Smith

As you know, your current lease expires on [the date given]. While we have been glad to have you here with us at

Jones Grove, we will be unable to renew your lease for another year. We feel we have exhausted every effort to make you comfortable in your home, and after receiving your certified letter yesterday expressing your dissatisfaction, our team feels the best for both parties would be to allow you to find a home that better suits your needs.

The letter went on to provide for two more months occupancy at her current rent if she needed the time, with a cut-off date near Christmas. Jones Grove had already credited her account with her deposit from years ago.

Smith seemed to be finished with her horror story of an infestation that hadn't been corrected. I asked if Mr. Jennings wanted to cross examine. Of course, he did.

Cross examination

Trey Jennings picked up a few documents from the defense table and approached the witness.

"You say there was a hole in the side of your apartment wall outside, correct?"

"Yes. It was there in that picture. It was the size of a lady's fist."

"This exhibit?" Jennings showed Smith one of the photographs she had entered into evidence.

"Yes. It was there," she said, pointing at an area in the shadows. "I don't see it in the picture, but it was there."

"I can't find it, either. Perhaps the Court has better eyes than mine," said Jennings. He changed subjects.

"Did you ever see these bugs?" asked Jennings.

"No, like I said, I never—I *couldn't* see them. That's the problem! They're called no-see-ums, I think people say. You can't see 'em!"

I'm sure my forehead screwed up a little. We were on a different page from "bird mites" in the biology book, now. No-see-ums is the common name for *Ceratopogonidae*, a type of small fly found chiefly in semiaquatic habitats. They are small enough to get through regular window screen, and they do sometimes bite human beings. When they do, they cause red, itchy bumps that last a few days. Maybe Smith had no-se-ums and not mites. But she probably would have seen no-see-ums. The name is not technically correct; certainly *Ceratopogonidae* are not invisible to the naked eye as mites are. They also don't eat sweaters.

Jennings was thinking the same thing, apparently, as he asked, "You mean like little flies?"

"Yes. They bite."

"And the flies ate your sweaters?" he asked.

"I don't know. Something did," she said.

"Did you ever see the little colored threads being flown through the air from place to place?" he asked. (I kept a straight face.)

"No."

"Now, Ms. Smith, I show you this document. Do you recognize it?"

She looked at it briefly. "Yes," she said, "it's where I asked for exterminators."

"And do you see below that where the response of Jones Grove is recorded?" said Jennings.

"It says they came on [a certain date]."

Jennings then showed her a photocopy from a log kept by the apartment complex manager where requests for maintenance and responses of the manager and maintenance personnel were listed, with dates. He didn't enter it into evidence but merely asked if she saw where she had put in a request and someone had come to her apartment in a reasonable amount of time and done something. Smith had to say in each case that she saw what the record said. She didn't deny the truth of the record, but she insisted that in spite of what they came and did, she still had the problem with bugs.

"Bugs, bugs, bugs!" she said.

Jennings cut his eyes to the bench for a micro-second, then moved on.

"Did you go see a doctor about the bug bites?" he asked.

"Not really," Smith said after a slight pause.

"Not *really?*" asked Jennings. "You did or you didn't, right?" he said, prodding her to be specific.

"I didn't," she admitted.

"So, you don't know what it was that bit you, do you?"

"No. I couldn't see them."

"Really, you don't actually know you were bitten, do you?" asked Jennings.

Smith got irritated. "I don't know what it would be if it wasn't bugs!"

"And the stuff you got from Bug Assassins didn't do anything?"

"No!"

"And what the maintenance men did didn't work either?"

"No!" she said, and harrumphed with frustration.

"And you rented a steam machine and that didn't do anything?"

"No, and neither did the steam machines the maintenance men used!" she said. "They didn't solve the problem, and I don't think they cared!"

Jennings let Smith calm down a minute. "Ms. Smith, you admit in your letter and in your testimony that Ashley was kind to you. Do you think she cared?"

Sniffle. Sniff. "Yes. She was the only one."

I was trying to predict Jennings's next question, and I kept hoping he would ask where Smith was living now; it had been several months since Smith's lease had been terminated and she had moved. I wanted to know if she still had a problem with bugs. Jennings didn't go that direction, however. Maybe he felt he didn't need to just for my benefit.

Mr. Jennings paused in front of Ms. Smith for a few seconds and asked one more question in a calm and low tone.

"What more did you want Jones Grove to do to help you?"

"I don't know. I just know they didn't get rid of the bugs."

Jennings stood another moment looking at her after her answer, glanced at me, then returned to his seat. Before sitting down he said gently, "That's all I have, your honor."

I dismissed Ms. Smith from the witness box and when she had sat back at her table I looked to Trey Jennings.

"Your honor, the Defense moves for a directed verdict. Ms. Smith has clearly not met her burden. She has offered no direct evidence there were any bugs in her apartment.

[While Smith had given the Court a CD in pleadings and a note saying there were pictures on it, she didn't present the CD or any pictures on it into evidence, other than the photos of bedding and the apartment's back porch. I wondered why she hadn't produced photographs of her bites, if she had them, but in the present circumstances I did not want to be seen as favoring the Plaintiff by prompting Smith for more evidence. If she had pictures, they weren't in evidence, and her time to put them there was now expired.]

Jennings continued. "Not only that, your honor, but Ms. Smith hasn't given any testimony of damages. She made a claim for $7,500.00 in her Complaint, but she hasn't mentioned any monetary damages on the record. Judge, we have Ms. Smith's own admission that Jones Grove responded to every one of her complaints, and while she is still unhappy, that alone is not enough reason for her to be awarded damages. My clients are sorry things ended the way they did, but they did all they could, and Ms. Smith just wasn't satisfied."

He paused, as if uncertain how to say what he wanted to end with.

"Your honor, we're not certain what the real solution for Ms. Smith is, but we believe she hasn't made her case to this Court that she deserves $7,500.00 in damages from Jones Grove, or any damages at all."

Ms. Smith seemed apoplectic and didn't respond.

THE JUDGMENT

In ruling on the Motion for Directed Verdict, I really combined that ruling with an off-the-cuff Judgment, referring to some notes I had made during testimony.

Plaintiff has not established, and appears not to be able to establish, the claim that her damages resulted from birds, bird mites, or any other cause for which Jones Grove is liable.

The principal claim, made in the Complaint itself, has not been sufficiently backed up by admissible evidence. Plaintiff brought no witnesses and does not have anywhere near expert testimony to identify the source of the problems she has experienced.

The Court also finds Plaintiff's testimony to be fundamentally flawed as to logic: that significant damage to her clothes and furniture and much else was caused by creatures that could not be seen. Yet she alleges the damage itself was major and sizeable. We have pictures of mattresses she discarded, but no evidence to corroborate her questionable assertion that they were ruined. Some evidence she gave to support her conclusion defies any explanation of being brought about by invisible pests, such as the transportation of black threads across a closet to a red garment and vice versa.

The Plaintiff's own testimony was that no exterminator ever found evidence of bugs of any kind in her apartment, yet she insists they were there.

Finally, Plaintiff admits that Defendant Jones Grove did respond to maintenance requests. They sent exterminators; they sent maintenance men; the manager herself came with others to steam clean the entire unit.

The Court must agree with Plaintiff Smith on this one thing, in fact: that the bugs in her apartment—see 'em or no-see-um—are not the sort that the exterminators could eradicate.

THE MOTION FOR DIRECTED VERDICT IS GRANTED, AND JUDGMENT IS FOR THE DEFENDANT. THE COMPLAINT OF PLAINTIFF IS DISMISSED.

Trey Jennings quietly thanked the Court. Rochelle Smith picked up her purse and a handful of papers and plodded out of the courtroom. Trey chatted a few seconds with his client, and then before leaving, he caught my eye. There was a hint of a sad smile on his face.

EPILOGUE

Not long after this case came to a close, Sgt. Rick Chadwick, a municipal officer—not the one who had responded to Rochelle Smith's apartment—came into my offices to ask me about her. He had been assigned to take a report from Smith about happenings at her present home, a rental house. According to Chadwick, Smith said there was a tremendous hole in her back yard, and she had fallen into it. (I thought of the sink hole in my own yard, ten feet wide and eight feet deep.) Her Chihuahua, Penny, had pulled her out of the hole. But the hole had caused her to develop cancer. Moreover, as a result of her accident she could no longer talk on cell phones anymore, only on land lines.

When she called police to come to her house to report all these goings on, as she explained to Chadwick, the officers who responded flew at her. Officer Chadwick asked her what she meant.

Smith said they "flew at me! Flew like birds!" And she demonstrated, flapping her arms as if she were a bird. "Like this! Just like this!" She wanted to file a complaint with their superior officer.

Yeah, that might bug me, too. But I'll leave it to you, my reader, to decide whether truth is stranger than fiction, or the other way around.

www.ingramcontent.com/pod-product-compliance
Lightning Source LLC
Chambersburg PA
CBHW031923190326
41519CB00007B/396